THE ROLE I PLAYED

SAMI JO SMALL

THE ROLE I PLAYED

Canada's Greatest Olympic Hockey Team

Published by ECW Press
665 Gerrard Street East
Toronto, Ontario, Canada M4M 1Y2
416-694-3348 / info@ecwpress.com

Editor for the Press: Michael Holmes
Cover design: David A. Gee
Front cover photograph by Heather Pollock
All photos courtesy of Sami Jo Small, unless otherwise noted.

To the best of her abilities, the author has related experiences, places,
people, and organizations from her memories of them. In order to
protect the privacy of others, she has, in some instances, changed the
names of certain people and details of events and places.

LIBRARY AND ARCHIVES CANADA CATALOGUING IN
PUBLICATION

Title: The role I played : Canada's greatest Olympic
hockey team / Sami Jo Small.

Names: Small, Sami Jo, author.

Identifiers: Canadiana (print) 20200248464 | Canadiana
(ebook) 20200248472

ISBN 9781770415652 (hardcover)
ISBN 9781773056104 (PDF)
ISBN 9781773056098 (EPUB)

Subjects: LCSH: Small, Sami Jo. | LCSH: Women
hockey players—Canada—Biography. | LCSH: Hockey
players—Canada—Biography. | LCSH: Women Olympic
athletes—Canada—Biography. | LCSH: Olympic
athletes—Canada—Biography. | LCSH: Hockey—
Canada. | LCGFT: Autobiographies.

Classification: LCC GV848.5.S63 A3 2020 | DDC
796.962092—DC23

The publication of *The Role I Played* has been funded in part by the Government of Canada. *Ce livre est financé en partie par le
gouvernement du Canada.* We acknowledge the contribution of the Government of Ontario through the Ontario Book Publishing
Tax Credit, and through Ontario Creates for the marketing of this book.

 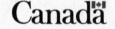

PRINTED AND BOUND IN CANADA

PRINTING: FRIESENS   5   4   3   2   1

·······

To Mom and Dad
Thank you for encouraging *play*

Contents

Introduction

The Canadian National Women's Hockey Team is one of the most successful teams in all of sports history. Not just women's history, but *all* of history. The team won four straight Olympic gold medals from 2002 to 2014 and were World Champions for 14 straight years from 1990 to 2004. I was just a small cog in its operation, serving as a goaltender for 11 years, from 1997 to 2008. The most incredible aspects of being on this team were the people I was fortunate to meet and the adventures we took together all around the world.

This book took me nearly a decade to complete. I wrote the rudimentary bones of the book in just under a year, took another two years to research and fill in the blanks. I then had a baby while working full-time and doing what some will say was playing professional hockey and others will say was toiling away in obscurity.

Regardless, the book got put on the shelf while life took over: I dedicated myself to once again becoming the goalie I knew I could be, while working full-time as a professional speaker to earn the primary income for our family, while my husband pursued his Olympic dreams. Our laundry was filled with sweaty workout attire and baby clothes covered in spit-up — but I loved every moment.

When my daughter started kindergarten, I dusted off the manuscript and thought, *Now what?* Thankfully, I had many I could call on for support, a vast network accrued over a lifetime of incredible opportunities.

With every story I wrote, I felt the raw emotions of those experiences all over again. I am thankful for the incredible support of my husband, who had to listen to me recount stories of big saves or bad games years later. I am sorry I often went to bed angry at having been cut from a team or sad that I had lost a loved one several decades ago.

The words written in this book are my recollections of events, but by no means do I accept them as fact. The mind can play tricks when we attempt to remember how life unfolded. Often, I'd write a section, then go back and watch game tape only to realize that situations did not transpire as I remembered them. Ultimately, the emotions in this book are real; while the facts may be disputed, I saw events from my perspective, and I am not too proud to realize that others will have different takes on the same story.

My good friends and long time teammates Jennifer Botterill and Cheryl Pounder and I all work as professional speakers, sharing stories of our successful team, but all the stories are different. The moments we accentuate are different and the people that had the greatest influence on us are varied.

I wanted to showcase my teammates, yes, but I didn't want to write their stories: those are theirs to tell. These are my stories, from my perspective, about the events as they happened to me.

This is a story of hope, belief, and persistence.

To my goalie partners over the years, I owe you an immense debt of gratitude. I'm sorry you are often portrayed as the antagonist in this book. We were in constant competition. Only one goalie can be in the net. And I always wanted to play, but I learned everything I know from watching you. I often envied you in our competitive environment, but observing your skills, your professionalism, and your love of the game was a joy and my greatest honour is having been your teammate.

To my defencemen, I'm sorry I had to highlight your mistakes in this book. Often your mistake followed by my mistake led to a goal and this book is about a lot of goals. But know that I appreciate the thousands of good things that you did that went completely unnoticed by most but me. You are the true unsung heroes of the game.

I apologize to the coaches that are not always depicted in the best of light in these pages. In my bubble as a player, I didn't have the maturity to see my coaches as people, with real lives, with real emotions. I've gained greater understanding with time, perspective, and the realization that I was not the only one you had to worry about. Through sport, you taught me valuable life skills. Every story needs villains, but I hold no grudges and hope you won't. I have the utmost respect for each of you and the difficult decisions you had to make.

I am thankful to my first editor, Jacqueline Larson, who went back to the drawing board and taught me how to write and to Deirdre Norman and Kate Reddy-Taylor who were invaluable with their feedback. Also, thank you to all who were willing to spend time reading and rehashing moments that happened long ago. And thank you to Dave Bidini, the incredible musician and author, for putting me in touch with great people at my publishing house, ECW Press.

Ultimately, I want you, the reader, to understand what made our team successful. I want you to appreciate the various personalities that created the fabric of our team and how each person had an impact on me, how we impacted each other. We were all thrust into different roles throughout our careers, struggling to maximize our potential while still contributing to the team.

········

In 1997, during my first year with the National Team, I was asked to write a short message to the rest of my teammates travelling to an away game. I chose the quote, "To win the game is great. To play the game is greater but to love the game is the greatest." In the end hockey gave me the greatest reward of all: I truly love the game.

PART I

Becoming a Hockey Player

SEPTEMBER 1997: MY FIRST OLYMPIC TRYOUT

I'm alone in a large dressing room in Calgary, goalie bag at my feet. The room smells of the men's league players from last night. I can hear the constant buzz of the refrigeration system. Nothing about this scene is new to me, aside from trying out for a women's team.

This evaluation will seal my fate. I don't know who will be with me on the ice. Play well today, and I stay to try out for a spot on the first ever Canadian women's Olympic hockey team. Play just okay, and I'll resume my life; catch tomorrow's flight to California and start my senior year in engineering at Stanford University.

I'm on a full track and field scholarship to throw discus and javelin, but surprisingly I'm here in Calgary to be a goalie. Today is a special tryout just for me — Team Canada selected the rest of the 28 girls back in May. I didn't know about those tryouts as I was playing on a men's club team at Stanford away from scouts, away from the limelight, and away from women's hockey.

This room is eerily empty. I sit on a wooden bench, a solitary grey practice jersey hangs behind me. It has the Team Canada hockey logo on the front. I've never earned the right to wear a National Team jersey before; the one I wore for successive school pictures doesn't count. I leave it on its hanger, not daring to move the sacred object until I need it.

Ripping the luggage tag off the straps, I lob them into the garbage at the centre of the room. I unzip my bag and occupy myself by pulling out various pieces of armour needed for practice that starts in approximately 45 minutes. I'm not used to having this much space or time.

Never at a practice this early, I poke my head out of the dressing room, but there's no one in sight. The actual women's National Team dressing room is at the end of the hall, but I see no movement. I feel like I'm the only one at the rink today. Heading back into my room, and with nothing else left to do, I start to dress.

1989: TRAILBLAZER — MY LIFE ON BOYS' TEAMS

The St. Vital Victorias Bantam AA boys' room is loud with chatter, jammed with my 13-year-old male teammates at various stages of gearing up. Playing hockey, I've never known anything but a room full of boys. I'm always the only girl.

The boys who arrive after me run to the bathroom to put on their under-gear clothes. There's nowhere private for me to change so I cleverly have the garments I will wear to play hockey on beneath my street clothes.

The room is almost full, but my bag and I squeeze in next to Jamie Bettens, one of the few guys I hang out with outside the rink. He's always been my champion, and his mom is one of my biggest fans.

I've been teammates with many of these guys since we were little, so this isn't embarrassing for me. What is routine for me was probably awkward for the new guys for the first few weeks of the season but now it's normal. I hunch towards the wall trying to conceal my sports bra from my team, and quickly change my t-shirt.

I begin to suit up amid the chaos. My hand digs through my bag for my garter belt; I stand and slide it loosely around my hips. I pull up my red, black, and white wool hockey socks and sit back down clamping them in place.

Despite the loud music, boys shout back and forth across the room to each other. Taunts are part of the routine, and I'm often privy to insider information.

"What's with you and Jenna?" yells one of my teammates to our captain.

"Don't *you* want to know," he shouts back slyly.

The more equipment I have on, the more I engage in the room's clamour. Playing hockey since the age of five, I have always been comfortable being "one of the guys." Like most of my teammates, I dream of playing professionally in the NHL.

Neither of my parents were hockey people before my brother, Luke, who was my idol, signed up to play as a six-year-old; I wanted to do everything he did. When I asked if I could play too, my dad, without hesitation, went to the local community club and stood in line with the other parents.

"Can I sign up my five-year-old daughter for the hockey team?" He asked. My brother and I had taken skating lessons dressed in full snowsuits since I was two.

"Are you sure?" said the first man decked out in a blue and white Norberry Community Centre hockey jacket.

My dad looked down at my hopeful face and nodded.

"I don't see why not," said the other gentleman as he turned, shrugging at his peer, and then nodded to my dad.

My mom tried to help me dress at home for my first practice, but I already knew how. Studying everything my brother did, I was determined to be independent.

"I can do it myself," I said to her pulling up my woollen hockey socks, my face beaming with anticipation.

Officially part of a team, my mom watched her daughter, the only girl at every practice, from the snowbank at the outdoor rink at Norberry. Joy beamed from my rosy cheeks as I glided across the ice. My dad, in his plastic Micron skates, was one of our coaches that first year — perhaps more like one of the helpers, lifting kids doing snow angels to their feet. I never wanted him to help me; I wanted to show him I could skate all by myself.

Neither one of my parents pushed me; in fact, they often had to curtail my activities, since I wanted to be a part of everything. "So driven," they would say about me to other parents.

Always driving me and my brother to activities, they often signed up as volunteers. I never really thought about what it must have been like for them to watch their little girl on the ice with boys, and the flak they must have taken for allowing their daughter to play.

Years later my dad told me someone in the registration line told him that if he signed me up for hockey, that I'd likely never have children, my uterus would be damaged from skating. Of course, my dad ignored the ridiculous comments, kept his cool, and always remained supportive of me. I grew up knowing they were both proud of my brother and me, regardless of the activity, as long as we tried hard.

"You starting today?" asks Jamie quietly beside me. I nod yes with the confidence of a future Olympian despite being the only female player in the Manitoba Bantam AA league.

I grab my last pieces of gear. Jamie taps his stick against my pads, the ritual to wish a goalie good luck. The more equipment I have on, the more confident I feel. I pull my hair back in a low ponytail and slide my helmet on. I slip my hands into my catching glove and blocker. Fully armoured, I feel powerful and capable of greatness. It's game time. I make my way towards the door, reach for my goalie stick, and lead my guys on the ice.

SEPTEMBER 1997: MY FIRST OLYMPIC TRYOUT (CONTINUED)

I continue to disrobe in the vast, empty room, giving each one of my clothes their own hook. The feeling of anxiety as I wait for practice to begin is almost overwhelming. I've grown up in boys' dressing rooms, and now in my first real chance to play with women, I am alone.

When I first arrived, the National Team equipment manager, Robin McDonald, greeted me and led me to this room. He then left to tend to some tasks but said he would come get me when it was time to go on the ice.

It doesn't take me long before I'm fully suited up. I feel like a gladiator preparing for an unknown battle. And I wait.

After what seems like an eternity, Robin knocks at the door.

"Time to go."

I pull my hair back in the habitual low ponytail and slide my helmet on. I slip my hands into my catching glove and blocker. Fully armoured, I feel powerful and capable of greatness. I make my way to the door, reach for my goalie stick, and start the long solitary walk towards the rink; every teammate I've ever had, every game I've ever been a part of, every coach I've ever had, and especially two parents who believed their daughter deserved to play, have all made these steps possible.

AUGUST 1997: BELIEF — THE PRACTICE (TWO MONTHS PRIOR)

Focusing on the blade of the player's stick as he crosses the blue line, I can see every line of tape. He's a big, strong guy, maybe plays Junior hockey somewhere. I can tell just by the way he skates that he's good.

His stick bends and flexes in exactly the right position mere millimetres from the puck. A snapshot is coming. I ready myself, flex my knees, and lower a bit in my stance. My pads move apart slightly, exposing my five-hole.

I can see the puck's rotation as it sails towards me. My body knows what to do. I kick out my right leg as my weight falls to the ice. I absorb the puck with my outstretched toe. I haven't told my toe to do that — it just knows. We've been through these motions thousands of times together.

The puck ricochets into the corner, narrowly avoiding the lineup of players waiting for their turn in the drill. In one fluid motion, I am back in the ready position and prepare for the next player.

This time it's a woman. I can't tell whom — I don't know these women well enough yet. It's the second drill of practice, and there are only six or so women on the ice scattered amongst the guys. This player is much smaller than the male shooter and I must play this differently. I found that out the hard way earlier in practice.

Accustomed to a lifetime of playing men's hockey, I understand how most guys shoot. They use their strength to control their shots, often trying to overpower the goaltender. I know what to look for and when to anticipate the shot. Women are stealthier. They don't have the power the men have so they hold on to the puck longer. They use angles to their advantage and find openings with pinpoint accuracy.

For the past week I'd been on the ice at the Olympic Oval High Performance Female Hockey camp in Calgary. I had seen a flyer for an Elite Women's Hockey Camp, but since the dates conflicted with an international track and field competition for which I was gunning, I didn't sign up. When I didn't throw as well as I had hoped and failed to qualify, I called up my long time friend Gillian Russell from Winnipeg and asked if I could stay with her in Calgary.

I was looking forward to training with some of the top female hockey players in Canada, but the skill level was not what I was expecting; I was the oldest by four years and with a much more extensive hockey background.

Someone at the Oval camp apparently saw my skill because here I am at a rink somewhere in the heart of Calgary training with a bunch of professional men and six of the women who are about to try out for Canada's first women's Olympic hockey team. The first Olympic tournament for women's ice hockey is six months away, but until this morning, I had no idea team selection was imminent.

Hayley Wickenheiser, a.k.a. "Wick," picked me at 6:00 am in her tiny VW Rabbit. I was nervous, unsure what to expect. I'd dragged my Stanford roommates to watch Wick and Team Canada play live at the 1995 Pacific Rim Championships a couple years ago in San Jose, and this morning I am getting the opportunity to play alongside them. Wick's only 19, but already she's been on the National Team for four years. Originally from Shaunavon, Saskatchewan, her family moved to Calgary when she was 11. She played a ton of boys' hockey and was also fortunate enough to play with women at the new hotbed for women's hockey, the Calgary Oval, under the guidance of the Olympic coach, Shannon Miller.

The woman skating towards me takes a couple of strides more than the last guy did, and it changes her angle of attack. She's closer. I have less time to react. I shuffle ever so slightly to the right to maintain the correct angle. Trying to make this as hard as possible for her, I take up as much of the net as I can. She cocks her stick straight back. The puck freezes in time, alone on the ice. I engage my quadriceps, lower my position, and steady my gaze.

I can see the position of the blade of her stick. A lifetime of studying this exact moment allows me to read the stick and know she's aiming high. As she brings her stick down, she transfers all her weight to her front leg, creating torque. Her stick first connects with the ice and then with the puck. She launches the puck in my direction. Anticipating where she'll shoot, I still have to scramble to get my limbs in position.

I swing my right blocker hand to my side, angling it in front of the puck. The blocker is a finicky piece of equipment. The puck must hit it at the perfect angle or bad rebounds occur. I have this shot figured out, but it's coming fast. At the last second, my blocker catches up with the puck, and I watch as it hits my outstretched hand directing it nicely into the corner.

No time to spare, I refocus on the next shooter. There's always another shooter, another opportunity. Each situation is different, but on every shot, I learn something new, building up a catalogue of techniques. Every moment leads into the next and as practice ends, I realize I played with some of the best female players in the world, and I held my own.

••••••••

Three weeks later and I am on a call at my desk in my childhood bedroom in Winnipeg as Wally Kozak, mentor coach for the women's Olympic hockey team, explains how try outs work for the National Team.

"Twenty-eight girls from five different cross-country evaluations have already been chosen to 'centralize' in Calgary from September until the Olympics in February in Japan."

Prior to Wally's call I had been packing my belongings for my flight back to California for my senior year of university. My bags sit open on my bed, piles of clothes surrounding them.

Wally's gentle voice is serious.

"You impressed me at the morning skate. Where do you play?" he asks.

There is a large map laminated onto the top of my desk. I give Wally a brief description of my background in hockey, how I play for the Stanford men's team but am on scholarship for track and field. I slowly trace the outline of Japan with my finger as Wally continues. Less than a week ago, I had never heard of Wally Kozak, but now he holds my future in his hands.

"You are good enough to be here. How did you get so good?"

I hesitate. "Uh, I don't know. I watch pro goalies every time I can, and I read a lot about technique."

"You mean you've never had goalie coaching?"

"Well, not really. I've gone to camps in the summer, but not the last couple of summers because I've been competing on the national junior team for track."

"Can you come back to Calgary for an evaluation?" Adding that he is the mentor coach to the Olympic coach, Shannon Miller.

". . . I'm not sure. I'm supposed to be starting classes at Stanford in two weeks."

"I want the other coaches to see you play." He is persistent. "You do things on the ice that you can't teach. You're athletic and you battle. You can make this team. Just come back to Calgary."

What would my parents say? I can't just drop everything and head to Calgary, can I? Wally continues to talk, as I ponder potential solutions.

Who is this Wally character? He doesn't even know me.

Wally has a belief in me that even I don't have.

"Can you come back to Calgary?" he asks again.

The Olympics have been a lifelong dream.

"Ummm . . . Yes. Yes, I can."

SEPTEMBER 1997: LIFE CHANGES COURSE (BACK TO PRESENT)

My first tryout went well. It was only me and some shooters on the ice, with the National Team coaches evaluating in the stands. The coaches, still unsure, invited me back for another evaluation the following day, and then another a few days later. I was then thrown into an exhibition game playing for the local club team, the Calgary Oval X-Treme, against Team Canada. Based on what I assume were good performances, the coaches asked me to stay, to officially be "centralized," to live and train full-time in Calgary and try out for the Olympic team.

I had hoped I would get this news but didn't plan for what it meant. Now I must call my Stanford track and field coach, Robert Weir, and tell him I'm not coming back to school while I attempt to make an Olympic hockey team. I feel like I'm disappointing him, letting the whole track and field team down.

Sitting near the fireplace hearth at my new residence in Calgary, I eye the rotary phone next to the sofa, trying to find the guts to pick it up. Holding a calling card in one hand, I stare at the numbers.

While the last two weeks have been challenging and exhilarating, not knowing if I was officially on the tryout roster left me in limbo. I prepared every day for the news that my time trying out was done, that I would be returning to Stanford. But early this week, the coaches released goaltender Isabelle Miner and gave me her spot.

Four goalies are left: Manon Rhéaume, Lesley Reddon, Danielle Dube, and me. Only two will go to the Olympics.

I was staying on my friend Gillian's couch, but two days ago, when I found out I was staying, I decided to move in with teammate Nancy Drolet, from Drummondville, Quebec. Fortunately, I went to French immersion because Nancy grew up in a very Francophone environment. She's been on the team since 1992 and scored the overtime winner at last year's World Championships. We've finished our workouts for the day, and she's lying on her bed, updating her diary.

In a moment of courage, I stretch out and pick up the phone to dial. It's an hour earlier in California, but likely Robert won't have left the office yet.

Robert is my throwing coach. He recruited me to Stanford, pushed to have me at the school, believed in my abilities, and convinced me that Stanford's academic program was above any other. He lured me with the knowledge that Stanford had a men's club hockey team where I could play if it didn't conflict with track and field. That sold me.

When Stanford's head coach discovered I was moonlighting on the men's hockey team, he immediately told Robert to put an end to it. Instead, Robert decided to make training so grueling that I wouldn't want to go to hockey. I did plyometric sessions until my legs felt like they were going to fall off and I showed up for extra workouts designed just for me at 6:00 a.m. But despite it all, I still went to hockey. The head coach, unrelenting, finally told Robert he needed to tell me I couldn't play anymore.

I fell apart as if I was missing a part of me. Robert saw my sadness and convinced head coach, Vin Lanana, that I *needed* to be a hockey player. "Hockey is a part of her," he told him.

At the time, I thought I had no future in the game of hockey, but I still wanted the opportunity to play the game that meant so much to me, even if it was just for fun. On scholarship, track and field had to be my priority, and thanks to Robert's coaching, I competed internationally for Canada's national junior team while scoring points for Stanford at every weekend meet, representing my school at the NCAAs.

The phone is ringing. I am going to have to let down one of my strongest supporters.

"Hello, Robert Weir," a deep British voice answers.

"Hi, Robert." I'm trying to sound confident.

Am I giving up too much for a mere possibility? A full scholarship to Stanford is an honour and an incredible opportunity. I'm only one year away from graduating with a degree in mechanical engineering. *Is this sensible?*

As I stare at the fireplace, I'm suddenly losing my nerve. Last time we talked was late August immediately after the Canada Summer Games, a multisport event hosted in Brandon, Manitoba, my home province. He called to say how proud he was of me for winning gold in the javelin despite a nagging shoulder injury. He told me to take the month off, that I deserved the rest.

Now a month later, my world has completely changed.

I'm procrastinating.

"How is Winnipeg?" His voice booms.

"Good . . . great . . . I mean." My mouth is dry. I'm hoping he'll understand and not be too disappointed in my decision.

"Why is it 'good-great'?" He's aware I'm withholding.

"Ummm, I'm not in Winnipeg."

"Where are you? Back at Stanford already? Are you living with Amanda again?" he asks, referring to my roommate in my freshman and sophomore years.

"Errrrr . . . no . . . I'm in Calgary."

"Calgary? What's the name of the tower there? It has a great restaurant."

"Ummm . . . the . . . Calgary Tower?"

"Yes, when I played against Calgary, we'd always go up there. Scary though."

Robert is not only my throwing coach, he's a British Olympian who competed at the 1984 Games in the hammer throw. A scholarship took him to America while he competed internationally. He then took a hiatus from track and field to play in the Canadian Football League. Robert hadn't even played the game before his first tryout, but his massive size, speed, and strength convinced the coaches to take a chance on him. He went on to play for six seasons on three different teams: Ottawa, Toronto, and Hamilton. He then returned to the sport he loved, competing in the discus, for the UK, at the 1996 Olympic Games in Atlanta.

"Ummm . . . Robert . . . I won't be back at school this trimester."

Silence.

"I'm in Calgary playing hockey, trying out for the women's Olympic hockey team."

"Really? When did this happen?"

Even as I start to tell the story, it doesn't seem real. One day I'm carrying the flag for Manitoba at the closing ceremonies of the Canada Games thinking that winning gold in the javelin will be the highlight of my sporting career; the next moment, I'm living in Calgary trying out for the Olympics in hockey.

Robert listens quietly and then says, "What are your chances?"

I'm not sure. We talk about the team, about the coaches, and about what I'll need to do to make this team. We talk about how hard the training is, how different it is from any power sport training I've ever done, and how much I've learned in just a few weeks.

The extent of his hockey knowledge is limited. He once asked about the start time for an upcoming Stanford hockey game: "What time is the puck-off?"

But none of that matters. He understands athletes and, most importantly, he understands me. "Sami, you're stubborn. You're athletic and you're coachable. Listen and learn and care about the process. Be a student of the game. Absorb the details. Believe you deserve to be there. I believe in you."

He should have gone off about how I was squandering a scholarship to one of the most prestigious schools in the world for a shoestring of a possibility. He should have told me this was unacceptable and to get on a plane back to school immediately. He should have, but he didn't.

Stunned, I can *hear* his smile. He believes in the Olympic Games, and he believes in me. That's all I need. As we hang up the phone, he wishes me luck, and my new life officially begins.

I am now a *real* hockey player.

2

Improbable Circumstance

NOVEMBER 1997: BACK TO REALITY

I'm trying to sleep for just a little longer, but the California sun fills my car. It's two months since my first Olympic tryout. I cover my face with my sleeping bag until the sun forces my eyes open. It must be after 9:00 a.m. as the Stanford Stadium parking lot is full. I'm lying as flat as I can in the back of the hatch of my blue Mazda 323 that I've nicknamed the Blue Bomber, after my hometown football team.

Nearly all my personal belongings are packed around me, minus my hockey bag which I've left in the old throwers' weight room down by the track. I sometimes sleep there, but there's a chance of being spotted by morning lifters, and I don't want to have to answer questions.

The Canadian Olympic women's hockey team let me go two weeks ago. Despite being with the team for only a few months, it still hurt. Being in the boardroom with the coaches is still a blur. I keep having flashbacks of seeing our physiotherapist, Carrie Smith, waiting for me outside the giant door that led to our change room.

In her sweetest voice, she directed me upstairs. She didn't say much as we navigated through Hockey Canada's offices. She knew what was waiting. I hadn't had much interaction with our head coach, Shannon Miller, a former police officer; she was still an enigma to me. Carrie seated me across the boardroom table from Shannon, who was flanked by the assistant coaches, Danièle Sauvageau and Ray Bennett.

"Sami, it's been a pleasure having you around."

I smile and nod, still unaware of what was about to happen.

"You've pushed Manon, Lesley, and Danielle to be better." I smiled as Shannon looked back down to sheets of paper on the table in front of her, pausing a little too long.

Her right eyebrow lifted as she refocused on my gaze.

"I'm glad we know about you now. You've shown that you can play at this level." Her focus turned down again and there was another long pause. "But I'm sorry to say, we are going to go with the veterans. We are releasing you from the Olympic team."

My face was still hopeful as the news registered and manifested itself physically in my body. Smile through the pain — that's what my mom taught me. Shannon looked down a moment, and then squarely into my eyes as hope slowly oozed out of me.

Following the coaches' lead, I stood as they stood, then shook their hands.

"Thank you for the opportunity, and good luck," I said with real feeling but a somewhat fake smile, shaking Ray's and Danièle's hands. Shannon's was last. Her gruff exterior cracked, and she gave me a big hug. Leaning in she said, "Don't give up on this dream."

The coaches escorted me to the door where Carrie waited.

"Carrie has your plane ticket back to California," said Shannon.

Carrie seemed so distraught to be the messenger as we walked back to my car.

"I'm so sorry, Sami — this is awful," she said, handing me the ticket as we approached the door. "Good luck with everything." I nodded, and smiled, unable to speak.

And that was it. I packed my bags, called my friend Gillian to drive me to the airport, and my dream vanished.

That morning, the team had left for the 3 Nations Cup in Finland. I spent the entire day alone in the Calgary airport as my flight to San Francisco was delayed nearly nine hours. My brother, Luke — enrolled in optometry school an hour and a half across the bay at University of California Berkeley — greeted me with a gigantic smile at the San Francisco airport. He wanted to know every detail about tryouts, what it was like, who the top players were, and so on. He'd had his own four-year scholarship to TCU in Texas as a swimmer and had been to Olympic trials in 1992. When his final senior meet at the conference championships didn't go as planned, he opted to end his swimming career. This has always been *our* dream.

We are sharing our parents' car, but since I'm homeless, he's letting me use it full-time for now.

Writing in my notebook, I make a note to drive up to Berkeley for a visit this weekend.

Sitting in the front seat of the Bomber, I can see some early morning joggers getting laps in on the track. I've only been gone a couple months, and already everything seems different. The new track and field stadium here at Stanford is done. My friends are nearing graduation.

At the end of the last school year, during the Stanford housing random draw, I drew into the same residence with my friends: Diana Tellefson from my dorm and Gina Heads and Katrinka Jackson from the track team. I was supposed to live with Diana this year. We roomed together, with Amanda Van Houtte, last year at Toyon residence. But when I stayed in Calgary, my housing spot was given away. Diana had a single, and I had no place to live for the year.

I stay some nights with Diana in her tiny dorm room and some with a throwing friend, Monique Bradshaw. However, my friends are engrossed in their senior year classes and I don't want to get in the way. I mostly sleep in my car. I like the solitude. The car's Manitoba plates stick out in California, but Blue Bomber is my command central.

My stomach's rumbling, but I've already missed breakfast with Diana. She's been sharing her food plan with me. We haven't been caught yet, and it certainly saves me money.

I continue writing, making my list:

1. Shower
2. Find my bike
3. Go visit my brother

4. Find a place to live
5. Go to the registrar
6. Call Coach Ferrari

That's a big enough list for today.

Still in my Cardinal-red sweatsuit, I search the back of the car for something suitable to wear. Grabbing a small grocery bag I pack a few essentials. Next stop is the showers over at the Stanford's Arrillaga sports building.

Most mornings I wake up with the sun. I'm in an amazing location, without any pressures or classes. Slowly I move back to the reality of Stanford. Back to being a thrower. Talking to the registrar I re-enrol in classes. They won't start until January so I have time. I'm enjoying the freedom, the lack of organization, and the ability to train in the gym at any time of day.

•••••••

My car is my home for almost three weeks with some intermittent stays with friends. Then one day, I am standing in line waiting for some food with Diana, and immediately behind me is an acquaintance from the club sports world, Bobby Blunt. He's a member of the Stanford Rugby Club and I vaguely know him from the club sports: last year, I was nominated as the president of the Club Sports Council and Bobby was going to be on the board.

After briefly catching up, I tell Bobby about my predicament.

"I need a roommate. You interested?"

"Oh my gosh, yes. Where is your place?"

"Just off campus, behind Escondido Village. You can come check it out later today if you want." I take down Bobby's details and agree on a time.

Walking back towards Diana, I see her smiling from ear to ear.

"He's cuuuute," she says with a sly grin.

"Is he?" I turn and look back at Bobby. "More importantly, I think I just found a place to live."

The next day I park my Bomber in front of Bobby's house on Hanover Street and move in my stuff. Bobby, being very generous, gives me the one room in his rented 600-square-foot house. Prices for real estate in the Bay Area have skyrocketed, so having a roommate helps him too. Bobby moves into the living room where his futon serves as both bed and couch. Almost everyone at Stanford has four years of housing on campus, but Bobby is doing a fifth year master's in mechanical engineering.

The house will be a 10-minute bike ride to my classes. My life in Calgary and the whirlwind adventure of trying out for the Olympic team begins to seem like a distant memory as life starts to settle. Everything is in place for the new trimester to start in January, right after Christmas in Winnipeg.

DECEMBER 20, 1997: AN UNEXPECTED CALL (TWO WEEKS LATER)

The hardwood floor I'm sitting on is cold, but sunshine floods the living room. The phone receiver jammed to my ear, I'm trying to focus. On the other end of the line is Ray Bennett, assistant coach with the Canadian women's Olympic hockey team. This is his first year coaching women's hockey, coming from men's college hockey. He has a kind voice.

My flight home to Winnipeg for the holidays is tomorrow. I can see piles of my clothes scattered around my room through the bedroom door.

I'm surprised to get a call from Ray, and I can barely hear him. After some pleasantries, he gets right to the point.

"Would you be interested in coming to the Olympics as our third goalie?"

Silence.

I immediately stand up, my eyes darting around our small house. I pull the receiver so hard it knocks the phone right off its ledge.

Ray asks again.

Bobby's in class, so I pull the phone over to his futon and sit down next to his multi-coloured Mexican throw blanket. My face goes scarlet; I want to scream, but I've got to hold it together. *Stay focused. Stay in the moment.*

"Ummm . . . yes?" I respond, as if I'm asking him a question.

My mind is spinning. *Am I going to the Olympics?*

Ray slowly outlines what will happen from now until February when the team departs Calgary for the Olympics in Japan. I'm trying to stay with him. "Our team will finish our preparations in Calgary. We have a five-day break for Christmas and then right back to it. We just named the team yesterday, so everyone here is excited. We are coming to San Jose mid-January. You can train with us for a few days there if you like?"

"So, I'll stay here in California until then?" I ask quizzically.

"Yes, you'll meet up with us in San Jose for a few days, and then meet us in Nagano in mid-February. Our manager Glynis Peters will send your plane tickets and your Olympic clothes in the mail."

Olympic clothes? I repeat silently to myself, still in disbelief.

I wasn't even the last goalie cut. When they released me, there were still three left. Manon Rhéaume, Lesley Reddon, and Danielle Dube. *Did one of them get hurt?* I don't dare ask.

I didn't even know that Canada could bring three goalies to the Olympics. My mind is racing.

"Welcome aboard and see you in San Jose," he says enthusiastically as he ends the conversation.

I stare into the space in front of me, the phone dangling in my hand. Am I really going to the Olympics?

Slowly I dial my parents. My mom answers.

"I think I'm going . . . to the Olympics?"

· · · · · · ·

Christmas in Winnipeg is a mix of training and visiting with friends. New goalie gear covered with maple leaves arrives at my house. It's beautiful, and I can't believe it's free. News starts to spread among my friends, and a mixture of excitement and disbelief permeates nearly every encounter.

Once back at Stanford, I start classes and try to explain to each professor that I am going to be gone for three weeks of a three-month trimester. Some are incredibly supportive, while others tell me it might be best to take their class when I can be fully committed. I stay enrolled anyway, knowing I need to pass enough classes to remain eligible for the track and field team when I return. After all, track and field is still a priority.

1990: MENTORS — BADMINTON

M. Cyr, my gym teacher, is poised to serve the badminton shuttlecock, or birdie, to me while my partner, Kathryn McKenzie, waits, racquet high in the air. We are the reigning high school conference girls' doubles champs. He stares right at me with a mischievous grin, and he sends the birdie flying over my head.

My feet scramble to follow the footwork pattern he has ingrained into our memories. I turn sideways, shoulders open, arm high in the air, prancing backwards. I'm in the perfect position at the back of the court. I look high in the air, and I attack the floating birdie just as he's taught me. Shifting my feet, I whack the birdie, follow through, and scurry back to the centre of my court.

Gérald Cyr has been my gym teacher since grade six at École Norberry, and I've always looked up to him, and admired him. He excels at every sport. He never lets us win, relishing pushing our limits, and he has taught us not only the importance of practice, but also the importance of fun.

The birdie's not deep enough to be a challenge for him. I've set him up perfectly. As Kathryn and I both ready ourselves low, I can sense impending doom, yet still I tell myself I'm going to return his smash. *This time I'm going to do it.*

He swings full force and then at the last second stops his racket for a sneaky short shot. I lunge, my racquet fully stretched out.

Someday I'm going to beat him, but as the birdie ricochets off my racket into the net, I realize it won't be today.

As he taps his racquet, he says, "Bien essayé," grinning, proud of the effort and knowing he's moulded us into the athletes we are.

JANUARY 1998: MEETING THE OLYMPIC TEAM

The sun warms the Bomber as I drive California's Route 101 this chilly January morning. I've taken the day off school. As Bobby rode his bike to his classes, I packed my hockey bag into my car and made my way through Bay Area traffic, forty-five minutes south to San Jose.

Olympic team equipment manager Todd Jackson welcomes me at the front doors and escorts me down to the dressing room. It's strange to see the girls again. It is wonderful to be in the dressing room, albeit surreal, but even better to be skating with the team.

On the ice, I watch every move that Manon and Lesley make. I have no idea what happened to Danielle Dube; she was still there when I was cut but I don't know the girls well enough to ask.

I wouldn't say they are my heroes, but they're close. Lesley was playing for Team Canada at the Pacific Rim Championship I watched a few years ago in San Jose in '95. She's from Mississauga, Ontario, and the girls say she's by far the best goalie playing women's club hockey. She played at the last World Championship Final in '97, winning in overtime.

Manon is famous. Originally from Beauport, Quebec, she became renowned for being the first female to play in an NHL game; however, she was controversially cut from last year's World Championship team in favour of Danielle Dube.

It's a bit odd being around Manon because I've read a lot about her. But she is down-to-earth and so helpful to me as I learn new techniques. Both goalies have incredible work ethics. Manon is calm, yet singularly focused when she steps into the net. Lesley never stops working. When she's not involved in the team drills, she's doing movement drills off to the side.

Both are also incredibly fit; however, they're much smaller in stature than me. At 5 foot 8 and 185 pounds, I feel like a giant next to them. We are very different athletes. When I first joined the team back in September, at our first off-ice workout together, the trainer had us run a two kilometre warm-up. I was exhausted while both Lesley and Manon were near the front of the pack, easily talking, not even breaking a sweat. However, when we went into the gym, my throwing background meant I could easily bench press 165 pounds, while both Manon and Lesley were just adding small weights to the bar.

In the dressing room at the end of practice, I ask if anyone wants to tour the Bay Area.

"Oh my gosh, can I come, too?" asks Vicky Sunohara. "Can we go to Candlestick?"

Jennifer Botterill wants to come so we all hop in the car. For a few hours before our evening team dinner, I play tour guide. I drive my teammates (it's still strange to say that) through the tech headquarters of Sunnyvale and Mountain View en route to my school in Palo Alto.

Vicky's in the back seat talking non-stop about how hard the last couple of months of training have been. She wears her team-issued black fleece jacket. She's an entertainer, acting out stories like a puppeteer. Tomorrow the team takes on the Americans at the Shark Tank — home of the NHL's San Jose Sharks. The Canadians lead the pre-Olympic series six games to four, with three games remaining.

It's nice to be reunited with Jen. At 18, she's the youngest member of the team, *and* she's from Winnipeg. To begin her Olympic quest, she finished high school at a sports school in Calgary while playing club hockey for the Calgary Oval X-Treme. She gained her tryout spot through a regional camp back in May and then shortly before Christmas officially made the Olympic team. She's taking a year off before starting university at Harvard next fall.

"How's your brother doing at Cal?" She asks.

"Great, it's just on the other side of the Bay, so we get together on occasion. And he's playing for Cal's hockey team, so I get to play against him. How's your brother doing?"

I grew up playing hockey in Winnipeg against Jen's brother, Jason, who went on to win three straight World Junior Championships with Team Canada.

"Good. Their Michigan team is getting ready for the NCAAs." She is three years younger than I am, but we still found ourselves competing against each other in school sports in Winnipeg. The Botterills then moved to Calgary when Jen decided to finish high school there. They were so warm and generous they invited me over for Thanksgiving. Her mom, Doreen, is a two-time Olympic speed skater, and Jen's dad, Cal, is a famous sports psychologist working with Olympians and NHL teams, but most importantly, they are genuinely nice and welcoming people. We often reminisced about Winnipeg. They were my home away from home.

Despite a shower, my face still glows from this morning's vigorous workout. From the back seat, Vicky asks, "How far is Candlestick?" referring to the stadium where the San Francisco 49ers play football and the Giants play baseball. She's a huge football fan.

"I don't think we'll head that far north. It's up closer to San Francisco, and we might not make it back in time for dinner. But over there is Apple's headquarters."

Both girls' heads swivel. I point out the obvious Silicon Valley sights as the car slowly rolls through Bay Area traffic towards my school.

"How'd they tell you?" asks Vicky, revealing how the team is very much in the dark about my role.

As I recount the story, and my last few months, I ask about the team, the cuts, and their last few games.

I try not to ask silly questions. I am constantly reminding myself that this is real. *I actually skated with Team Canada today.*

"Crazy — they cut Angela James?" I say as we take the exit for Palo Alto. Angela is said to be the Wayne Gretzky of women's hockey, and I had read about the controversial cut in the newspapers. She and Geraldine Heaney had taken me under their wings for the short time I was in Calgary, and I was floored that she didn't make the team.

"Yeah, who knows," Vicky says as she gives some dramatic theories based mostly on gossip, but still scintillating.

"Wow, now this is California!" she exclaims, motioning to the palm trees that line the street.

I liked Vicky the minute I met her. Her enthusiasm is contagious, and she seems to want everyone to be happy. She's had me and Jen in stitches the entire ride. From Toronto, she has some of the best hands in the game making her a great set-up person who can also score.

Vicky played at the first official World Championships in 1990 as well as the first unofficial one in 1987. She went to play university hockey at Northeastern, however this was long before women's hockey was organized at the NCAA level. She dominated but got homesick and, after two years, opted to return to Toronto. Hockey became an afterthought in her life, and it wasn't until 1997 that she returned to the National Team.

As we drive down Palm Drive, I am in awe of these women — real Olympians.

3

A Lifetime of Anticipation

FEBRUARY 7, 1998: OPENING CEREMONY — NAGANO

I've only been in the Olympic Village in Japan two days, and it's already the morning of the Opening Ceremony. I am not at breakfast with my teammates; instead, I'm waiting at the gender-testing lab. Our team physiotherapist, Carrie Smith, accompanies me, explaining what I'm going to have to do.

"What? I have to prove I'm a girl?"

Carrie calms my nerves as she explains that the procedure simply requires a swab of the inside of my cheek to test for X-X chromosomes. I can still feel my freshly inked Canadian Olympic tattoo that I got last week. I'd been a little apprehensive, but Monique, my friend from school, took me up to San Francisco after one of our classes and sat through it with me. *The mark of an Olympian.*

The receptionist attempts my name with a strong Japanese accent. Her white gown suggests she may also be one of the nurses. She smiles, bows, and escorts me alone to the first station where she provides me with a questionnaire. I still can't believe I'm at the Olympics, let alone undergoing some test to prove that I'm female. *If I am the third goalie and there's no chance I'll play in games, why go through this trouble?* I don't ask those questions.

Carrie has already been through this with the other 20 women on the team, but because I arrived two days later, I go through the experience on my own.

With the testing done, I rush back to my room to scan my Opening Ceremony attire. I see a bowl of dry cereal I picked up yesterday and scarf that down as I look at the clothes I've hung on the back of my door in preparation for today. I finish eating, disrobe, and slowly put each piece of clothing on based on the specific order given to us.

I peek out of my room into the hallway to see if any of my roommates are ready. Not yet. I have my own room but share a common area with five other teammates. I double-check the list to make sure I have on all the pieces of clothing I need. Our uniforms, made by Roots, are already the talk of the Olympics.

Black fleece pants with red piping? Check.

Black boots with an ingenious maple leaf tread? Check.

Red mock turtleneck with Olympic rings logo? Check.

Nagano scarf? Check. Red poor-boy hat? Check.

I examine myself in the mirror one last time and smile ear to ear. I proudly present myself as a real Olympian. I'm not sure I feel real, but this uniform suggests I belong.

Out in the hallway, I can hear a voice. Lesley is fidgeting with her hat, looking at herself in the hall mirror, twisting it in different directions trying to figure out how it's supposed to fit.

"Looks good, Lesley," I say as I sneak past her.

Poking my head in the next room I see Judy Diduck and Cassie Campbell sitting with their feet up, laughing and joking while also most likely sweating profusely under layers of fleece.

Judy, a defenceman from Sherwood Park, Alberta, holds a three-inch plastic princess figurine in the air and with a huge grin says, "Princess is ready for her big moment."

I don't know too much about the figurine, but I heard Judy bought it at some McDonald's on one of the numerous road trips the team took across the country. Judy seems like the team practical joker, always making people laugh and injecting energy into every interaction. She leads the warm-ups as well as most cheers. Princess has become a mascot of sorts, making her way into countless photos, including, if you look hard enough, the official Hockey Canada photo.

I didn't even make that photo.

Cassie is a defenceman from Brampton, Ontario. She was the poster girl at last year's World Championships in Kitchener and has been featured in many of the news clippings my mom mailed to me at school. My parents are very excited for me and this opportunity, and my mom was constantly cutting articles out of Canadian newspapers and magazines with reminders about the upcoming Olympics.

Cassie's constantly making sarcastic jokes and seems to like to have a good time. I'm in awe around her. She's warm, charismatic, and magnetic. She's one of the few female athletes in Canada with major sponsors, and I feel amongst stardom in her presence. Cassie's like the cool girl at school that everyone gravitates to.

I make my way towards the common area where I find the huge grins of Hayley Wickenheiser and Geraldine Heaney. The nine of us (including Princess) make our way outside.

Canadian athletes from all the other sports have already congregated. I find Jennifer Botterill with her roommate, Becky Kellar. Becky's from a small town southwest of Toronto called Hagersville. When we first met, she said to me, "You know, where the tire fire was?" I hadn't heard of Hagersville or the tire fire, but she sure was proud of her town.

Seeing Wally Kozak across the field, I run over to embrace him. His belief in me is the reason I'm here. Despite being a mentor to our coaches, he's helping coach the host Japanese women's hockey team and is dressed in Japanese regalia. We quickly catch up and I head back to join my teammates.

Not all our team is walking in the ceremony. Sadly, Danielle Goyette, from Saint-Nazaire, Quebec, learned last night that her father passed away at home in Quebec. He had been afflicted with Alzheimer's. I can't imagine how incredibly hard this day must be for her, being so far away from home, having to choose between attending the funeral and being with family or staying and pursuing her dream. Stacy Wilson, our captain and one of Goyette's good friends, decided to stay back in the village and support Goyette as she grieved and struggled with this decision.

The rest of us make our way to a holding area just outside the stadium. Anticipation fills the air, though the ceremonies don't start for another hour, and the athletes won't march for at least another two. Hurry up and wait — that's what today feels like. This is different from *big game* nervousness because I can't mess this up. I mingle with the other athletes, chatting with Canadians from other sports, and find the ice dancers who were on my flight from California. I'm an Olympics junky, consequently seeing all these athletes up close and personal is a bit unnerving — I do my best to mask my awe.

From the holding area, we're summoned to walk towards the Minami Nagano Sports Park Stadium. We approach it like bees to a hive — the stadium is packed. The pulsating noise travels like an echo, and in less than an hour, we will be inside the stadium *and* on television for the world to see.

Underneath the stadium, we are in the shadows. Athletes fill the distance as far as I can see. In front, above the heads of my teammates, is the Canadian flag, held high by Jean-Luc Brassard, a freestyle moguls skier and Canada's flag bearer.

You'd think that mere moments before we enter the stadium in front of the world, we'd share words of motivation among friends, but no. We've exhausted most of our conversation. In the dimness, we simply wait. Words are distractions. We are moving slowly closer to our moment.

Greece always enters an Olympic stadium first, an honour for having hosted the first Games. Countries are then introduced in alphabetical order. Lining the tunnel are entertainers in various stages of dress preparing for their cues. Young Japanese kids stare wide-eyed in their white powder-puff costumes.

I can sense we are close. Off in the distance, I can see the opening leading inside the arena like a bright guiding star. The roar of the crowd gets louder. The hallway is wide enough for only three or four of us. We lose touch with the group in front and run to catch up. Hurry up. Wait. All I can see is the bright opening. Slowly we move. The narrow hallway opens into a larger staging area. One of the organizers is yelling something in Japanese into a headset. She holds a clipboard, and her hands direct others who run into action. It seems like hundreds of elements are meshing under her orders.

The Canadian mission staff has laid out the marching plan a dozen or more times in the last four hours, but now it's for real. We squeeze into rows of eight. I don't like my spot in the middle. I want to be on the edge. I dreamed about walking into the stadium on the edge. I see our chef de mission run down the line of athletes. As soon as they are out of sight, I move. There's chaos in this area and no one notices. I'm about five rows back from our flag.

Team Canada veteran Geraldine Heaney is directly behind me. I turn and give a precocious smile. She scored an incredible Bobby Orr–like goal in 1990 that continues to make the evening sports highlights. She is a playmaking defenceman, often joining the rush. Heaney is in great shape and runs like she could easily complete a marathon but, being of Irish descent, which she has reiterated numerous times to me, she also likes to have a few beers. Geraldine and Angela James took time to include me while I was at tryouts in Calgary. They went out of their way to ensure I felt welcomed, and while I didn't really get to know them well, I am forever grateful.

Another veteran, France Saint-Louis, our oldest player at 39, is on my right. She and Heaney have been members of Team Canada since its inception in 1990. Both have played nearly their entire lives likely never imagining this could be a reality for female hockey players.

Spinning around I find Jen. I wave for her to come up. I grab her elbow and pull her next to me. I ask her if I look all right. She reciprocates. Hats are on straight, logos in the right spots. We wait.

1984: PRIDE — WATCHING ON TV

I'm on our gold plush family room carpet, legs stretched out under the coffee table. I am eight years old and wearing my Team Canada quarter-length sleeve mock hockey jersey — my favourite shirt. I've spread papers out like a university student studying for exams. The Opening Ceremony for the 1984 Los Angeles Summer Olympics plays on TV as I squint to make out the details. I frantically write on the papers, documenting everything.

I draw out the flags of each country as they march into the stadium. At commercial breaks, I ask my mom where a country is on the map.

My mom has a degree from the University of Toronto in geography and has the atlas beside her, ready to point out even the smallest countries. The procession is too fast, but I know we are taping the show on our Betamax. I can go back later for the countries I miss.

"Where is Cameroon?" I keep writing and drawing.

My brother at 11 is much wiser than I am. He knows so much about the Olympics. I follow his gaze. Canada is coming out soon. We are both swimmers for the Manitoba Marlins, and he already talks about the Olympics as a future dream. He holds nearly every Manitoba age-group record. I look up to him and at almost every turn try to emulate him. I go fast in the water because he goes fast. I play hockey because he plays hockey. Because he wants to go to the Olympics, I want to go too.

I hear the announcers proclaim "Canada" and look up to a sea of white and red.

I picture myself in the procession, waving to the crowd.

"There's Alex!" my brother says with glee as Canadian swimmer Alex Baumann appears on screen carrying the flag for Canada into the Los Angeles Memorial Coliseum.

"I think that's Victor Davis and maybe Anne Ottenbrite?" I write their names down. I know my brother will be there someday, and I'll point him out in the crowd as he marches in. I know their names because my brother has their posters on his bedroom wall.

As Canada walks around the stadium, my dad is in his usual spot on the couch behind the coffee table.

"What it must be like to walk into that stadium . . ." my dad says, leaning closer to the TV as my mom comes and sits next to him, taking a reprieve from making dinner. I can see the pride in my parents' faces; this is a significant moment.

FEBRUARY 7, 1998: OPENING CEREMONY — NAGANO (CONTINUED)

Our group is idle. Waiting. Jean-Luc steps forward with the flag, separating himself from the rest of us. He will march a few paces in front. I watch as the Japanese sumo wrestler who will lead our contingent joins Jean-Luc. A small girl dressed as a snowflake accompanies him. I take my final picture on my disposable camera by lifting my arm high in the air, and then tuck it into the team-issued red fanny pack hidden under my jacket. Organizers physically push us into straight rows of eight.

Jean-Luc's movement ripples back to us. This still doesn't feel real. I try to stay in line with my row, marching almost in unison. The ground is white, the stadium is white, and the crowd roars.

I hear over the loudspeakers, first in English, then in French, then in Japanese, "Please welcome: Canada."

The crowd erupts as we take our first tentative steps into the stadium. We follow Jean-Luc, but I soon lose sight of him as I take in the crowd. I see other athletes wave, so I do too. I don't know who I'm waving to. I'm trying not to wave like the queen, trying to make it real. I'm trying to act natural, but nothing is natural about this situation. I am beaming.

I can't see the TV cameras, but they must be on us. What are my friends doing right now? It's 3:00 a.m. in Winnipeg. My parents are for sure watching. I wave to them through the camera, thinking to myself how proud they must be. I hope my brother is awake in California. I smile at Jen beside me and yell, "This is awesome!"

The announcer has moved on to the countries behind us as we make our way around the stadium. I look for Canadian flags in the stands and wave in their direction. Waving at something makes me feel less strange. I am actually on the other side of the TV screen, being broadcast to millions.

Our journey around the stadium takes about five minutes, but I feel a lifetime of memories flood back to me. From my beginnings as a swimmer, to the countless school and community sports I played, I'm grateful for all the incredible coaches and teammates I've been fortunate to have had. And most of all, I think of my parents and my brother, walking these steps with me, despite being thousands of miles away.

I can hear the crowd roar as they introduce each country. Jean-Luc disappears, and I spin around one last time to appreciate my circumstance. Someone is pushing me from behind, herding me to a seat. I want to sit beside my hockey teammates. I hold my position and push through. I find a seat next to Jen and Becky and drop down. Athletes scoot past me. My heart still races.

Am I an Olympian now?

FEBRUARY 8, 1998: BEST SEAT IN THE HOUSE

It's game day, and I walk along the sidewalk of a neighbourhood in Nagano. The air is still warm enough that I don't need my toque. My Team Canada boots leave maple leaf imprints on the wet walkway. There's snow on the ground, but grass pokes through.

Our team arrived at the arena nearly an hour ago for our first game against the host, Japan. Riding the bus with my teammates from the Olympic Village to the arena, I then made my way to the dressing room.

Everyone looked busy. The coaching staff, Shannon Miller, Ray Bennett, and Danièle Sauvageau, were off in a separate room going over game notes, tweaking match-ups. Carrie, our athletic therapist, was going over last-minute medical checks with our massage therapist, Holly Mair, and team doctor, Dr. Louise Walker. Our equipment manager, Todd Jackson, rushes around, ensuring all the equipment is ready and skates are sharp — all this happens while our GM, Glynis Peters, seems to be engrossed in dealing with media inquiries alongside our media relations manager, Joanne Gray.

I'm the only one without much to do, though I don't want it to seem that way. I chit-chat with the girls as they get into their warm-up clothes, then pretend I am needed somewhere else and find the nearest exit for my own little adventure.

I tucked my camera in my backpack before we left the Village. I'm still enrolled in Photography 101 at university, and I need to get some good black and white shots.

As I walk the streets, the sky is still bright, and I can't help but think I really should be in class in Stanford, California. *How fortunate am I?* I have an hour before I want to be back. I make my way to the main street, my boots crunching the snow. Flags adorn every lamp post and I grab my camera to take a picture of a McDonald's with Japanese writing. Familiar things in foreign lands seem strange. I can tell locals are pointing at me. This makes me proud — *I am an Olympian. I marched in the Opening Ceremony so I must be an Olympian.* I nod and smile as locals take my picture. I walk taller, prouder than when I left the rink.

I can see the Aqua Wing Arena way off in the distance. No one would miss me if I didn't make it back in time for warm-up, but I don't want to miss a thing. Despite not knowing my place, I feel like the most fortunate sports junky in the world. I'm a tourist at the Olympics with an all-access behind-the-scenes pass.

4

Stars All Around Me

FEBRUARY 10, 1998: DAY OFF

Jen, Becky, and I walk down the side streets of one of the Nagano districts, sneaking through back alleys. We play the "remember when" game of telling stories, each one more unbelievable than the next.

"Remember when Nike gave us an entire bag of free clothes?" Becky shouts.

"Remember when the Canadian Olympic Committee surprised us with new BlackBerry phones?" Jen countered.

"Remember when I chatted with Wayne Gretzky about hockey in California, or asked Curtis Joseph about his goalie gear, or when my goalie idol Vladislav Tretiak pulled me in tight for a photo . . . *maybe a little too tight?*" I quickly add. We laugh.

"Remember when we watched Catriona Le May Doan skate to a gold medal, *live?*" says Becky in disbelief.

Becky, Jen, and Kathy McCormack from New Brunswick are the only rookies on the team. And me, I suppose. Becky just graduated from Brown University where she played alongside one of the top American players, Katie King.

Kathy, a big strong forward from Blackville, New Brunswick, attends University of New Brunswick where Lesley Reddon is doing her master's degree and played for the men's CIAU team, the UNB Varsity

Reds from 94-96. Along with Thérèse Brisson, who is a professor of kinesiology at UNB, and Stacy Wilson, originally from Salisbury, New Brunswick, all four play for the Maritime Sports Blades winning a silver at the National Championship in '95 and a bronze in '96.

The tournament started with an easy 13–0 victory over Japan. Wally did all he could to keep his team in the game. It was 0–0 after the first period, but by the second period Japan was so fatigued they couldn't get it out of their zone. Despite the lopsided victory, the home crowd was in love with Vicky Sunohara. Signs all around the rink read *Sunohara*. The lone Japanese Canadian on the team, she is the toast of Nagano, the Japanese nationals seeing her as their hero. Her dad, who'd passed away a few years prior, was from this area, and many of his family have come to see Vicky. She even went with her mom, a Ukrainian Canadian, to a Sunohara family gathering where they celebrated the heroine.

This Olympics has only six teams. We are the top seed and will play against all the teams in this tournament. The top two teams will then play for the gold medal.

In the second game, we faced China. Guo Hong, known as "The Great Wall of China," stood on her head but we still came away with a 2–0 victory. Danielle Goyette scored one of our goals, on top of her hat trick against Japan. Thus far, she's been our best player, despite her grief.

There are no games today, so Jen, Becky, and I decide to venture out of the Olympic Village and into town.

I met Becky when I officially joined the tryout roster back at the end of September. I was living at my friend Gillian's in the eclectic part of Calgary known as Kensington Village. My daily commute to the rink on the train was on the same line Becky took. She's fun to be around, calm, and easy to talk to. We often saw each other on our commute. She was living with another teammate, Tammy Lee Shewchuk, from Montreal, who was on a year's sabbatical from Harvard University. Unfortunately, Shewchuk didn't make the team, but I was excited when I heard Becky did.

It's surreal to be walking the streets of Nagano with two real Olympians. I try not to embarrass them, but I love recounting their big plays, or team-saving moments. These are the fun moments for me. *What must it be like to be on the ice?* I so desperately want to ask, but I don't want to sound ridiculous.

Sitting on my goalie bag outside a locked door at the University of Manitoba's rink, I'm 15 years old. It's 6:30 a.m. and I've tucked my head inside the neck of my jacket trying to shield my face from the cold November wind sailing across the prairies. My jacket isn't providing enough insulation. The wind is ripping through my sweatpants, and I'm regretting not grabbing a toque when my friend Susie Yuen picked me up in her Jeep this morning. I long for the snuggly-ness of my bed that I was in a mere 30 minutes ago.

The days here in Winnipeg are getting shorter and the morning sun still hasn't completely shown itself. My hands in my mitts, I fiddle with my goalie stick, huddled on top of my bag, hoping that Susie has found an open door somewhere on the other side of the building. Susie's bag nestles against mine, and occasionally I glance up through the glass panes looking for signs of life inside.

I see nothing but unreachable warmth. I love these practices because most of the players are University of Manitoba alumni or guys looking for a good scrimmage to get them ready for their pro seasons, including my teammate Jamie Bettens's older brother Mike. He plays pro in Europe. Susie and I are the only girls. I'm heavily outmatched, but Susie thinks I'm good enough to be here.

Susie is 10 years older than I am. In my eyes, she's a superstar, having already played at the first ever World Championships in 1990 with Team Canada. The World Championships in women's hockey are every two years, and she's training to make the next Worlds' team heading to Finland in April. I have a picture of Susie on my bedroom wall hoisting the World Championship plate right beside a picture of female sports star Abigail Hoffman and great Russian goaltender Vladislav Tretiak.

I jokingly say that she is my "Little" Big Sis, because at only 4 foot 11, I already tower over her; but get her on the ice and she plays anything but small. She holds her own with these guys, never giving an inch, always playing hard.

I first met Susie earlier this year, prior to leaving for the Canada Games with my Manitoba team. She came and chatted with us, and I was captivated. When Susie asked me to come and play with her, I jumped at the opportunity. We've been training together all summer, and I'm learning how hockey players train. She is exactly where I want to be. I love listening to her stories, hearing about her teammates, and as she talks, I don't just think about the possibilities, I plan for the future. I glance up to see some feet through the doors and they instantly thrust open as Susie bounds out. I quickly stand, excited to get inside. I grab both our sticks, and head inside towards the dressing room reserved for us.

FEBRUARY 14, 1998: GAME AGAINST USA

Today we play the last round robin game, against Team USA. Even though this is a "meaningless" game on the score sheet, it always means something when we play them. The teams are evenly matched. We have played each other 13 times this season in exhibition games and the series is 7–6, barely in our favour.

As warm-up begins, I am sitting next to defenceman Fiona Smith. The Nagano Aqua Wing Arena area reserved for Olympic athletes is at rink level right across from the players benches and close to the penalty boxes. Fiona is a nimble, quick defenceman from Edam, Saskatchewan. She is capable of joining the rush or making a nifty breakout pass, always creating something. She'd much rather be playing but she took a hit to the head in the last game, against Finland, and hasn't been feeling right.

After our day off, we played Sweden who had stunned us less than a week earlier in a pre-Olympic exhibition match with a 1–1 draw. Lesley Reddon started the third round robin game in net for Canada and, despite a few bad bounces, looked good guiding the team to a 5–3 victory.

The following day we played Finland who almost upset Canada in the semis at last year's Worlds. The Finns are perhaps the best team, other than Canada and the USA, in the world. Manon Rhéaume played and was solid in a 4–2 win.

Fiona and I watch the conclusion of the warm-up and leave our jackets to mark our territory before heading to the dressing room. I feel bad for Fiona, but I like having her with me. I've missed so much of the year, and it's nice to be able to hear about the team from her. I ask about players, about positions, and lineups. As we make our way through the media gauntlet, I'm all but invisible next to a star defencemen sidelined with an "undisclosed injury."

"Sami, keep walking, just pretend we're talking the whole time," says Fiona, who doesn't let me stop despite the many questions shouted in her direction.

Once in the dressing room, the air is light. Both teams have already qualified for the finals, so there isn't much pressure. France Saint-Louis, always very focused, goes over some last-minute Xs and Os with her linemates. Vicky, sitting in her stall, has her corner in hysterics, as usual. Everyone seems relaxed yet excited to play.

As soon as coach Shannon Miller finishes her pre-game speech, Lesley walks past me. I tap her on the pads and wish her luck. She nods, smiles, and bobs her head to let me know she is ready.

1987: MOTIVATED — TRACK PRACTICE

It's a hot, sticky Winnipeg day, and I am riding my 10-speed bike behind two of my best friends, Adam Salem and Dermot McDonald, as we pedal towards the University of Manitoba. Dermot lives at the end of my street, and Adam lives one street over. School is out for the summer, and we often go on adventures.

Dermot's mom passed away when he was only five years old, his dad was left to raise him and his twin brother, Declan, and their older sister. Dermot is often at my house, before school eating cereal at our breakfast table and after school walking home from the bus stop together. He has a ton of energy, like Tigger from Winnie-the-Pooh, often wanting to explore the neighbourhood.

It is a long ride for an 11-year-old over the busy Bishop Grandin Bridge, but we are on a mission to watch a boy from our school, who has joined the Takus track club.

I love track and field days at school. We are at École Norberry, a French immersion school, but our divisional meets are held at the local English high school because they have a full-sized track. This year, Adam won all the distance races, as he usually does. Ever since we joined cross-country, he's been the best runner in the school. Dermot won the high jump, and I won some of the girls' races but excelled in the field portion of the day.

At the Bisons outdoor track and field complex on University Drive, we park our bikes in the bushes. We have no plan. We don't want to be caught spying or get into trouble, so we slowly climb the stairs into the grandstands. As we enter the seating area, we lie prone on the ground, attempting to be invisible.

What we see is incredible. The stadium is filled with athletes. Coaches bark orders, check their stopwatches, and measure jumps and throws. In the hot sun, we slip around the far end of the grandstands and climb down behind a hill. Peering over the rise, we can see sprinters as they explode out of real race-starting blocks. They look so professional. The entire stadium is a dizzying array of athletes running, jumping, and throwing. I think to myself, *This is how you get better. This is how real athletes train.*

"Can you ask my parents if I can join?" Adam whispers to me. "If you tell them you're doing it, they'll let me." His dad is an engineer from Egypt, and his mom is from the Philippines, and both seem to value good grades at school, which maybe is why they think I'm a good influence on Adam.

"Could you imagine if we got to train on this track?" says Dermot as we pedal home.

The whole way back, Adam, Dermot, and I try to figure out a way to join a track club. We leave our bikes in my garage and head to the park behind my house. We bring a tape measure, some hockey sticks, and some bricks and proceed to make hurdles. We are constantly in a state of play and learning, pushing each other, creating new games and new obstacles, and dreaming that someday we too will be like the athletes we saw on the *real* track.

FEBRUARY 14, 1998: GAME AGAINST USA (CONTINUED)

Our team comes out strong. The score is tied 1–1 after the second period, but we appear to have everything under control. As we make our way back to the room to hear coach Shannon Miller's between periods speech, I say to Fiona, "This looks too easy."

Fiona quickly counters, "Yeah, but Lesley shouldn't have to bail us out so much. We're letting mental mistakes creep in." Fiona's right: despite a 1–1 tie after the second, we are not playing our best hockey. Lori Dupuis scored early in the first on a pass from Vicky, but we are having mental lapses, not supporting each other on breakouts and making passes that are just out of reach.

In the dressing room, Shannon sounds angry. She's not impressed. She yearns for perfection, and we are still far from it. There is no laughter in the dressing room anymore. No one wants to make the next mistake.

Fiona doesn't feel good as we sit back down in our seats for the third period. "Did you notice the room was silent? That's not us. We look nervous."

Despite Fiona's worry, we score with ease. The Americans are rolling four lines, letting everyone touch the ice. Casually, they even switched their starting goalie, Sarah Tueting, for Sara DeCosta halfway through the game.

Six minutes into the third period, we continued our momentum and Canada is up 4–1. The Americans are playing a physical game; perhaps they are trying to send a message for the finals.

Slowly, like a singer with an itch in her throat, we start to derail. Fiona's premonition proves fatal, and we can sense the momentum shift. Our team is playing not to lose. Instead of the pre-game warm-up's smiling faces, I see the fear of failure. An American barrage ensues, and despite Lesley's best attempts, nothing seems to be working. The Americans find the net an incredible five times, including an empty net goal, to secure the game.

Fiona and I are in disbelief. I feel sick to my stomach for Lesley. The team gave up on her. Ricochets, deflections, bouncing pucks — we have all the excuses, but the Americans have the scoreboard and the mental victory.

Maybe the loss will be good for us. Maybe that fiasco is the spark we need. Despite it being Valentines Day, the handshake at the end of the game is anything but loving and it turns into a skirmish, when apparently an American player goads Goyette with a taunt about her father's death. Players push and shove each other until the refs intervene while an agitated Goyette skates off the ice.

There were some positives to the game such as Vicky's line, with Jayna Hefford and Lori Dupuis scoring three of our five goals. We outshot them for the game and had a shot total of 21–13 in the third period, but we had some bad luck. We need to focus on the good.

Now, going into the Olympic women's final, despite Canada having won all four World Championships ever played, we find ourselves in a strange situation. We have become the underdogs.

5

The First Ever Women's Olympic Hockey Gold

FEBRUARY 17, 1998: GOLD MEDAL GAME

The third period of the first ever women's Olympic hockey final is about to start. The Americans lead 1–0 on a power play goal by Gretchen Ulion, but I still have faith.

I make my way to the athletes' section behind our net, at the Big Hat Arena. We played our previous round robin games across town at the Aqua Wing, but this rink is much bigger. Fiona Smith is back in the lineup, so am alone. I find my row and squish through the other spectators to my open seat.

Sitting directly behind me are about a dozen players from the Canadian men's hockey team. All of them are All-Stars in the NHL, but here they are just Olympians. It's odd to see them dressed in matching Team Canada outfits. Eric Lindros, a star with the Philadelphia Flyers, is inquisitive.

"Here, we saved your seat. What did the coach say? How'd the girls look?"

"Good . . . I think. They were kind of quiet . . . Coach was harping about support and told them to shoot more."

Eric nods, but the play starts, so the conversation halts. There was more to the dressing room conversation, but it was for our ears. Down by a goal, coach Shannon Miller did what she does best: not Xs and Os, but inspiration.

She presses play on a video depicting generations of women playing before us. Each Canadian National Team and a series of images of women who helped make this Olympic dream possible.

"So many women have battled throughout history so we could have this Olympic moment," Shannon Miller exclaims as the video ends.

"The American team has not respected us, they have attempted to derail us, trash talked us, but we are bigger than that, we are classier than that. No matter what happens, you must hold your head high, skate with pride together. This is not just for you, but also for an entire generation to follow you."

As she finishes, France Saint-Louis, respected by everyone in the room, leads us one last time in our team chant, and at the end we all yell "Together!" in unison.

I can't get comfortable. My seat is four rows up from the glass. Athletes from other Canadian sports teams and other nations surround me, chatting with each other, but no one has as much riding on this game as I do. That's my team.

Manon Rhéaume is on the ice directly in front of me. The play is in the neutral zone, but I still see her head turning, focused on the puck. She has made some big saves this game, but Sarah Tueting, the American goalie, has too. The only American goal came on the power play just a couple minutes into the second period, but Manon didn't have much of a chance — the US power play moves the puck amazingly well. Both teams have had their opportunities, but the goalies have been the stars thus far.

The light reflects off the Plexiglas as the Americans put pressure in our zone. Manon is in her ready position. She is the reason this game is only 1–0. She shuffles around her crease at a perfect angle for every shot. My body flinches, mimicking her saves.

Manon got the start for us today. I'm not sure if the coaches would have started her if we hadn't lost our last round robin game to the Americans 7–4 two days ago. I don't know the politics behind the starts. Lesley Reddon was in net that game, and I feel bad for her, relegated to the bench today, the scapegoat in the loss. Lesley was the goalie in the '97 World Championship Finals last year in Kitchener when Canada won in overtime. Manon didn't even make the team last year, but she was the starting goalie at both the 1992 and 1994 World Championships, so she is no stranger to this action.

Manon has been a hero to a generation of female athletes because of her opportunity to play in the NHL. She played a period in a pre-season game for the Tampa Bay Lightning, and it made the quest for professional hockey a dream for many of us.

None of the female stars get much recognition outside female hockey circles, so coming into tryout camp, like most Canadians, I knew Manon's name from her NHL debut. Last year she was cut from the team — it seemed as though she and Shannon Miller would never see eye to eye. But Manon battled back and is now starting for Canada in the Olympic final. She's been proving critics wrong her whole life, and here is another chance to do just that.

1992: INSPIRATION — MANON RHÉAUME

Sitting nervously in the sound booth of Manitoba's French radio station, CKXL, I am 16 years old in grade 10 at Collège Jeanne-Sauvé. I have been on the radio several times being interviewed about participating on Canada's national junior track and field team, and I was recently the Junior Jets reporter on CBC. However, although I am in French immersion, I have never done a full radio show speaking only in French.

To add to the stress, the hosts are set to call up one of the best female goalies on the planet, Manon Rhéaume. I sit with my giant headphones on in front of a large microphone, watching the two hosts as they take direction from the producer, André Brin. Suddenly the intro music plays and in French they start: "I'm Jacques Lévèque and I'm here with Charles LaFlèche. In studio we have Sami Jo Small, a local goaltender with the St. Vital Victorias, and on the telephone we have Manon Rhéaume, who has made national headlines because she became the first ever woman to play hockey at the Junior level with the Trois-Rivières Draveurs. I believe she is about to report to an Ottawa Senators camp. Is Manon there? Good evening, Manon."

"Yes, hello, but just one correction, it's not the Ottawa Senators — it will be the Tampa Bay Lightning."

"Wow, well that's way more interesting, at least you'll be able to head to the beach too." Manon laughs. "Well, Manon, perhaps you could help us out for any listeners who are not totally up-to-date. Can you give us a brief history of your career to date?"

"So, I started playing hockey when I was five years old, like most of the little boys that lived in my neighbourhood. There was no girls' team, so if I wanted to play, I had to play with the boys. It was the same evolution as most other boys and in fact some of the boys I played with are now playing in the NHL or the Major Junior leagues."

I listen intently to every word Manon says. She seems smart and speaks with such elegance. She continues, "Last season I was the alternate goalie on the QJMHL's Trois-Rivières Draveurs. I did the training camp with them and ended it with the best goals against average. I returned to Junior Tier II, and I would get called whenever there was an injury to the Major Junior goalie."

"Manon, I just wanted to remind you that in-studio right now we have Sami Jo Small. She is our Manon of Manitoba." I feel my face turning red, but at least Manon can't see it. I try to play it cool.

"Bonjour."

"And Sami Jo follows your career closely," adds Jacques, putting me even more on the spot.

But Manon's seasoned at interviews and instantly makes me feel like a peer.

"I think it's really fun to see there are others scattered everywhere. When we are young, we don't have a chance to start with the girls, so we have to start with boys. It's fun to see there are other girls in other places attempting to break through the glass ceiling. Because it's not easy. There's still a lot of prejudice out there, and it's been there since I started playing and it will be there for a long time. Whenever a girl has a chance to crack a lineup on a team, it's great. When the Draveurs gave me my chance . . . it's probably not a lot of other teams that would have given a girl a chance like that."

I listen carefully as Charles and Jacques go on to ask how the guys accept her, if they try to hurt her, and, of course, the question I get all the time, how the change rooms work. Manon is a pro in her answers, politically correct, but funny. *She's even better than I imagined.* I can't believe I'm actually talking (kind of) to her.

"Manon, do you see that eventually it will be more accepted?"

"I think that more and more there's an improvement in women's hockey. Now there's a World Championship and hopefully, someday, there will be an Olympics. So, if it evolves like this, I'm sure that young girls will get to start playing on teams with other young girls. That will help a lot to have more players because lots of parents don't want to send their daughter to play hockey with the boys. I think because I had two brothers, I was used to being around all boys, so it didn't bother me. But there are lots of girls who wouldn't be comfortable. Women's hockey is evolving, and at the same time, people are seeing more and more that women can play hockey. So, seeing girls play with boys is way more accepted now than it was before."

I'm staring at the giant black microphone, picturing Manon on the other end of the phone. I smile and nod as she talks as if she's directing her answers just to me. The radio hosts steer the conversation towards the differences between men's and women's hockey, while I picture Manon on the ice, battling with the Draveurs.

Charles asked the next questions. "Tampa Bay, it should be a great experience?"

"Of course . . . I have the opportunity, and I'm going to take it. This happens once in a lifetime, and if I don't take it, I'm sure I'd regret it someday."

"Can we talk briefly about World Championship hockey? How do we pick the National Team? Is there a formal process? Does each province supply a certain number of players?"

Manon goes on to describe the process.

Manon turns the conversation to me, "Sami, you play with a boys' team?"

"Yes, I think like you?" I say, embarrassed that I have just compared myself to the great Manon Rhéaume.

"She's our Manon." Charles jokes.

"That's fun. Don't give up. You never know when you'll get an opportunity. When you get the chance, take it and show them what you're capable of."

"Yes, of course." I grin as if I've just heard the wisest words spoken.

"Don't give up. And I hope everything goes great for you."

"Thank you so much."

I am still beaming, even more assured about my future in hockey. I'm thinking about how our trajectories are similar: *If Manon can do it, then maybe I can.* The radio hosts push the conversation towards *Playboy*'s invitation to Manon to be in their pages. She answers graciously about it not coinciding with her morals and redirects them back to hockey.

"Manon, of course we'll hear about you in the fall, but then after that do you think you'll play at the national level?"

"With the National Team, if it goes to the Olympics in 1994, of course that will interest me to have that experience. It would be the ultimate hockey experience. I've been to the World Championship, I've played Junior, and I will have been to an NHL training camp. That would nicely end my career. I won't be playing hockey my whole life. I've already started working at RDS [TSN] to be a reporter. I'll put more energy into that because that's what I want to do."

"Thanks so much, Manon. I know you have to go shortly. And good luck in Tampa Bay."

Manon responds, "And I just wanted to say good luck to Sami Jo."

"Oh, thank you so much and you too," I say, as politely as I can.

FEBRUARY 17, 1998: GOLD MEDAL GAME (CONTINUED)

We seem calmer, playing with a renewed sense of purpose, but still we can't beat their goalie. As the puck careens through the neutral zone, Danielle Goyette collides with Shelley Looney, and the referee's arm goes up. Who is the penalty on? Us or them? As the ref's arm comes down, she points to Goyette, and once again we must try to combat the lethal American power play.

The bright lights of the arena make it as if I'm watching this game on TV. The crowd is exuberant if not exactly the most hockey knowledge-able. Whistles get louder cheers than goals or hits. As the Americans ice the puck, the entire stadium enters into a melodic, harmonized chant, a Japanese tradition.

"Faceoff! . . . Faceoff! . . . Faceoff, faceoff, faceoff!"

Team USA sets up with the puck in their power play formation and sends it to Sue Merz who, on the point, sends it down low to Manon's left, to Jenny Schmidgall. From my vantage point, I can see an open American player, Shelley Looney, to Manon's right. *But can Manon see her?*

"Cassie, behind you!" I shout, trying to alert our defenceman Cassie Campbell.

Schmidgall leaves it for Gretchen Ulion down low. Ulion scored their first goal and is always a threat with the puck. Ulion passes the puck back to the point to an awaiting Merz who quickly fires it to Looney on Manon's right. Manon reads the play, but Looney, all alone, deflects the shot-pass over Manon's pad.

2–0 Team USA, with only nine minutes left to play for the gold medal.

We're running out of time. With just over four minutes left, we finally get a power play. On the ensuing play, Wick out-battles an American behind goalie Tueting to retrieve our puck. Wick's been working hard all game, and all tournament. She's an emotional player who plays on the edge. She is so intense. It's not strange to see her in her dressing room stall alone, quietly staring straight ahead, grinding her teeth as she rocks back and forth. During the round robin game against the Americans, I walked into the dressing room between periods to see our doctor stitching up Wick's elbow. Blood all over her elbow pad, but she refused to stop. She's tough.

She sees Goyette alone in front of the net. Goyette one-times Wick's pass. Goyette rarely misses from that spot and cuts the American lead in half. Geraldine Heaney joins them in the celebration but it's stoic. There's still a hill to climb.

2–1 Team USA. Four minutes to play.

It's only fitting that Goyette scored. She's led us in scoring all tournament, and she's been the centre of controversy since she arrived. First she lost her father the day before the Opening Ceremony, then words were exchanged in the handshake after our round robin loss to the Americans; allegedly American Sandra Whyte said something regarding her dad, and Goyette left the ice heated, causing the media to exacerbate the issue. Nevertheless, she has still managed to carry our team.

We ache for more. The American goalie, Sarah Tueting, is standing on her head. She played at the 1997 Worlds, but didn't play the final; here she's putting on an incredible performance. The intensity is palpable as bodies fly in all directions.

With just under a minute left, and the score 2–1, Manon skates out of Canada's net for an extra attacker. Our coach has Jen on the ice. That's a lot of confidence put into Jen, and I want her to be the hero. We attack, but Tueting covers the puck, and Shannon Miller calls a time out.

Our team gathers around Coach Miller, looking at her whiteboard. I can't see what she is writing, but I assume it's a faceoff play with the puck deep in the US zone and some last-minute words of inspiration.

With 54 seconds until the final buzzer, Nancy Drolet is out to take the faceoff on Tueting's left. She has young 20-year-old Jayna Hefford on her right, while Wick and Stacy Wilson line up on her left. Thérèse Brisson, a defenceman, also lines up on her left, overloading that side, hoping Drolet will win it back to Judy Diduck, alone on the blue line, for her cannon of a shot.

Unfortunately, we don't win the draw. American centre, A.J. Mleczko, wins it, but the puck gets tied up in the corner and luckily once again the faceoff is to Tueting's left.

This time Drolet wins the puck back, but the Americans are all over us and force the puck into the neutral zone where no Canadians await.

As the final seconds tick away, American Sandra Whyte solidifies her team's lead, firing the puck into our empty net. The American crowd explodes. Our girls on the bench stare blankly into oblivion, attempting to mask their emotions.

The final buzzer sounds. I feel gutted for our team as I watch the Americans throw their gloves in the air and rush Tueting. The first gold medal in women's hockey . . . and it's not ours. I leave my post and make my way down to the players box to be with my teammates. I inch past the row of Canadian NHLers behind me, all with sympathetic faces, not knowing what to say. Music plays throughout the arena as the Americans continue to celebrate.

I walk down the long narrow hallway adjacent to the ice surface, past a table filled with Olympic medals surrounded by ceremonial staff and women dressed in kimonos. I try not to linger, but the medals look so brilliant.

I emerge into the Canadian players box just as the medal ceremony is about to begin. Shannon Miller's there standing beside her assistants, Ray Bennett and Danièle Sauvageau, but the bench feels lonely. I take a seat at one end, trying not to be in anyone's way.

The Americans line up in front of me, holding hands, exuberantly awaiting their gold medals. I stare at my teammates lined up parallel to the blue line to my right. Some Canadian players weep while others stand stoically staring off in the distance. Manon hasn't even taken off her helmet. The Americans, like excited kids on the last day of school, receive their medals first. They put that first ever gold medal around American captain Cammi Granato's neck and she breaks down.

The silver medal presentation is next. Our team is distant, apart, and in agony. Stacy Wilson, our captain, is first in line, her hands on her hips. She bites her lip as she fights back tears. Stacy has been a pioneer in our game, constantly fighting for girls to have a chance to play. The sadness is palpable. Assistant captains, Thérèse Brisson and Danielle Goyette, stare at the ice in front of them. As the ceremony continues down our line, some girls can battle back emotion to provide a smile and handshake and some cannot. My heart aches for my friends. Nancy Drolet grabs the shoulders of the two girls beside her and gradually the Canadians grow closer in grief, arm in arm.

"The Star-Spangled Banner" fills the arena. The feeling of failure permeates our blue line. As the anthem ends, our team heads back into the dressing room, right past me. I sympathetically tap each one on the shoulder as they walk by, but I'm nearly invisible to them in their sorrow.

The dressing room had been prepared for victory, but there is none. I see the disbelief in my teammates' faces as I walk in the room. I sit beside Jen, her eyes red and swollen, and ask to see her medal. I feel its weight, its significance.

Coach Miller starts to speak, her voice quivering. "The journey has been difficult, no question, but I am proud of each of you, proud of us, and proud of this moment in history."

Some players linger longer than others, unwilling to take their gear off, unwilling to make this moment real. I sit for a while, eventually heading towards the bus, not knowing what else to do.

FEBRUARY 17, 1998: CALLING HOME

Two hours later, our bus drives to Canada Olympic House where friends and family await. I hang out downstairs for a bit. My anguish at not playing seems small compared to my teammates' misery. Eventually I head upstairs to call home.

As I call my mom, I start to feel sorry for myself, and begin to tear up. I'm sitting in some kind of control room. There is a row of rotary telephones lining the wall. I can barely speak through the tears. I know she woke up in the middle of the night with my dad to watch the game.

My mom tries to find the right words, but what can you say to your daughter when her dreams are crushed? Our team has just lost the Olympic women's hockey final, but all I can think about is me. I'm sad about not playing and mad at myself for being selfish.

It's early in the morning in Winnipeg, but my mom tries to stay upbeat. She thinks I'm sad we lost — and deep down I *am* sad for the girls that we lost — but right now selfish feelings consume me.

"At least you have a silver medal." My mom tries to ease the hurt.

"I didn't get . . ." I can't finish my sentence. The beige phone slips on my tears. There's too much saliva and words can't find their way through. I bring the phone back to my ear, wipe my face with the sleeve of my red Team Canada fleece.

I'm mad at myself for feeling this way. My teammates are the ones to have the right to feel crushed, to be sad and disappointed. *What right do I have? I didn't actually play in the game.*

After the loss, I thought, *Should I join my team? Should I just sit in my seat?* There was no discussion with the coaching staff regarding my role. I just did what I thought would help.

When I accepted this role, I saw myself as an Olympian. Coaches teach you how to score goals and how to make saves, but no one teaches you how to sit on the sidelines.

"I didn't get a medal," I blurt out.

Tears stream down my face; I can't hold it together.

"We'll get you one, don't worry," my mom says.

I know she means well, but this is something even my mom can't fix.

PART 2

6

Hockey's My Future

The Olympics behind us, we're into a new season. It's been 10 months since Nagano and we are off to our first international tournament of the year, the 3 Nations Cup. The National Team has seven rookies, seven players that didn't directly experience the heartbreak of Nagano and 13 players with holes in their heart. The mix creates the duality of wanting revenge juxtaposed with excitement and naïveté.

Our team takes over the back of the plane and are seated by position. Because I'm the first goalie on the roster, rookie goaltender Kim St-Pierre, from Châteauguay, Quebec, is on one side of me and our new assistant coach, Ken Dufton, is on the other. Manon is out the mix because she's pregnant.

"How are your classes at McGill?" I ask Kim in French, as I pull out a book from my backpack.

"Yes, fine, thank you," she says back in English, with a shy grin.

I turn to my right to see Ken's grip on the armrests unchanged since takeoff.

"Ummm . . . you okay?"

"I just want this to be over," he says, beads of sweat forming on his brow.

"Ken, how are the Aeros doing?" I am referring to the team he coaches in the newly minted National Women's Hockey League and trying to take his mind off flying.

He nervously plays with his eyebrow as he tries to calm himself. Never one to mince words, he says, "Great, we're fifteen-and-oh. Best team in the league."

I open my physics textbook and start to dig in. The flight is long, but I'm excited that I'll get to play some games. With numerous rookies, including staff, I almost feel like a veteran. *Almost.*

•••••••

We land in Helsinki and make our way by bus across the interior of Finland to the small town of Kuortane and a complex built specifically to train elite athletes.

The inside of the rink looks like a sauna, but the temperature feels like the tundra. Gorgeous wood planks surround us, but the temperature is well below zero Celsius. We settle into training, learning Team Canada systems while attempting to bond quickly. With only a few hours of dusk/daylight every day and new foods to contend with, it's tough on a lot of the team. But equipped with my Finnish/English travel dictionary, I relish the travel experience.

As there are only three teams in this tournament, Kim and I will play one game each against both the Finns and the Americans.

In the middle of playing my first game of the tournament against the Americans, I'm almost too green to be nervous. There's only 30 or so people in the crowd so this doesn't feel like an international game, but the pace of the play is quick. I settle in quickly, playing with poise. Unfortunately, one of our rookies, Toronto Aeros player Sommer West, went down early in the first period with a shoulder separation, and that put a damper on the mood between periods.

We haven't recovered. The Americans, with a mix of veterans and rookies of their own, are outplaying us; however, I am seeing the puck well and controlling my rebounds.

It's still 0–0 heading into the third period. During centralization last year, I played in two international games, both shutouts and both against Sweden. *How great would it be to continue my career with a win against the Americans?* Just as the thought passes through my consciousness, Goyette continues her dominance from Nagano and scores a goal to give us the lead.

The play is fast, but I'm in the zone, following the play and ensuring I cover the puck every chance I get. It's intense, and yes, I have new teammates, but it feels no different than any other important game and I often forget that I'm playing the Olympic champions.

With only four minutes left to play in the game, we are still in the lead. *Hang on, Sami. Focus. We can win this.* As American forward Katie King, one of their strongest players, barrels down the wing, I ready myself, knowing she has a great shot. Katie's been beating our defence wide all game. As she looks up, I know I have this. She shoots. My knees hit the ice, right on cue as the puck ricochets off my black leather pad. Unfortunately, King is the first to react, and she gathers up her own rebound that has careened too far out of my reach. With one sweep she capitalizes.

Suddenly, it's a 1–1 game with just under four minutes left.

I can feel my face get red; I'm embarrassed I let in a goal. I turn and grab the puck out of my net for the referee. I replay the goal in my head. *Next time I need to hold my ground. No more goals.* I refocus for the faceoff knowing my team is going to need me to perform in these last few minutes.

The Americans are pressing. I'm not sure if there's overtime or it ends in a tie, but I just need to get our team out of this period. Blocker save, kick save, I'm doing my utmost.

With under a minute to play, we finally get the puck in the American zone. A point shot leads to a scramble, and rookie Mai-Lan Lê from Montreal pounces on a puck shot from Lori Dupuis, beating their goalie Sara DeCosta.

I breathe a sigh of relief. The team pours off the bench to celebrate with me in my crease.

We win 2–1. We've beaten the Olympic champions.

I love to compete; I love being in the game. For the girls that lost in Nagano, I know that beating the Americans is a big deal, a small form of vengeance, but for me, it's simply motivational fuel to want to play more.

·······

Kim plays the second game, against Finland. I set up at the end of the bench in the backup goalie's regular spot. I'm freezing. This rink is bitterly cold. Unable to move from my spot, I get colder and colder as the game wears on. As we finally secure an 8–4 win, I can barely cheer because my lips are blue and frozen.

The following game, Kim is up again because our opponents are the Americans and it's her turn to play them. This time, instead of the regular long johns and t-shirt under my gear, I layer up with a pair of sweatpants and my giant yellow hooded sweatshirt. I put on extra players socks over my arms under my jersey and wear my neck warmer. I also make sure to grab the biggest mitts and coziest toque I can find. I snuggle myself into the end of the bench, all toasty warm as the game starts.

The Americans score quickly to start the game. I try to encourage my teammates, it's still early. The game is a back-and-forth affair, and we are getting great opportunities in their end, but can't find the back of the net.

The game is back and forth, but unfortunately, the Americans beat Kim again at the 16-minute mark of the first period. It's only 2–0, not an insurmountable lead, but we need some energy, we need to capitalize.

Without warning, our new head coach, Danièle Sauvageau — an assistant in Nagano — screams, "Sami, you're in!" and gestures towards Kim.

I look around to make sure she's talking to me.

What's happening? Is she pulling Kim?

"Sami, get in there!" she repeats. Danièle is a former undercover cop from Montreal and is fully versed in the stern man-voice she's just laid on me. I'm startled into action.

Robin McDonald, the team's equipment manager, hurriedly brings me my glove and blocker. I pull off my toque and neck warmer and reach my hands into frozen goalie gloves. I scramble to get my helmet on, adrenaline pumping. As I make my way to the net, my yellow hooded sweatshirt flaps behind me.

Fear must have been the spark we needed, because our young team plays with a new sense of purpose. Jayna Hefford scores to bring the game within one.

The period over, I make my way to the change room, trying to avoid eye contact with the coaches. I feel bad for Kim — *only two goals and she gets pulled?* Her first game against the Americans. It doesn't seem fair.

Ken Dufton, the defence coach for this tournament, pulls me aside before I can escape into the room. He shakes his head disapprovingly at my layers of clothes. "Make sure you do what you have to do to be ready for this period."

I frantically take off my equipment as my teammates stare. I have no time to laugh — we're down 2–1. Most can't believe the coaches pulled Kim. I must disrobe nearly completely to get my sweatsuit and all the extra layers off. I hurry to put all my gear back on before the coaches come in. I'm not only completely warmed from a period of play, but now am sweating from speed dressing.

I'm used to having my brain go from zero to one hundred in the blink of an eye from a lifetime of training, and running from one sporting activity to the next, and now more than ever that preparation comes into play.

Our team rallies, and I manage to keep the Americans at bay while relishing my second opportunity to play against such a formidable opponent. The Americans outshoot us in the second, but Mai-Lan Lê is on the board again, scoring late on a pass from Karen Nystrom. We head back into the dressing room after the second period with a draw. New game.

"Sweet pass, Nystrom," I say to her as she takes her helmet off. Nystrom, a gritty winger from Scarborough who has been a member of Team Canada since 1992, always seems super serious, but she gives me a wry smile. It feels like my game. Like my team to lead. I am such a different person when given the reins.

"Let's do this," I say to no one in particular as Danièle finishes her pep talk.

As the third period starts, defenceman Cheryl Pounder scores a nifty goal, and we lead for the first time. I tap my posts as I smile.

The action is never-ending. Veterans have angst and rookies want to prove their worth. We battle too hard and are sent to the box. Not once, but twice. As we attempt to kill off the five on three, the puck heads to Sue Merz at the point. I battle to find it through a mélange of skates. Merz fires it towards our net. I can't see it. She thrusts her arms high in the air as I see the netting move behind me.

Back to a tie, 3–3, as the third period ends.

I skate towards our bench. The team circles around Danièle as she goes over the plan for overtime. I join the huddle, but I know my role — just stop the puck — thus I don't intently listen as she maps out a faceoff plan. As she finishes, I find Pounder.

"Great shot," I say, excited she scored. Pounder is my age and lives in Mississauga. She made the World Championship team in 1994 as a 17-year-old, but was left off the roster in 1997 and didn't centralize for Nagano. She's great defensively and so tough in front of our net, but it's a rarity that she scores. I am really happy she put the puck in the net here.

I laugh and joke with my teammates before the 10-minute overtime starts, almost forgetting this game decides the 3 Nations Cup champions.

As I skate to my net for OT, I think to myself what a privilege it is to be playing the game I love, wearing a Team Canada jersey, with a championship on the line. I love that the game rests squarely on my shoulders. It's an incredible feeling.

1989: HAVE FUN — MY DAD

I am walking up the steps of the entrance to St. Vital Centennial Arena for a game with my boys' AAA peewee 12-year-old team, the Winnipeg Warriors. Snow covers the tops of the steps, but salt has been thrown down to make them less treacherous for the daily throngs of hockey players. I'm walking just slightly in front of my mom and dad.

My parents converse loosely as I rush to get inside. I'm excited to play today. Yesterday's game, my goalie partner played, but today I get to play, and I'm pumped.

I have my hockey bag slung over one shoulder and my white Cooper goalie pads over the other. I am balanced out by the two goalie sticks I carry in my hands.

I turn sideways to manoeuvre my heavy equipment into the facility. My mom holds the door open in front of me but tries not to be too obvious. She knows I like to be independent. I push through the second set of double doors, and the familiar sights, smells, and sounds of my home rink come flooding back to me. I have a brush cut; my number shaved into the side of my head like most of my teammates. I smile as I enter, knowing many will look at the strange sight of a girl with a hockey bag. Finally, through the doors, I see my teammates' parents filling the lobby. Most gather to the right of the entrance, which is my cue that our team's dressing room is in that direction. One last set of doors separate me from the stairs that head down to the dressing room. I am excited to see my teammates.

Other parents smile at my parents, Rod and Pat Small, who are a welcome addition. My dad, easygoing, always has an elaborate story to tell, and my mother eternally chuckles, sighs, and then rolls her eyes at his jokes. My father is an entertainer, likes to be the centre of attention — we have that in common. Dad jokes are his speciality. Being an optometrist by day gives him plenty of fodder for his stories. He and my mom are both dressed in neon ski jackets. My dad's glasses are ever-changing; he is always up on the latest style. My mom's glasses are all the rage, with a coloured tint built right into the oversized rims.

As my parents stop to chat, I proceed towards the stairs. Decked out proudly in my puffy white Winnipeg Warriors jacket with "Small" on one sleeve and "#1" on the other, I don't look back. Turning sideways one last time to fit through the doors, I glance back at my parents with a smile on my face.

"Good luck," my mom says, smiling in a protective, motherly kind of way.

"Have fun and stone 'em," says my dad with immense pride as the door shuts.

They say the same thing every game, but it's reassuring knowing they will always be cheering, proud of their "girl in the net."

DECEMBER 1998: 3 NATIONS CUP, FINLAND (CONTINUED)

Overtime is about to begin. I settle into my net and face the centre dot. I hit my right post with the top of my stick and my left post with my glove, centring myself between the pipes. I then push lightly out to the top of my crease, tap my stick on my skates, and I'm ready to go.

Unfortunately, overtime proves nothing.

The refs exchange looks. I skate to my bench wondering, *What now?* My coaches look unsure. This is Danièle's first time as a head coach, Ken's and Karen's first times as assistant coaches. They are conferring. I ask my defencemen seated on the bench what's going on. Her face tense, Pounder says, "Sami, I think it's a five-player shootout."

"Oh great," I say with a sheepish grin, but internally I'm excited. The coaches try to figure out our shooting order. There is no final, so, despite another game against the Finns, if we win here, we will be the 3 Nations Cup champions.

I don't want my team to be nervous. I skate down the bench, smile at my players; I want them to know I'm confident, even though I've never done a shootout before. At the collegiate level and even in minor hockey, if a regular season game ended in a tie, it was counted as a tie. If a playoff game ended in a draw, we played overtime until someone scored.

The shootout starts.

The in-arena announcements are in Finnish, so I don't know one American player from the next as they skate towards me. I let them guide the dance. My body knows how to react.

"Stone 'em," I repeat to myself as the whistle blows.

The first American tries to go five-hole, but I shut it just in time. As she skates to her bench, I realize that it was Cammi Granato, one of their best players. Good thing I didn't know that before she shot.

I keep skating back to the bench between shots as is customary in international play. The second American scores, but Nancy Drolet responds. The third American scores, but Cassie Campbell evens the score. Two more shooters, and I manage to stop them both, but so does their goalie, Sara DeCosta. We remain tied.

Overtime and five shooters, and we are still tied.

The conclusion will be a sudden death shootout. Whoever scores first wins. The American shooter lines up at the centre faceoff dot. The referee looks at me and then whistles to signal the player to begin. I stay on my goal line until she crosses the blue line, as instructed by the officials. This player is small, but she's coming at me with speed. I attempt to match her speed but also hold my ground. She fakes left, but her stick still cups the puck. I don't fall for the trick and follow her to the right giving her no room to tuck the puck in my net.

I take my seat on the bench as our sixth shooter lines up: rookie Amanda "Benny" Benoit, from Welland, Ontario. She uses almost the same move as the American but freezes DeCosta shifting to the right and puts the puck in the gaping net for the win. I skate the length of the ice as our team rushes off the bench.

We've won! I jump and I scream as we pile on top of Benny, a smile permanently affixed to her face.

FEBRUARY 1999: THE CALL

I return to school and life in California with a new training regimen from Team Canada. I rejoin my Stanford hockey team, but we're not as strong as we once were. We've lost coach Ernie Ferrari, who led us to Stanford's best finish, a third place my freshman year at the American Collegiate Hockey Championships (ACHAs).

While we've been close in most games, often splitting weekend games with our PAC-10 rivals, we don't have many wins. We don't have the same talent we had my first couple of years; however, it does mean I get to see a lot of shots.

Playing men's hockey is all I've really known. I love the challenge and the pressure, knowing that how I perform will reflect all of women's hockey. I love that I get to train away from the National Team coaches' evaluating eyes, to toil away in obscurity, able to work on my weaknesses without anyone knowing. No scouts watch my games; I get to just play.

I live off campus for my final year with my former roommate Diana, and our dormmates, Corey Karlin and Susan Wu. I still have hopes of making the national track and field team, but my shoulder is still nagging me. I have already had one surgery to repair it, and the doctors are talking about another. I have pain when I throw javelin, but rather than ruin another season, I opted last year to just throw in competitions, finish out my collegiate career, and deal with the discomfort. Pain and struggle marked my track and field career and despite getting to compete at the NCAA championships, scoring in nearly every meet for Stanford, my potential often outweighed my performances.

Last year, I didn't complete my classes in the normal four-year span due to missing so much time for the Olympics, causing my four-year scholarship to end. I begged and pleaded with the athletic department to allow me to come back the following year, and they relented, offering me an athletic department grant in exchange for work in the media relations department.

It's still February and a call comes into our rented house in Redwood City from Danièle Sauvageau, now Team Canada's head coach. I think I like her. She's a former RCMP officer and Montreal cop with a tough exterior, but also seems to engage her players.

"How's hockey in California?" she asks in her thick French accent.

"We're in the middle of the pack, probably outside a berth to the Nationals, but for our final weekend we'll play against the University of California at Berkeley for what's known as the Big Skate."

"The big skate? You win a skate?" she asks as if perhaps what I had said was lost in translation.

"Well, kind of. Berkeley is our biggest rival, and in football they play 'The Big Game,' so in hockey we play 'The Big Skate.'" I opt not to explain further. Neither Berkeley nor Stanford are very strong this year; however, my brother, Luke, after being accepted into their optometry school, decided to play for our cross-bay rivals. The Big Skate is for bragging rights, but I don't explain all this to Danièle — it's a family thing she's bound not to understand.

"Well, I guess, good luck in . . . 'The Big Skate,'" she says with a confused tone.

There's a pause.

"I am calling to congratulate you on making the World Championship team."

I realize that this call is not just a catch-up session, but in fact *the call* I've been waiting for since I first watched Susie Yuen and the entire Team Canada in pink jerseys play on television at the 1990 World Championships.

"Welcome to Team Canada."

Goosebumps run up my spine as a smile floods my face.

"Thank you . . . thank you so much."

I hang up the phone and scream for Diana, who is in the other room. Corey and Susan come running too.

"Guys, I made it! I made Team Canada." They rush in for a giant hug, making me squirm while they laugh and congratulate me. None of my roommates have any sort of hockey background, but they've watched me play and have been my biggest fans. Diana makes us all a celebratory dinner of empanadas and other Mexican treats, and my Stanford friends help me celebrate a Canadian childhood dream come true.

7

What a Feeling

The World Championship is in Finland, but first I must fly from San Francisco to Toronto for a pre-Worlds camp with Team Canada. Every camp or tournament, I fly in a day early because of the distance. My goalie partner for Worlds is Kim St-Pierre. She and Lesley Reddon both competed for Canada in January on a team that I was not a part of, in a four-game series against Finland in Ontario and Quebec. I guess Kim outduelled Lesley.

Kim is a very strong goaltender, but I can't believe Lesley is not here. Lesley's dedication to practice and her skill inspired me. She played in the last World Championship Finals in 1997 in Kitchener, in which Canada won in overtime, and I just assumed Lesley would be on this team for a long time. I am, nonetheless, happy for Kim, and her presence puts me in the position of "veteran goalie."

Our pre-camp is at the old Maple Leaf Gardens, a historic arena that will be torn down next year, so this is special. The coaches run us through some breakouts and forechecks and try to get everyone used to Team Canada's systems.

We have an exhibition game in Brampton prior to our departure for Scandinavia, which will be my first time playing the Americans in Canada. They are missing a couple of stars: defencemen Angela Ruggiero of Harvard and Tara Mounsey of Brown are still involved in their NCAA college playoffs, so the Americans play with just four defence. Our roster is short too, due to injuries. Vicky Sunohara and Lori Dupuis, who both play with the local Brampton Thunder, are out with ailments. They're missing a chance to play at home but will be travelling to Worlds. Laura Schuler, who played in Nagano, steps in to fill out a roster spot until Vicky and Lori are back. Karen Nystrom also suffered a season-ending knee injury, so the coaching staff brought in Mai-Lan Lê, our hero from the 3 Nations Cup, to replace her on the roster. Hayley Wickenheiser is back despite leaving yesterday's practice having lost an edge crashing into the boards. Wick is resilient; she attended the Philadelphia Flyers rookie camp in September and there's not much that will keep her off the ice.

The exhibition game is called the TSN Challenge, and will be broadcast live on TV across Canada. My family and friends in Winnipeg will get their first glimpse of me playing in a Team Canada uniform as I start for Canada in front of a packed 5,000-seat Brampton Centre.

We score two goals quickly in the first five minutes on their goaltender, Laurie Belliveau, a rookie from Yale. This relieves my stress and lets me ease into the game. Jennifer Botterill, currently at Harvard with American Angela Ruggiero, is missing her East Coast Hockey Association (ECHA) playoffs to be here. She's involved in both goals and is double-shifting at centre.

I battle to keep our team in the game, and with our few chances, we score another two goals to end the second period, forcing the Americans to pull Belliveau in favour of veteran Erin Whitten for the third. The Americans are strong and outshoot us in the first two periods, but I feel confident, able to see pucks and to smother them for stoppages in play. Local Brampton Thunder member Laura Schuler is like a bumblebee, relentlessly forechecking, likely hoping to prove to the coaches that she deserves to be back on the team next year.

Pucks bounce my way; with more shots, I gain more confidence. The packed pro-Canadian crowd screams loudly and cheers for every save I make. In the third period, Cammi Granato walks out from the corner unchallenged and slips the puck between my pads. I reach back to corral the slumbering puck, but it manages to squirt over the goal line before I snatch it up in my glove. I want that one back, but it was a nice play by Cammi, and it only makes the score 5–1.

The game ends 6–1, despite us being outshot by the Americans, 31–24. As I stand on the blue line with my teammates awaiting the player of the game presentations and the awarding of the inaugural TSN Challenge Plate, I take in the roar of the crowd. I can't help but think how this gives us huge momentum going over to Finland for the Worlds.

I think of which of my friends may be tuned in to watch on TSN, and of my parents willing me on, watching with clenched nerves as I made each save. I can't wait to get back to the hotel to call my boyfriend, Colin, and tell him about our victory when suddenly over the PA system I hear, "And the Esquire Player of the Game for Team Canada goes to No. 1, Sami Jo Small."

I'm snapped back to reality as Jen and Cassie, standing on either side of me, nearly have to push me towards centre ice. In disbelief, I skate over to the sponsors. I accept my award and exuberantly shake each one of their hands with a smile extending from ear to ear with sheer joy. My face beet red, I turn to skate back towards my teammates, but they mob me halfway, laughing as they hit me with mock punches and facewash me with their smelly gloves.

•••••••

On our way to the World Championship in Finland, we make a pit stop in Sweden for some exhibition games. We have the youngest ever average age for a national women's team. We have four National Team rookies with us who have never competed at a World Championship or Olympics for Canada: Mai-Lan Lê, Caroline Ouellette, Amanda Benoit, and, of course, my goalie partner, Kim. We also have Cheryl Pounder and Nathalie Rivard, who are both World Champions but were left off of the Olympic team last year.

Head coach Danièle Sauvageau had been an assistant coach since 1996, but took over the head coaching role this season and will now be at the helm assisted by two rookie coaches new to the national team; Ken Dufton from the now called Toronto Beatrice Aeros (after signing the largest endorsement deal in women's hockey) and Karen Hughes from the University of Toronto.

While in Sweden, Kim and I both start an exhibition game against the Swedes. I use my start to get used to the larger European ice and the different angles of attack. Our coaches also give us some freedom as we do some team building playing tourists at the Swedish Royal Palace, walking the streets of Stockholm.

MARCH 1999: WORLD CHAMPIONSHIP — FINLAND

For my second trip to Finland this season, we're in Espoo, a suburb of Helsinki. The World Championship tournament begins easily enough. Kim starts the first game and we beat Switzerland 10–0, and then I am in net for a 13–0 win against Germany. I'm not sure who Danièle was going to start in the following game, but Kim tweaked her neck in yesterday's practice, so I'm called upon to start the third game against the Finns.

Team Finland is good, and in front of a huge, pro-Finnish crowd, they have a lot of energy. Canada has never lost to Finland at the World Championship, but the games are usually close. Finland is the next best team to Canada and the USA and has both speed and skill.

The Finns take three penalties in the first period, but Tuula Puputti, the Finnish goalie, is strong, making huge saves, stymieing our power play. Six minutes into the second period, Vicky Sunohara finally scores on a breakaway, thanks to a trademark feathered pass from Jayna Hefford. We've beaten Puputti, but there's still no breathing room in this game. The rest of the second period sees a reversal of roles as we take five penalties. The Finns have an excellent power play trying mostly to set up Emma Laaksonen on defence with her powerful shot. I attempt to stay square to the shooters, do the little things right, and cover the rebounds.

Between periods, Danièle urges us to stick to our game plan and stay out of the box.

Midway through the third period, on a rush down the wing, Hefford, with her incredible snapshot, riffles the puck over Puputti's shoulder into the top of the net. Exuberantly, she smashes into the glass behind the Finnish goaltender. As she celebrates, arms in the air, she is engulfed by the four other players on the ice. I smile 200 feet away in my crease, relieved to be up by two goals. I spin around and proceed to take a sip of water from the bottle on the back of my net with a mixture of confidence and awe of Heff's shot.

Surprisingly, as I turn back towards centre ice, the play is still going on, Finns have the puck, and they're skating four abreast crossing the centre line heading towards me. *Did we not score?* I'm snapped into action and pull my gloves back on. I try to find the centre of my net, and push to the top of the crease preparing for the onslaught.

Vicky, who had been celebrating with Jayna, notices the play and scrambles to get back as she yells at the other players, but it's too late. It's me against the Finns.

Tactically I want them to make an extra pass to potentially screw up. Sometimes a single person on a breakaway has a better chance of scoring than four in the clear: too many options.

As the Finns cross the top of the circles, they scatter to openings. The puck makes its way from a high player to a low player attempting to skirt behind me. I've read the play and make the save leaving a big rebound, a second shot ensues, another rebound, but Vicky manages to get back and swipe the third rebound harmlessly away.

"So sorry, Sami. Why the heck was that not a goal?" she says standing in my crease as the play continues. "Heff, you scored, right?" Vicky screams out. "Sami, cover it up if you can, I need off this ice," she says panting.

With no video replays, Vicky and Jayna argue to the referee that the puck went in top corner and shot out just as quickly. The ref denies it.

We narrowly escape the game with a 1–0 victory, despite the Finns nearly matching us shot for shot at 21 to our 27. Our motto for the tournament from coach Sauvageau is "Protect the House." Be vigilant on defence. A shutout could not have been more fitting. The win ensures that we will play in the semifinals against the Swedes, and not the powerhouse Americans.

We finally get Fiona Smith back for the semifinals. She didn't play the first three games, out with another concussion suffered in our last exhibition game. Kim gets the nod for the semis against Sweden as I take my seat on the bench, cheering our team to an easy 4–1 victory that sets up a climactic final game against the Americans.

•••••••

I'm walking towards the ice for the second period of the World Championship Finals. No goals have been scored. The Americans' best chances both came from one of their top forwards, Katie King, blasting down the left side, but I held my ground on the first shot and then was lucky on a screen shot that careened off my shoulder onto the top of the net.

The black rubber matting below my skates gives me some grip, but it's still hard to walk in bulky goalie gear. We're in our red jerseys. My equipment is almost all black but for a white maple leaf split in two on my goalie pads. I'm wearing the upper-body equipment I made in my engineering class at Stanford. I feel like a gladiator.

We kill off a penalty to start the second. Three minutes later, they have another power play. I remind myself to focus on the puck. I make more saves, mostly on point shots, but both Granato and Ruggiero sneak through for wide open shots in the slot that I must be acrobatic to stop.

Just after the nine-minute mark of the second period, King again creates a scoring chance. This time she does a give-and-go from the corner with speedy forward Jenny Schmidgall deceiving my defenceman. To complete the play, King makes a nice saucer pass over a Team Canada stick and finds a wide open Schmidgall in front of the net.

Schmidgall's all alone in front of me as big power forward Caroline Ouellette tries to swing low to help cover for the defence but can't make it in time.

Shuffle. Push. Shuffle.

I stay with Schmidgall. I try to outwait her. Calm turns into panic as she drags the puck uncontested across the front of the entire crease from my left all the way to my right. She's quick, and I realize I'm behind. She has the open net, so I make the split-second decision to dive with a two-pad stack to cover the opening. Schmidgall still has the puck. With me lying on the ice, she sends the puck up and back towards the opposite top corner. I reach out with my hand, then my leg, but I narrowly miss. The puck goes in.

1–0 USA.

I stand and try to look positive for my teammates. I watch the replay on the Jumbotron hanging from the rafters at centre ice. Great shot and almost a lucky save. So close. I don't look at the bench. I look to centre ice. I tap my pads with my stick. I replay the goal in my head. *Could I have played that differently? Would I make a different choice?*

Sweat runs down my face. I breathe, look down at the ice, and then look up. The ref drops the puck, and the play starts again. There's no sense dwelling on the last play. I can't make our team score, but I can certainly prevent the Americans from creating a bigger lead. The pressure doesn't let up, but Erin Whitten, the American goalie, is also making key saves.

Whitten played men's pro hockey in both the East Coast Hockey League and the Colonial Hockey League. She was the starter for the American team at the last three World Championships and centralized last year with the American team for Nagano. I think she should have been on the Olympic team, but coach Ben Smith went with two young goalies, Tueting and DeCosta. Whitten's getting her chance to prove herself again.

Shortly after the 11-minute mark of the second period, Sunohara, Hefford, and Ouellette step back on the ice for an offensive zone faceoff. I like this line together. Vicky and Jayna have played together for years on their club team, and Montrealer Caroline Ouellette seems to complement them well, finding them space to create synergy.

Vicky wins the faceoff, and Ouellette taps it back to Thérèse Brisson at the point. She has perhaps the hardest shot on our team. She shoots so hard that forwards rarely want to stand in front.

Brisson winds up and blasts the puck, narrowly missing the left post. A scramble ensues behind Whitten's net. She tracks the puck from one side of the net to the other. Vicky, still behind the net, with superb hand-eye coordination, taps the puck through some skates. Whitten looks to panic and slides to the left post unsure where the puck is, but the puck has bounced to Ouellette on the opposite side.

Aggressively, Ouellette wraps the puck around the net on her backhand. Whitten can sense this and attempts to slide back, but she's out of control. Ouellette finds a narrow opening and tucks the puck in, just barely crossing the line before Whitten gets there.

Stillness washes down my chest as I smile. "Yes!" I murmur and grip my stick secretly fist pumping to myself. All alone at my end of the ice, I have no one to cheer with. But that's okay — I don't want to get too excited.

Hating to be outplayed by another goalie, I'm relieved we are now even. Tie game. New game.

With one deep breath, composure fills my body again. Canada is giving up lots of chances down low, but calmly I kick them all away.

Cassie Campbell, who was recently switched from defence to forward, skates down the wing and takes a slapshot about five feet away from Whitten. I know Whitten doesn't see it, but her glove is in the right spot, and she catches the puck. Chaos ensues. Punching and shoving, these teams really do not like each other.

Both teams have good chances, but when the second period ends, it's still tied 1–1.

I smile in the dressing room as I catch my breath preparing for the all important third period. I think of what this moment will mean to *this* team and the retribution from Nagano this will provide for many.

I picture us as World Champions and instantly think of other exciting team victories I've had. I've been fortunate to have won several team titles over the years.

1993: TEAMMATES — VOLLEYBALL

Standing at the net, I wait for the serve. "Let's go. One more point," Stacey Ross, our setter, yells as she claps her hands in the third and final set of the Manitoba Provincial AAA Volleyball Championships.

My parents are up in the stands of our packed Collège Jeanne-Sauvé gymnasium. My teacher and classmates cheering us on.

The ball thumps towards our side of the net. I have the captain's stripe on my No. 13 jersey and am a right side power hitter. I watch as Kathryn McKenzie bumps the serve from the back row to Stacey Ross. Her hands stretch high in the air; she lowers her body beneath the ball.

Only in grade 11, Stacey and Kathryn have become close friends of mine over the course of the last two years of volleyball, often carpooling to and from practice. Most of my friends are boys, but it's a pleasure to have girls who share my love of sports. I have such respect for their work ethic and their athleticism.

Besides myself in grade 12, there are only two other graduating seniors: Karen Good and Stephanie Simpson. We have been together since kindergarten. Many students left French immersion in high school but we stayed and will graduate with a class of only 42 students. Unfortunately, Karen and Stephanie have to watch this final set from the bench as younger players play in their usual positions. Their composure in such a difficult situation is commendable.

Stacey sets the ball, floating it towards the power position; I've already started my approach. Left, right, left. I jump as high as I can and shift my body to avoid the block. I can't jump remarkably high, but I have long arms, a family trait that's served me well as a goalie. Power is not my problem. My weakness is accuracy.

Our coach, M. Ragoonaden pushed us to our physical limits before and after school, made us tired, and then worked on our technique. He has put in a lot of time moulding us as athletes mentally and physically. He said if we could get it right under physical and mental duress, we could get it right under the pressure of a big game.

Stacey sets me a perfect ball out wide. In the air, I can see my opening cross-court. I swing, not too hard, turning my wrist to find the opening. It's in.

We've done it!

I rush my teammates, and then I remember Stephanie and Karen and turn. They've already made their way off the bench with euphoric smiles and arms high in the air. Screaming we embrace as Provincial Champions.

MARCH 1999: WORLD CHAMPIONSHIP (CONTINUED)

The third period starts with a 1–1 score and this time we have the player advantage with American Tricia Dunn in the penalty box. Wick, who is normally a forward, but with her vision and incredible shot can quarterback a power play, starts on the point with Geraldine Heaney. Jennifer Botterill's out on forward with Goyette and Drolet.

We win the faceoff and gain possession in the American zone. Goyette has the puck down low in the corner. She looks up and sends the puck back to Wick at the point. Jen heads directly in front of the American goalie, Whitten, as Goyette and Drolet skate into position, off to each side, awaiting a deflection. Wick puts her full body weight into a blast. Jen screens Whitten as the puck makes its way towards the net. Goyette desperately reaches and manages to get a stick on the puck redirecting it miraculously through Whitten's legs and into the back of the net. Goal for Canada.

We've got this. I tap my posts as I watch my team celebrate in the other end.

We lead the World Championship Final 2–1.

Wick exuberantly heads to our bench in full stride, high-fiving each person on the bench as she skates by. She thrusts her arm in the air in my direction, screaming the whole time. I have no idea what she is saying, but don't care. I excitedly thrust my hand back at her.

Still in the third, two minutes later, Goyette and Drolet are out again, this time with their regular linemate Amanda Benoit, to take a faceoff in the American end. Drolet beats Schmidgall clean on the puck drop and shovels it back to Heaney, known for her accuracy. Benoit gets tied up as Drolet heads to the net. Heaney's blast goes right through Benoit who is causing a screen on Whitten. I can't tell if the puck is deflected, but amazingly, her shot winds up in the net.

Only Heaney and France Saint-Louis, the matriarchs of our sport, have been on Team Canada since its inception in 1990. I'm incredibly happy Heaney scored — if we win today, it will be their fifth straight World Championship. After the team celebration, Heaney, with a giant smile, skates all the way back to include me in her elation.

"Yeah, Ger!" I say as she exuberantly high-fives me on the skate by.

3–1 Canada.

Focus, I tell myself. *Don't be too cocky — there's still 10 minutes to play.* Lots of time still. I watch as the clock ticks away.

Sometimes you want time to speed up and it does anything but. More stoppages gives me more time to think. All the sports I have ever played, every other team I've been a part of, and every coach, every teacher has prepared me for this moment.

We play a dump-and-chase game, opting only to send one fore-checker in towards the American zone, trapping them there. We are playing with poise and seem to be in control.

Only three minutes remaining. The US regains their jump. They won't give up. I must stay focused. I make saves on Mounsey and Ruggiero. I know my team is counting on me. The Americans pull their goalie, but then accidently ice the puck. Whistle. Time out for the Americans with only 53 seconds left.

I skate to the bench.

Danièle goes over our plan. Wick, Dupuis, and Campbell will be on forward with Brisson and Heaney on the point. I only pay slight attention to the play Danièle is drawing up. I smile confidently at Jen on the bench, and she joyfully smiles back.

The play starts and the Americans have six attackers buzzing all around me. I hold my goal line and try to find the puck as my team does a great job of keeping them to the perimeter. The puck careens behind the net and finally I sneak a peek at the clock.

Three . . . two . . . one.

Heaney grabs me and suddenly the team is on top of us. Pandemonium.

The pileup is all legs, arms, and screams.

We are World Champions.

The pride of playing my best game when it matters most is hugely satisfying. We came together quickly as a team, accepting our roles and never losing sight of the end goal. *World Champions*.

Chills run down my spine as I'm presented with the Directorate Award as the top goalie of the tournament; however, what's most important is the Championship Plate. That is what we came here to win. We celebrate long into the night. As far as sporting moments go, *this* electrifying experience is my new highlight.

The following day, tired, hungover, yet pumped with adrenaline, I make the long trek back to Toronto with my teammates, and then on to San Francisco and Stanford. There's no time to rest — my final exams for this trimester start in 11 hours.

8

Hard Work Pays Off

I never thought I'd make it this far. It's been three months since I became a World Champion. It's been a challenging five years as I juggled engineering while competing in two sports, but here I am sitting in Stanford's Roble Gym about to (maybe) become an engineering graduate from one of the most prestigious universities in the world.

I will be walking across stage today, but at Stanford, we have the odd tradition that you can "elect" to graduate whatever year you like, which means you can walk the stage, but only official graduates who have completed the course load will have their degree in the folder handed to them. I redo the mental checklist. *Did I pass all my final exams? Did I take all the right classes? Do I have enough credits? Did I pay all my parking tickets?*

In high school, I graduated near the top of my class, was the co-valedictorian and class president. But going to school with some of America's and the world's best and brightest often made me feel I was left in their dust. I had to study more; I had to work harder to acquire knowledge.

I watch as the rows in front of me are marshalled up to receive their diplomas. The main graduation including all the faculties was held this morning at the huge football stadium and featured Stanford's infamous "Wacky Walk" where students dress up in costume or adorn their graduation robe. I wore a red maple leaf on the top on my mortarboard so my parents could see me from the stands.

I'm getting slightly nervous as the letters L though R are called, knowing that I will be in the next group. My brother couldn't make it as he's doing an optometry rotation at the University of Beijing in China. However, my parents and my grandparents have flown in from Winnipeg. My dad's parents are getting older, but they still managed to make it here. Yesterday, my grandpa, who is an optometrist like my dad, gave me his father's engineering rulers and squares and told me how proud he is that I am following in his father's footsteps. *I just hope I actually get my degree today.*

My grandma is quiet but feisty. She raised her two kids, my dad and my auntie Margaret-Ann, to be independent. Often mischievous, my dad liked talking his way out of trouble. My dad played on the Kelvin High School basketball and football teams and amazingly, my auntie Margaret-Ann, three years his senior, played softball and school sports at a time when not many women did. Dad says his sister was his hero. She was often the best athlete amongst all the boys in the neighbourhood. I'm sure this is why my dad saw the value in me playing sports when most girls my age weren't allowed.

My family is somewhere in the bleachers at the back. I haven't looked yet to see where they are. My friend Monique, a fellow thrower, who graduated in product design last year, is sitting with them. We worked non-stop on our project design projects and we have become the best of friends these past few years.

My boyfriend, Colin, is also here. He flew in from England. We've been together just over a year, and despite the distance he's been my rock. My current housemates, Diana, Susan, and Corey, are here too, with proud smiles, even though they graduated last year. Student after student walks the stage and shakes the professor's hand.

1990: PERSEVERANCE — RUNNING

It's 7:00 a.m. and indoor cross-country running practice is about to begin inside at Collège Jeanne-Sauvé. There's still an hour until my grade 9 classes start but it's -33 Celsius outside, so we have to run in the school.

I'm on my last loop of the corridors. Each one is supposed to be faster than the last. My legs are burning, and the stairs await.

I started the laps with my friend Adam Salem. We only have 30 seconds of rest between each lap, but after the first couple, he speeds up ahead and I run alone.

Adam often comes and knocks on my door after school and asks to train together. In the winter, we put nails in the bottom of our shoes down in my dad's workroom, so we have traction on the snow. I am never as good as he is when it comes to endurance, but he never stops asking me to train.

I climb the stairs, my heart pounding and I'm panting. At the top of the stairs, the hallway is empty. I consider walking — no one would know — but my brain keeps yelling, *One more step!*

The corridor is dimly lit, almost yellowish, but I know our coach, M. Bérubé, waits at the end, stopwatch in hand. *Don't give up.* I sprint. I haven't got much left, but I want him to see me giving it my all. Maybe I can make it under time. I'm close. I lunge past the imaginary finish line.

I collapse at the waist, hands finding my knees. The world goes black for a second, and I'm struggling for air. I slowly regain consciousness and stand to see Adam in the corner stretching, his shoes almost too heavy for his skinny brown legs. Adam wanders over, not saying a thing, and hands me his water bottle. We turn at the end of the gym and make our way back to M. Bérubé.

Coach looks up from his clipboard to tell me my time wasn't faster on the last lap. Adam and I continue to walk around the gym, cooling down as M. Bérubé gathers his stuff and follows behind us.

"Adam, I'm going to be faster tomorrow," I say, regaining my breath.

"That was pretty tough today," he says back. "But yeah, tomorrow let's go faster."

JUNE 1999: STANFORD GRADUATION (CONTINUED)

"S though Z, please stand up." The woman with a clipboard ushers us against the wall. There are 15 or so students in front of me. I scan the crowd for my parents, but see only the glaring lights directed at the stage.

Only 10 students left in front of me. Counting always calms me, makes me feel prepared.

I didn't set out to be an engineer. I was going to be a doctor. Smart people become doctors, so that's what I was going to do, just like my dad. Then in my second year, I enrolled in Mechanical Engineering 101. I only enrolled because I had heard it was fun, but it changed the course of my academic life. The class was a lot of work and kept me up all hours, but I loved every minute of it.

We made objects, problem-solved, and figured out how things worked. My heart led me to the wood shop, the metalworking studio, and the product realization lab. The math and physics were tough, but I also took art and photography classes and eventually settled into the faculty of product design. In the final project of my senior year, I designed upper-body goaltending equipment for women that helped win me a World Championship. I was hooked.

Five students in front of me. I scan the stairs, check that my gown and cap are on right.

In my first year, my grades earned me the Dean's Award, but then classes became harder. I had to retake many classes and was embarrassed to show my transcripts to my parents. When I was called into the track and field coach's office, I promised the head coach that I would improve. I didn't know how, but I had to. *Had I bit off more than I could chew?* I had no time; I was either in class, studying, at track practice, in rehabilitation for my injured shoulder, or on the ice. They tried to make me quit hockey, but I just couldn't give it up; I promised Robert Weir, my throws coach, I could do it all.

I had no time for my friends or a social life and seriously contemplated changing majors to something easier. The only times I went out was when my brother and his friends visited from Berkeley or my roommates and I were celebrating a major milestone. Hopefully, what I had forsaken was all worth it.

Deep down I knew I could do this. What did it matter if it took me forever to become an engineer at one of the best schools in the world?

I tentatively step up the two stairs to the stage. I'm next.

"Samantha J. Small, Engineer," echoes on the intercom.

I walk slowly towards my faculty of product design advisor, Rolf Faste. He looks more like Santa Claus than a professor. His face is all smiles as his hand reaches out for mine. I want to give him a huge hug but I'm not sure there's a paper inside the folder he hands me. I can hear my entourage in the stands, my friends whooping and hollering, and my parents, I'm sure, clapping through the tears.

I want it all to be worth it. All the struggles: studying for hours in the library; the cuts on my fingers from my X-acto knife and burn marks on my hand from hot glue guns as I built projects late into the night; the days spent outside training in the hot California sun or in the weight room; the evenings spent at the ice rink in Redwood City. There were the extra study hours, the days I didn't ever feel like I got enough sleep, and the times I had to say no to going out or hanging out with friends. There were the times spent carting heavy books on planes and buses, snatching moments to study; the tests I failed or barely passed; and the times I didn't think I belonged among the best and the brightest. I want it all to matter.

I smile at Rolf and continue the length of the stage. I sneak a peek into the stands, hold up my folder, and hear my supporters roar. We are marshalled back to our seats, the folder firmly clutched in my sweaty hands. I don't want anyone to see my disappointment if my degree isn't in there. I shuffle through the rows of graduates back to my seat. I look left, I look right, no one is watching. I slowly open the folder.

My diploma stares back at me.

I am an engineer from Stanford University.

9

New Environment

NOVEMBER 1999: MOVING TO TORONTO

Staring into our fridge there's little more than condiments and pickled beets. Colin and I haven't eaten since training early this morning, and we're are famished. I graduated five months ago, and have moved to the Greater Toronto Area (GTA), north of the city, to a basement apartment in the suburb of Woodbridge.

We trained today at York University, a 15-minute drive from our place. I often tag along on Colin's track and field training sessions and use the gym in the corner. This is the first time in my life I don't have a schedule. I've started volunteering at the local Mississauga Valley Community Centre helping my teammate Donna-Lynn Rosa with their lunch program. But besides hockey practice, my days are mostly free.

Colin makes his way to the bedroom adjacent to the kitchen. Our apartment is less than 400 square feet, so he's never far away. In this mostly Italian suburb, above us live the owners of the house, a family from Nigeria. We rarely see them as our life consists of training, eating, sleeping, and fighting the endless traffic in the GTA.

With the fridge door still open, I contemplate something I can assemble. It's hard to stay on top of groceries when Colin eats so much. I check the almost-bare pantry. I was instantly smitten with Colin when I met him at Stanford. He is tall and muscular, with a melting accent. Over from Europe, he trained at Stanford for a month alongside my coach, Robert Weir, and I was taken not by the bravado that he puts on for others, but by the sensitive side that he seems to show only to me.

We forged a deep connection even after he returned home. It was the kind of stupid love you read about in romance novels. We wrote letters to each other every day, and I counted the days until we could be together again. I'd never been in love before, and I never knew how all-consuming it could be. My friends made fun of me, and I knew they weren't his biggest fans, but it hurt to hang up the phone with him. For the last two years, our relationship has been long distance, as I pictured what our life would be like together.

It's not exactly as I imagined, but it's still good. We're certainly never at a loss for words, and I can tell him everything. He's an instant friend in a sea of new faces. I follow him to his training sessions, and he follows me to my practices and games. We spend nearly every minute with each other.

"How about spaghetti?" I shout, hoping he'll hear me. I don't have the heart to tell him it will have to be plain.

I don't hear a response. I walk towards the bedroom door. I repeat our disappointing dinner option.

We are living on the $800-a-month funding assistance, also known as carding, that I receive from the Canadian federal government for being an elite athlete. I had some savings built up, but we've already gone through that. Our rent is $600, so it doesn't leave us much wiggle room. Colin owns a house in England, and he pitches in from his savings but, as a full-time athlete, also doesn't have much income coming in.

"Oh, Sami, come here." He looks down at me with a big smiling reassuring face as he grabs me in his arms and says, "Love, don't worry, we'll be all right. I'll call my brother tomorrow. See what I can get sorted," he says with empathy, knowing that I worry. "How about I run out and grab us something for the pasta?" This makes me smile. I know we don't have the money for this, but right now, I don't care.

"Can you grab milk for the morning too?" I ask as if I'm requesting a present for Christmas.

I head back towards the kitchen as Colin grabs his parka. I fill a pot with water and place it on the element. Our only remaining Canadian money sits in a change bowl near the door. Colin grabs a handful and with a grin is out the door.

After I strain the pasta, I grab two bowls. I make his heap much larger than mine and leave them steaming on the counter while I head to the couch and flip on the TV and await his return.

JANUARY 2000: TSN CHALLENGE — BUFFALO/TORONTO

I play for the Brampton Thunder of the National Women's Hockey League (NWHL), a league in its second year of existence, combining teams from Ontario and Quebec. Brampton's owner, Susan Fennell, persistently called while I was at school in California, trying to convince me to come play on her team. I desperately wanted to play men's semi-pro, but my calls were met with trepidation by team owners, therefore Brampton seemed like my best bet.

Susan is credited with starting the NWHL and was serving as the commissioner. I love her vision for the future of women's hockey. While we don't make any money, she has helped in every other way she can. Susan had a sponsor pay for my hotel room when I first arrived and took my parents out for dinner when they flew out to visit. Susan wants the best for each player, and I feel like I joined the Thunder family.

Unfortunately, my life since graduating from Stanford now only revolves around sport. When is the next practice or how was the last game? While in school, I was used to playing on two varsity sports teams while trying to cram in an engineering degree. I had friends outside of sport and somehow found time for extracurriculars.

Now I'm just a hockey player. My balance is off.

I have too much time to think about my performances, and my expectations of myself are through the roof. My mood always reflects my last ice session.

Our first Team Canada camp of the year was in October at Teen Ranch, just north of Toronto. More than 50 athletes participated; however, I was ill most of the week, and missed another day to spend time with my mom who had flown in for her aunt's funeral. I had to miss the wedding of my former Stanford roommate, Bobby Blunt, and my Stanford throwing friend, Katrinka Jackson. It was a tough week but by the end of it I was on the mend. The highlight was on the final day, when I came in third in the slapshot skills competition despite cumbersome goalie gear.

I did also get to see Manon again, who returned to play after giving birth to her son Dylan. Our relationship grew after the Olympics. She lives in Sacramento, not too far from where I went to school. My final year at Stanford, in '99, she invited me out to play roller hockey on her pro team, Team Mission. Last year, we won the North American Roller Hockey Championship (NARCh) in her old stomping ground of Las Vegas where she'd played pro with the Knights in the AHL.

I wasn't selected to be a part of the 3 Nations Cup tournament in Montreal in December as the coaches opted to split up my goalie partner, Kim St-Pierre, and me at different tournaments. It's unfortunate we never get to go to both. The other goalie at the 3 Nations was the Calgary Oval X-Treme's Lorenda Beuker, but Kim played in the final.

Kim had a fantastic performance in a 3–2 shootout victory over the Americans in her home province and Jayna Hefford scored the winning goal. But the tournament was truly highlighted by a shootout goal from Angela James. After controversially being cut from the 1998 Olympic team, she returned for one last memorable moment. After the game, in the media scrum she told reporters, she's officially retiring from the National Team.

It's January and my tournament will be the TSN Challenge. This year it's a two-game series against the Americans, one of which will be hosted by the NHL during their All-Star weekend in Toronto. My goalie partner for the two-week traning camp and games is Marie-France Morin from the NCCP Ottawa Raiders team in our league. "Franky" is an awesome goalie partner. She's extremely supportive and likes to chat. She's small in stature, but I've never seen another goalie as quick. Her speciality, the two-pad stack, is executed to perfection, often stymieing opponents while playing boys' hockey growing up in Ottawa.

Marie-France starts our first game in Buffalo. We play at Colby College, which is also the alma mater of one of my Brampton teammates, Meaghan Sittler, who is playing for Team USA. Marie-France is on fire, but our team is not. Not only do we accidently lock our own player, Judy Diduck, who was a scratch for the game, in the dressing room for an entire period, we lose 4–1.

My parents are in the stands for today's game back in Toronto at the new Air Canada Centre, home to the Toronto Maple Leafs. My brother has flown in from California. My agent, Jane Roos, is here too. I signed with her last year, and she's been a huge help securing events and sponsorships. Colin is here, and so are my Brampton Thunder teammates.

I make my way to my net, water bottle in hand. The arena is jammed with a young, enthusiastic crowd of nearly 15,000. I have never played in front of this amount of people. It is loud. I set the water bottle on top of the net. Same place as always. Waterspout facing the other goalie on the right side of the net. I scrape my skate blades forcibly across the crease, trying to scuff up the smooth ice. I try to make this feel as normal as possible in front of what seems like a circus in the stands. My legs are shaking, so I kneel and stretch a bit until the referee signals me from centre ice. Despite my jittery legs, I'm ready to go.

1994: RESILIENCE — PLAYING FOR STANFORD'S MEN'S TEAM

"You're a whore," shouts a drunken University of California Berkeley (Cal) supporter directly over my shoulder.

It's the PAC-10 men's hockey playoffs, and I've just made a save, smothering the puck for the referee. This arena is an awful place to play in — I wish we were playing at home — but Cal finished higher in the standings and earned the right to host.

I'm an 18-year-old freshman, in my first year at Stanford. The ice surface is oversized, made for pleasure skating, and my angles are all off. A disco ball hangs from the rafters and the boards are painted black on the bottom, which is a goalie's nightmare because it conceals the puck. The stands look like giant stairs for standing rather than seats. Nearly 1,500 screaming fans are jammed into the arena, including, on adjacent sides, both the Stanford and Cal bands — complete with giant wrap-around massive tubas.

Most of the fans are dressed in the blue and yellow of Berkeley. Conversely, a few, including some friends from my dorm, have made the trek across the Bay Bridge and don Cardinal red. My brother flew in this weekend for a visit from Texas, where he's on a swimming scholarship and doing his undergrad in environmental sciences. He's my most loyal fan and is proudly wearing Cardinal red, standing beside my freshman roommate Amanda Van Houtte; dormmates Diana, Susan, and Corey;

and my throwing friends Gina Heads, Michelle Breaux, and Katrinka Jackson. Our fans are poised behind our team bench with the Stanford band blasting directly behind them.

I use the word *bench* loosely because it's actually just the first step in the stands. There's no box around us. Nothing separates our team from the rabid Berkeley fans, nothing protecting us from the beer cans hurled in our direction. Never have I played in a place so unsuited for hockey and yet filled with such passionate, crazy fans. The Cal band is to my left, conducting cheers for the students, who for the most part are enjoying a night out complete with road beers and other alcohol. Most of the spectators have no idea about the rules of the game, but they love the aggression. They cheer every hit as loudly as they cheer a goal.

And they jeer.

"Small, you're a sieve!"

"Who let the f**king girl on the ice?"

I try not to flinch when the taunting directly behind me doesn't subside. I've never been one to let a crowd get under my skin. At least while the play is on, I don't hear them, but we're between whistles now awaiting a faceoff in my end, and they are getting the rest of the crowd involved.

"You suck, Small, and you're good at it."

My team, the Stanford Cardinal, is up 2–1, and it's midway through the second period. I have a love/hate relationship with playing at Berkeley. It's such a great rivalry, the games are always intense and tight, but this rink is atrocious.

I avoid eye contact with any fans. As I reach back to grab my water bottle from the top of my net, I stare at the mural on the far end of the arena. It's a northern outdoor scene complete with pine trees and snow-capped mountains. Instead of Plexiglas like most arenas have, this rink has wire fencing, similar to the outdoor rinks back home. As I sip from my bottle, I see our coach, Ernie Ferrari, giving last-minute instructions to our captain, Luke Winter, as he hops over the boards for a line change.

Ernie has been a mentor to me this year. He is an extraordinary coach who volunteers his time to travel the West Coast with us. Despite his initial apprehension, I think he was swayed because he has a young daughter that plays and now has included me with vigor on the team. He has high expectations and isn't afraid to tell me to play better. He knows track and field must be a priority, but still pushes me every practice.

Our captain, Luke Winter, skates towards the right faceoff circle in my zone as I turn to put my water bottle back on top of the net. The netting sags slightly as I point the nozzle towards the other net. Luke settles himself into the faceoff, just as the fans directly behind me yell yet another inappropriate comment. Luke starts too soon, the ref waves him out of the circle. Restart.

As Luke stands and turns, he eyes up the Cal students behind my net with a look in his eye that says he's going to kill each one of them in the parking lot after the game. These guys are like my brothers. Stefan Teitge, whose skill with the puck makes it seem like he has Velcro on his stick, steps in for the faceoff, trying to win the puck back to Eric Haug, a tall lanky defenceman who, like Luke, is a transplant from Minnesota.

I ready myself and look to see how their team is positioned. With only a 2–1 lead, I need to stay focused. We've put together one of the best seasons Stanford men's ice hockey has ever had, but this Cal team is strong. The winner of this game will be crowned PAC-10 champions and will also earn a berth at the American Collegiate Hockey Association Championships in Colorado next month.

Forget the crowd, just play the game.

JANUARY 2000: ALL-STAR GAME — TORONTO

Once the puck drops at the Air Canada Centre, I tune out the crowd and settle into the game. The Americans get some quick shots on net and dominate the first 10 minutes of play. They have injuries and are playing with just 10 forwards instead of the usual 12. Most of their team is now centralized in Lake Placid, including our Brampton Thunder teammate, Sue Merz.

We find the back of the net first. Local Beatrice Aeros member Amy Turek, in her first game with Canada, hops on a Thérèse Brisson slapshot to put us up 1–0.

With seven minutes left in the first, we are on the power play. I watch the play like a fan as Thérèse Brisson winds up from the point with Cassie Campbell in front. Cassie gets a piece of the puck, but American goalie Erin Whitten makes a great save. Defenceman Angela Ruggiero is there to clear the puck, and she fires it down the ice. Heaney bats the pucks out of the air, but only just enough to slow it down.

I see their player Karyn Bye slip behind Heaney and rush towards the open puck at our blue line, but I think I can beat her. I take a calculated risk and start skating full speed towards her. As I get closer, I realized I wrongly anticipated the speed of the puck. I'm not going to make it. Bye is going to get there first. I'm already well past the hash marks, so in a final effort I Superman dive in her direction. I miss the puck, but clip enough of her skate to send her flying. The crowd goes nuts as I scurry back to my net. My mother probably just had a heart attack in the crowd, and my dad is probably laughing his head off. I smile with a sense of relief while laughing at myself as the play continues.

The US finishes the period with two power plays, but I do my best to find the puck and cover it at every opportunity. The ref continues to call penalties. This time the Americans are called for two quick ones in a row to give us a two-man advantage. Head coach Melody Davidson sends out Wick with Delaney Collins to quarterback the five on three. That's a lot of confidence in Collins, who is playing in her first big games for Canada. She is agile and plays with her head up, always capable of finding an open player. We put Goyette, Hefford, and Dana Antal up front. The puck moves swiftly around the perimeter, eventually ending up on Goyette's stick to the right of Whitten. Alone in front she accurately snipes it between Whitten's pads.

2–0 Canada as we head to the dressing room at the end of the first period.

We explode further in the second period to create a 5–0 lead. Erin Whitten is not getting any help. The Americans look tired and depleted. Despite a decisive win yesterday against us in Buffalo, they can't seem to put together two passes in a row today.

We come out on top, 6–0, and the passionate crowd fills the arena with cheers right until the final whistle. Six different Canadians score. Wick has three assists and is named player of the game for us.

My Brampton Thunder teammate Meaghan Sittler, who is fighting for a spot on the Worlds' team, is named player of the game for the Americans in front of her dad, a legend for the fans in this arena, Toronto Maple Leaf great Darryl Sittler.

Stay Focused

APRIL 2000: THE DECISION

It's the day before the finals of the 2000 World Women's Hockey Championship in Mississauga. The tournament is proudly hosted by the Ontario Women's Hockey Association, the largest women's hockey organization in the world, run by Fran Rider and Pat Nicholls. Mississauga Mayor Hazel McCallion, who played professional hockey in Montreal in the '40s, has made this tournament on home soil very special. She, along with OWHA, was instrumental in pushing women's hockey to be included at the Olympic Games.

The World Championship final is tomorrow and assistant coach Karen Hughes, with her shy, friendly face, escorts Kim St-Pierre and me to the coaches' room. It's been three months since my huge win at the NHL All-Star Game. We have just finished our semifinal game against Finland. Kim played and we won a close one, 3–2, the home crowd cheering every time we touched the puck. In the round robin against Finland, the Americans had to come back from a 3–1 deficit going into the third period but then easily made it through their semi against Sweden, setting up a Canada — USA final. Karen walks us the length of the hallway underneath the stands at the Hershey Centre.

Kim stopped 25 shots today and made key saves at opportune times, but as we walk towards our fate, I'm not worried. She played well, but not well enough to usurp me from my spot. We've won every game I've played in and I haven't let in a goal with Team Canada all season. Kim was great in December at the 3 Nations Cup in Montreal, playing before her hometown crowd dramatically by winning a 3–2 shootout against the Americans, but I won at the TSN Challenge in January, 6–0, and I haven't let in a goal in this tournament or in the pre-tournament games.

I'm confident.

"You guys wait here." Karen enters the room alone, leaving us to wait. Both Kim and I are in dress clothes, wet hair pulled back into ponytails. I try to keep the mood light as we wait.

"You played great today."

"Merci beaucoup," she says with a timid smile. I can see she's nervous. She wants to play tomorrow's final as much as I do. I'm sure she feels she deserves it. I sat at home in December and watched Kim in an interview after the shootout win when she indicated she wanted the number-one goalie job. I wouldn't have ever said that on national TV, but I do think it.

Karen re-emerges into the hallway, "Okay, both of you come in."

Both of us? Maybe our head coach, Melody Davidson, is not going to tell us about the starter for tomorrow's final. Maybe Mel hasn't made her mind up. She wouldn't have us both in the room together?

The dressing room is stark white with a solitary grey plastic table in the middle. Hooks line the walls, but nothing hangs from them. Covering the table are papers, coaching notes, what may be scouting reports or lineups.

Mel sits facing the doorway as orange classroom-style chairs face her. Without looking up she motions. "Sit down."

She has a clipboard in her hand and frowns. This isn't unusual — she rarely looks happy. Only away from the rink will she let her guard down and smile. Around the rink, we all walk on eggshells. She never seems satisfied and I always feel I'm about to get into trouble or I've made her angry.

Kim and I sit down. My heart is racing. Mel's awkward silence intimidates me. Karen grabs a chair and sits off in a corner, joined by our other assistant, Wally Kozak.

This tournament has been an amazing experience thus far. The team has become close very quickly and playing the World Championship in Canada, unlike last year's in Finland, has meant that my friends and family can be here. My parents flew in from Winnipeg even though they were just here in January for the All-Star Game. They met at U of T, so it's a bit of a homecoming. My Thunder teammates are all here too, cheering for both their American teammates and us.

Colin had to fly back to Europe for a training camp and for his Olympic trials. He's becoming frustrating and I feel okay that he's gone home; it makes it easier to focus.

Mel is emotionless. She begins with "This choice hasn't been easy." My palms are sweaty, and I can feel my face getting red.

Kim stares straight ahead, hopeful. Mel continues. "Kim, you've had a great year with your McGill team, really proved yourself," she says, gesturing with her hands in Kim's direction with a slight hint of a smile. My heart sinks a little.

Mel turns to me. "And Sami, well, we expected more."

I'm shocked. What more could I have done? I played well in every Team Canada game, and even if I wasn't always my best with the Brampton Thunder, I played excellent when it mattered. It's a hard league, with good teams and great players. Kim's university league is second-rate compared to the National Women's Hockey League. She plays with younger players. The Canadian Interuniversity Athletic Union league is no NWHL. I play amongst the best in the world. It's not a fair comparison. What more did she want? Now I'm angry.

"But Sami, my gut tells me I should go with you for the final."

What? Wait. Am I playing? Did she just say I'm playing the finals? Relief sweeps over my body. My face turns back to its normal colour. I don't want to look at Kim. I don't want to see her disappointment. *How could Mel tell us together? This is cruel.*

Mel extends her hand to Kim and then to me. I don't want to look too excited — I know Kim must be devastated. I shake hands with Mel, turn, and follow Kim out the door. We walk in silence side by side, towards the bus that awaits us.

Just before we climb the stairs of the bus, I turn to Kim and whisper, "I'm sorry."

It's the gold medal game and I walk into the dressing room after the second period. Sweat runs down my forehead. This isn't how I envisioned the game. The Americans scored twice that last period, outshooting us 13–3 and now leading 2–0. We look like a team with no hope.

I sit in my stall at the front left of the dressing room, normally the home of the OHL's Mississauga Ice Dogs. I'm tired — it was a tough period. Two goals got past me. The first was a rebound by Tricia Dunn off a shot by rookie high schooler Krissy Wendell, after an uncharacteristic turnover in our zone by Geraldine Heaney. She rarely does that. The second, just minutes later, I had squared down on Sue Merz coming in from the point uncontested, only to have her shot niftily redirected by Karyn Bye, up and over me as I sprawled on the ice. I want them both back.

I look at my black painted goalie stick. I had to paint over the Louisville logo since they are not an official tournament sponsor. I turn the stick over in my hands and on the back I see a giant gold Kim St-Pierre autograph. I knew she was upset at not playing today. Before the game, I asked her to sign my stick so that a part of her would be with me on the ice.

I sit further back in my stall and hide, protected by the wood partitions. *Maybe Mel made the wrong choice.* I've never had this much doubt during a game. Maybe the team would have played better for Kim.

I lean forward, take off my upper-body gear. I'm soaked. I look down and take a sip from my water bottle and gather myself.

Smile through the adversity — Mom taught me that. The dressing room is quiet. We've never been here before. We've never lost a World Championship. Kelly Bechard, a rookie from Sedley, Saskatchewan, who plays for the Calgary Oval X-Treme, turns on the stereo. She's a natural playmaker. She's been playing on what, effectively, is our second line with veterans Hefford and Campbell and has been holding her own.

Maybe music is the spark we need. I head to the washroom, walking directly through the centre of the room, cumbersome in my goalie pads.

The first period had fairly even back-and-forth action. I got to play the puck several times and was battling well to find sight lines. Ruggiero took a "hitting from behind" penalty, a two and a ten, against Wick as she crumpled hard against the boards. Wick got up, but it looked bad. Already playing through pain, she'd suffered a shoulder injury late in the semi against Sweden and then got hit hard into the open American team's door during the second.

Having their dominant defenceman, Ruggiero, in the box in the second should have been to our advantage. The Americans have had several injuries this tournament and have moved forwards Jenny Schmidgall and A.J. Mleczko back to defence, but we haven't been able to capitalize.

I emerge from the toilet and walk towards my stall. I shout to no one in particular, "We got this." As I walk past Jen, I tap her on her shoulder. Ruggiero, originally from California, was her roommate last year at Harvard. Jen amassed an incredible 88 points in 29 games, winning the American Women's Collegiate Hockey Association Championship as a freshman.

She's been doing great this tournament on the top line, playing wing, though she's a natural centreman, alongside Wick and Goyette, but mentally it's a tough line to be on. Wick is hard on her linemates. Wick and Goyette are often at opposite ends of the bench because Hayley's intensity can be too much, with Jen somewhere in between. Wick's been training like a pro since the age of 14 and expects everyone around her to put in the same degree of effort.

Her unrelenting pursuit of excellence is often seen as selfish, but I know she's doing it for the team, to help the team win. Goyette is a stark contrast to Wick. She works hard and is a naturally gifted player but is best and most creative when she's carefree and in a positive state of mind. We need Jen to be their glue.

I take my seat. The mood is tense. The pressure is high. We can't let them beat us at home. I stare across the room at Wick. She's silent in her stall, swaying back and forth with a scowling grimace on her face.

Is she okay?

Mel comes into the room trailed by Wally and Karen. This is her first year at the helm, and there's a lot on the line for her. I can tell she's frustrated.

"That period was not an indication of how good we are." She stares deadpan around the room. "Each of you deserves to be here. Believe that and play like that.

"Is anyone having fun?"

Silence.

"This is supposed to be fun." She cracks a rare smile. "Embrace the crowd, feel their excitement, and remember to enjoy the game. It's just hockey, and you're good at hockey."

The intermission ends and I lead our team on the ice. The packed crowd roars as we emerge from the tunnel onto the ice for the third period.

We're better. We have jump. Thérèse Brisson, our captain, takes our team on her shoulders, injecting energy with an end-to-end rush capped off by a massive hit on Ruggiero. We get chances. The line of Shewchuk, Ouellette, and Drolet is humming, creating opportunities. The crowd is willing us to get one back.

The play is end to end. I make a save on their youngest player, Natalie Darwitz, only 16 and out of Minnesota. Remarkably, Darwitz was also on their team last year at Worlds. Delaney Collins just misses on a two on one saucer pass from Vicky Sunohara.

Delaney is one of our rookies. From tiny Pilot Mound, Manitoba, she basically grew up at the famous Athol Murray College of Notre Dame in Wilcox, Saskatchewan, where her dad coaches. She and Nathalie Rivard, our third pairing, haven't seen as much ice time today but every time Delaney steps on the ice she tries to ignite a spark.

········

Seven minutes into the third, a save made, I cover the puck ensuring a faceoff to my right. I've been corralling the puck well, ensuring no second chances for the Americans constantly buzzing in my crease. Mel sends out Jayna Hefford and Cassie Campbell, but this time moves Hefford to her natural right wing and has Jen take the faceoff. Jen looks at Cassie, then glances to ensure Jayna is positioning herself correctly. Jen characteristically lowers herself into a crouch and glides into the faceoff position against Darwitz.

Exactly as planned, Jen wins the puck forward, and Hefford grabs it and takes off. Her speed with the puck is insane. She jets down the right wing past American defender Jenny Schmidgall. It's a two on one but Campbell acts as a decoy. Hefford looks up and, just inside the American team's hash mark, she fires the puck a foot off the ground past DeCosta's outstretched blocker.

Jayna's arms thrust high in the air as she skates past Cassie and exuberantly leaps into Jen's arms, and all three embrace. Delaney and Nathalie join them in the mayhem. The crowd erupts, on their feet transforming their nervous energy to a thunderous roar.

2–1. Now we have a game.

We have the momentum. Becky gets a glorious chance walking in from the point that DeCosta just snags with her shoulder. I make a couple point-blank stops on Jenny Schmidgall, but then at the nine-minute mark, Hefford takes Cammi Granato hard into the boards in our zone and gets a penalty. She shakes her head as she makes her way to the box. Kill this off, just a setback. Excitement is in the air. *Sami, stay focused.*

1994: SAVOUR THE MOMENT — MAKING HISTORY

It's a cold February in Winnipeg, but spectators, photographers, and local news cameras have piled into St. Vital Centennial Arena to see history being made. I'm 17 years old, in grade 12, and I am playing in net for the home side. I put my elbow on the crossbar, position my stick on top of the net, and use my other hand to flip up my mask as cameras click to record the moment. *Stay calm.*

Behind me I hear the ref scream, "Let's go, boys. That's it, boys. All done," as he tries to squirm his way between the two large men entangled in fisticuffs. These players are huge compared to the average-sized 17-year-old male opponents that I face in the Midget AA loop. Likely in their early 20s, both are over 6 feet tall, have full beards, and look like men.

This is the MMJHL, the Manitoba Major Junior Hockey League. Both St. Vital Victorias goalies were hurt last week, and Coach Bob Thompson called up the two goalies from the lower league.

The fight is right behind my net. I take a sip from my water bottle amid more clicks of the cameras and try not to look in their direction. I'm the first girl to ever play in this league. *Focus on the next play.* No distractions. We're winning 3–1. Just keep my team in the game.

There's a player's glove lying dormant in my crease, a remnant of the fight.

One of the linesmen joins his referee partner as each now has control of a player. Both players' helmets are off, blood running down the side of my teammate's face as he tries to reach for his opponent.

"F**king stop running our goalie. F**k you, you big man," he shouts over the linesman who has him in a full bear hug now.

"Okay, okay, you've said your piece," I hear the linesman say, attempting to create space between the two fighters.

The crowd is going bananas. The fighters' energy fizzles out, and both search the ice for their gloves and helmets, escorted by the linesmen. I flip my helmet back down and position my water bottle on the right side of the mesh. Always on the right side for easier access.

"You're playing well," shouts a voice beside me. I spin my head around to see my opponent's yellow jersey in my crease, reaching over to fetch his errant black glove.

Confused, I realize I'm within a foot of the opponent towering over my 5-foot-7 frame. I can see his eyes. He repeats the words again, this time softer, "You're playing well," he says with a sincere smile.

"Thanks." I smile back, the whole interaction lasting about a second — perhaps he too realized he is part of history — before his skate to the penalty box, the crowd screaming expletives in his direction.

APRIL 2000: WORLD CHAMPIONSHIP — MISSISSAUGA (CONTINUED)

Lori Dupuis and Vicky forecheck hard, and we kill off the first minute of Hefford's penalty. Campbell and Bechard switch up at forward, but the US is able to set up in our zone. Their power play is exceptionally efficient. Their passing is hard and crisp. Schmidgall passes the puck to the point and Mleczko redirects it to her partner Ruggiero for a cannon of a shot. However, fortunately the D, Brisson and Heaney, have cleared the front of the net, and I see the trajectory all the way.

I deflect the puck in the corner. The cycle starts again. Crisp, fast. Schmidgall to Mleczko to Ruggiero down to low Granato, over to Wendell. She's wide open. I scramble, but Wendell loses the handle.

The penalty ends and Hefford's back out, more electric with each shift. This is her game. She is incredible at finding open ice when she doesn't have the puck, often streaking up right wing, flying right past the opposing defence. Her snapshot has tremendous power but it's her backhand that's a greater threat.

The clock is ticking. Seven minutes left. The faceoff is deep in the American end. Jen is once again on the ice centring, Hefford on her left and Campbell on her right. She wins the draw, and the trio cycle the puck down low. Behind the net Jen fights off US Olympic gold medallist Laurie Baker and wraps the puck around trying to stuff it in on DeCosta's left. She takes a couple of whacks at the puck, and it squeezes through the crease to an open Hefford. DeCosta reads it perfectly, making a kick save. But Hefford holds her ground, finding the rebound and lifting it over DeCosta's outstretched pad.

The crowd goes bonkers. Tie game 2–2.

With six and a half minutes left in the third period, we exchange chances with the Americans, but DeCosta, whose style is a combination of butterfly and stand-up, doesn't falter. Less than two minutes to play, and Mel moves Nancy Drolet up to centre Wick and Goyette. They create some chances. Neither team is satisfied with a tie. Everyone is pressing for the winning goal. The period winds down with a save off a hard shot from Ruggiero from the point, with King and Granato on the doorstep.

The US has outshot us 30–19.

Overtime.

Sitting in the dressing room between periods, I take a deep breath.

We re-emerge with confidence and momentum for overtime. Our legacy and how each of us remember this game will come down to which team scores.

Our team started together at a pre-tournament camp three weeks ago in Sarnia, Ontario. We've lived an entire lifetime in these past three weeks. We did team-building activities: learning to curl and make pottery, and speaking in the community and skating with local kids. We did whatever was asked of us to sell our game, all while training twice a day. We lost rookie forward Dana Antal to a leg injury in our second prep game. A tough loss as she's such a consistent player who can create space with every stride. Dana was centralized in '98 but she was released early. She has perhaps the most deceptive shot. Every goalie has their nemeses who they just can't seem to read. Mine are Dana and Tammy Lee Shewchuk. They just always seem to put the puck past me in practice.

Dana's dreams dashed, she has to sit in the stands for the remainder of the tournament, but she remains positive. I'm impressed with her willingness to participate in everything off the ice. Amanda Benoit, who was with us last year at Worlds in Finland, has filled the roster spot. She's a speedy forward and has meshed right into the lineup.

I feel mentally sharp and strong. Mel starts with Jen, Hefford, and Campbell up front and Brisson and Heaney on defence. They've scored our two goals and were on fire in the third period. Mel follows them up with Wick (now back at centre) and Goyette with Drolet still on her wings, with Kellar and Pounder on defence. Goyette narrowly misses sending this arena into a frenzy when she skirts the puck wide on her backhand.

We are dominating this overtime. The puck is in the American end as we cycle through three lines, each more relentless than the previous.

I don't want my emotions getting too high or too low. I just let the play unfold, completely in the zone. Then, just under four minutes into overtime, the ref's hand goes up calling a penalty against Hefford as she battled in front of their net sending the American defenceman to the ice.

Time to shine. Focus.

The American power play takes over passing the puck around the perimeter. Shuffle. Shuffle. *Where's Granato?* I turn my head to see her low to my left. *Always know where Granato is.*

Bechard finally clears the zone to end the penalty, as Hefford comes back on with her line.

USA has possession, and Schmidgall waits with the puck behind DeCosta while a new line comes on. She emerges from behind the net looking for O'Sullivan skating up the middle. Wick reads it perfectly and intercepts the pass just inside the blue line. She fires the puck on net with Goyette and Drolet chasing the rebound behind the net. American defender Chris Bailey attempts to clear the zone along the boards but Wick once again reads it perfectly and blocks the puck, knocking the play down to her feet. Her head down, she gets run over simultaneously by both Shelley Looney and Bailey. Kellar picks up the loose puck and wrist shots it high over the net. Drolet fetches the puck out of the corner. Drolet was the hero at the 1997 World Championship in overtime. She skates around the circle, Goyette providing support in the cycle down low. She sweeps uncontested into the middle of the ice. Drolet takes a quick slapshot just inside the faceoff dot. DeCosta goes down. The puck hits her upper body and then slowly, miraculously, careens over her shoulder. The puck falls in slow motion to the ice behind her. For an impossibly long moment, it bounces in front of the goal line and then magically, willfully, dribbles over the line into the gaping net.

Nancy's arms thrust high in the air as she skates into Becky Kellar's embrace and our bench clears.

It takes me a moment to realize this is real. I bend over giving myself a private cheer. I skate towards the pileup. Kim has skated from the pileup back towards me. We embrace.

"Kim, you deserve this too."

We turn and skate full force and jump on the pile.

What a wonderful sensation, the exhilaration of triumph: World Champions again.

Transitions

SEPTEMBER 2000: LIVING IN BRAMPTON

Sitting in our living room, we enjoy a rare night off from hockey. Despite the hockey season recently starting, we're watching Hayley Wickenheiser and Toronto Aeros player Sommer West play for Canada in softball at the 2000 Olympic Summer Games in Sydney, Australia.

I broke up with Colin over the summer. Nothing dramatic, the relationship just fizzled away. We had some great times and some great adventures together, but I just couldn't be in a relationship with him anymore. After the breakup, I decided to move in with my goalie partner, Stacy Kellough, and fellow Olympians Lori Dupuis and Sue Merz.

Joining me to watch the Olympics are teammates Ally Fox, Meaghan Sittler, and Samm Holmes. Ally is at University of Toronto, studying to be a lawyer. She's one of the smartest people I know. She's the one you call when you're fighting with a friend over some trivia. Meaghan is a kind soul, funny and charismatic, and a recent graduate of Colby College in Buffalo. Samm Holmes, from Mississauga, just graduated from the University of New Hampshire where she won a national championship. Both Meaghan and Samm were NCAA Collegiate stars and both are training full time, like me, to play for their national teams.

My roommate Stacy and her girlfriend, Jill, are here too. They sit on opposite ends of their couch, their feet pointed towards the middle, intertwined. They're throwing a soccer ball back and forth, lost in conversation, as if they are the only two in the room, making up rules to a game only they know.

I like Stacy and Jill together because they're open about their relationship. I can talk to them like a couple and not be fearful that I may insult them. Many of my friends and teammates live in secret, which must be strenuous. It's difficult not to say the wrong thing. Most of the time, I have no idea who is with whom, and I'm constantly lost, but I try my best to be supportive and to be an ear if anyone needs to vent.

All of us cheer on Wick and Sommer as Olympic dreams flash before our eyes. Despite playing for different club teams, they are still hockey players to us and we proudly cheer them on.

NOVEMBER 2000: A HISTORIC GOAL

My Brampton Thunder are taking on the Sainte-Julie Panthères from just outside Montreal, a regular season game in the National Women's Hockey League. We are better, but I've let my team down. I'm not playing well. With just under four minutes to play, we're up 5–3, but it should be 5–0. I'm more hurt than mad. I don't want to be on this ice anymore. I want this game to be over.

Yes, they have some good players, including National Team player Nancy Drolet. And yes, they made the NWHL finals last year, losing to Toronto's Beatrice Aeros; however, our team, this year, has much more depth. Their goalie, Marie-Claude Roy, a goalie with Canada's 1992 World Championship team and last year's playoffs MVP, is keeping them in the game.

I am almost solely responsible for all their goals.

After the Team Canada selection camp in October, the coaches once again split Kim and me for two separate tournaments. Kim recently got back from hers, the 4 Nations Cup in Provo, Utah, where she shut out the Americans in the final. *I need to be better.*

I really did prepare as if this was an important game. I woke up this morning looking forward to the challenge, did the same pre-game routine I always do: an activation in the morning, a pre-game nap, some visualization, and a good meal . . . but for some reason, my ego gets in the way. I see the other team isn't at our level, and I don't concentrate. I do things on the ice that are out of character. I lose focus easily.

I want to get over the embarrassment of playing poorly in front of our devoted Brampton fans. After the second period, our coach, Terry Richardson, yelled at me. It hurt, but I knew he was right.

All three goals were my careless mistakes. I was wandering outside of my crease, playing the puck without intention, inadvertently passing to their team, giving them great scoring chances. I got in the way of my own defencemen, and created chaos in our zone. I was a hindrance rather than a help. Luckily, my team has bailed me out, and we're winning despite my blunders.

Without Colin, I'm getting to know my teammates. We have plenty of talent from the National Team including Jayna Hefford, Vicky Sunohara, and Lori Dupuis who I think are currently the best line in all of women's hockey.

We also have plenty of former National Team members, including Olympians Karen Nystrom, a forward with grit and a huge wallop of a shot, and Laura Schuler who is a speedy, relentless forechecker recently returning from knee surgery. The two are polar opposites. Nystrom is wise, serious, studious, and thinks about the game like a tactician. Schuler is a prankster, outgoing and gregarious and the glue every team needs.

We also have National Team hopefuls: my good friend Samm Holmes, and Under-22 National Team members 17-year-old Krista McArthur and 18-year-old Teresa Del Monte.

In addition to those top Canadian players, the team includes Americans Jeanine Sobek and Meaghan Sittler, both currently on their National Team roster and hoping for a roster spot at the World Championship. Also, Stephanie Boyd, who, despite growing up in Canada, played for Team USA at the 1994 World Championships. Unfortunately, this season we won't have USA Olympian Sue Merz, as she is centralized with the National Team in Lake Placid.

Also on the Thunder is Justine Blainey, an iconic symbol for me ever since she won her battle at the Court of Appeal of Ontario as a 13-year-old winning the right to play on a boys' hockey team. I was

10 years old when she won her case, and because of her perseverance I knew I could continue to play locally without legal hindrance on boys' teams.

We have high hopes this season. The Beatrice Aeros have been the dominant team for years. Ken Dufton helped start the program in 1984 along with owner Colin "Big Guy" MacKenzie. However, two years ago, Susan Fennell, a former city councillor in Brampton, and recently elected mayor, started the Thunder to give women in the GTA another option for high-performance hockey. She started to build a franchise to beat the Aeros.

There's less than 30 seconds left on the game clock. The faceoff is in my end and Sainte-Julie has pulled their goalie for an extra attacker. They are intent on scoring two goals to tie this game.

As the ref readies to drop the puck, both centremen approach the faceoff dot to my left. Vicky takes the draw while wingers Hefford and Dupuis set up to her right. I tap both posts and glide into position. Tough defenceman and fan-favourite Donna-Lynn Rosa and youngster Krista McArthur are poised in front of me to protect the ambush. Sainte-Julie has put all but one player on the line of scrimmage. I know their plan is to win the puck back to the lone defenceman hovering at the top of the circle while the other five players will come barrelling towards me looking for a tip or deflection. They need a goal fast.

Vicky's always consistent winning faceoffs. Just before the puck drops, she looks at me to ensure I'm ready and gives me a nod. Vicky always makes me want to be better, if not for me, then for her. I lower myself into my ready position and focus on the puck.

Vicky wins it clean but instead of the puck jetting straight back to our defenceman, it angles to me. My first instinct is to pounce. In any other game with the score this tight in the third period, that's what I'd do, but I'm still in a bad mood that I can't shake, still angry at myself for the coach yelling at me.

I should cover the puck, but when I'm angry I make dumb plays.

I look down the ice. If I can get the puck safely out of the zone, the 25 seconds left should tick away. I thrust my blocker hand up my stick. My coach's words in the locker room are ringing in my head, "Don't make stupid plays. Be safe."

I look at the empty net. *I'm not being safe.*

Donnie and Krista have held off the onslaught, preventing any player with a black jersey from getting close to me.

I look down at the puck and wrap my catching mitt around the base of my long goalie stick. I've worked on my shot religiously for the past two years. My goalie partner, Stacy, and I are always passing the length of the ice when drills stop. I've made this shot thousands of times.

This might be my only chance. I lean on my stick and, like a football quarterback with a dozen big burly players coming to tackle him, I block out everything but the puck and the far net. I launch the puck in the air and propel it down the ice with the cockiness of someone expecting it to go in. Shock slows most of the players on the ice — the goalie has just shot the puck towards the open net.

Hefford skates as fast as she can down the ice. One of the fastest pure skaters in the game, she gets out in front of two Sainte-Julie defenders who also see what's happening. They're all trying to recover. It's right on target. Hefford battles the Panthères girls for position, trying to slow their progression.

I can no longer see the puck. Too many bodies in my way. Hefford's in a scrum with the two players in front of their net. Others have joined in the pushing and shoving. I can see the red light on indicating that we scored.

Did someone touch it before it went in?

Like not knowing if a hole in one went in from 250 yards away, I wait. Hefford fishes for the puck in the net with her hand, finds it, and lifts it high in the air. With her other hand she points at me. I smile and thrust my arms high in the air in celebration.

It went in. Now I'm surely going to get it from my coaches, but as my team rushes down the ice to celebrate with me, I'm too happy to care.

FEBRUARY 2001: TSN CHALLENGE — RED DEER/DENVER

As the third goalie for the first game of the TSN Challenge, I'm watching from high in the rafters in Red Deer, Alberta, as Charline "Charlie" Labonté, from Boisbriand, Quebec, plays against the Americans. The score is tied 4–4 with under two minutes to play in the game. The third period has been a bit of a Wild West with a combined six goals put past the goalies.

Hayley Wickenheiser scored first for us off a rush in the first period, and Cassie Campbell scored our second goal on a great point shot by rookie Isabelle Chartrand. I was thrilled for Cassie because she has been out with a concussion since the 4 Nations Cup tournament in November. Hefford tallied the third and Kelly Bechard scored our last midway through the frame to give us the 4–3 lead with seven minutes left. Unfortunately, with four minutes to play, Mleczko tied it up for the Americans.

Danielle Dube started in net for Canada and played the first half, helping Canada to a 1–0 lead. This is Danielle's first year back with the Team Canada program since her mysterious release in 1998, but she was impressive. I've always liked her calm style. She does a good job reading the play and doesn't overreact. In a scheduled move, Charlie came in midway through the game and now it's tied 4-4.

Unbelievably, with only 21 seconds left, after three point-blank saves by Charlie, Angela Ruggiero scores the go-ahead goal. Charlie's sprawled on the ice face down, nothing more she can do. My heart aches for her. The final score is 5–4.

Watching Charlie makes me realize the fragility of all our dreams. My game, my performance, my dreams, and, ultimately, my lifestyle are all dependent on other people. There are countless goalies in Canada aiming for this coveted spot. This was her first game against the Americans in a Team Canada uniform at the senior level, and our team did not play well in front of her.

•••••••

At the airport in Calgary, we await our departure to Denver for the second game of the TSN Challenge against the Americans, which will once again be part of the NHL's All-Star Weekend. I chat casually with Jennifer Botterill about the game. She's on leave from Harvard, where she won the Patty Kazmaier Memorial Trophy last year as the top player in the NCAA and is once again nominated this year. She played very well; however, offensively, our best line was Wick with young stars

Sommer West and Cherie Piper — both up from our newly formed Under-22 National Team program.

Jen created some great chances, even getting an incredible assist on Hefford's goal midway through the third period, but she's a bit down about the final goal. She was on the ice when the Americans scored. It was her linemate's giveaway in the corner. No one likes to be on the ice when the other team scores.

We make our way through customs dressed similarly in our black Team Canada tracksuits. Delaney Collins joins us at the other end of security. She's just grabbed some snacks for the flight. Delaney is a defenceman on the team and was on last year's Worlds team that won in Mississauga. She wasn't on for any of the five goals against today, which will certainly help with her coaches' evaluation.

"Botts, don't forget you played awesome in the series against Sweden," Delaney says to Jen, referring to the five-game series we played last week against the Swedes in the towns of Hanna and Cranbrook, in Alberta, and Kelowna, Trail, and Golden, in BC, in which I got two shutouts. It all counts.

•••••••

Arriving at Pepsi Center for the game in Denver is exciting. Home to the NHL's Colorado Avalanche, the festivities have already begun for the All-Star Game.

Fans pack the arena for our Canada–USA women's hockey tilt, making this one of the highest attended women's games in the States. Prior to the game, the men's Olympic coaching staff, including Pat Quinn and Wayne Gretzky, dropped by our dressing room for a visit and some inspirational words.

The game starts with a fast pace and lots of emotion. Because it's a short tournament, I wear my comfortable blue and gold Brampton Thunder goal pads. I battle; I make big saves; I manage to keep it a 2–2 game going into the third period. Krissy Wendell scored early in first on a power play, but Thérèse Brisson responded with a huge clapper from the point that found the back of the net. Wick scored late in the first period on a one-man rush, but Natalie Darwitz countered by putting one past me on a rebound in the middle of the second period.

Because we lost in Red Deer, we need to win this game in regulation in order to force overtime to decide the winner of the TSN Challenge.

We press hard, playing a four-man attack, trying to put one past the American goaltender, Ali Brewer, making our defensive zone suffer. We are sloppy, and the Americans capitalize with many odd-man rushes. They dramatically outshoot us in the third. I move after each puck and focus on squeezing each rebound.

We look tired. The last two weeks have taken their toll. Long bus trips through Alberta and BC, and demanding practices. Yesterday's practice was a killer and Danièle was not happy with our performance in Red Deer.

With less than seven minutes to play, Karyn Bye pounces on a turnover low in our zone. Bye's shot hits me through traffic, but I can't get enough of it, and it glances off me into the net.

3–2 Team USA.

After the goal, the Americans continue to buzz, and we just can't seem to generate any chances. The altitude seems to have gotten the best of us. I do my best to keep it close. I stop their top players, Cammi Granato and Katie King, on the doorstep, but we can't get the puck close to the American net. We end the game with a power play but are prevented from getting any pucks through.

We lose 3–2. My first ever loss in a Team Canada jersey, and it's gut-wrenching. It's hard watching the Americans accept the TSN Challenge Plate and grueling watching them celebrate.

I hate losing.

I know I played well, but with Team Canada, nothing matters but a win.

FEBRUARY 2001: COACH'S CALL

My roommate, Lori Dupuis, just got off her call with Team Canada's head coach, Danièle Sauvageau. She's in her room and I can hear she's clearly upset.

In the living room, I answer our white cordless house phone. It's been three weeks since the NHL All-Star Game.

"Hello?"

"Hello, is Sami Jo there, please?"

When I hear head coach Danièle's voice on the phone, my heart quickens. I run to my room and shut the door. Danièle spent last year coaching the Montreal Rocket in the QMJHL.

I think Danièle knows I speak French, but she never speaks in French to me. And I'm too nervous to willingly speak French to her.

"Kim played great at this year's 4 Nation, let in no goals, but she struggled too, with McGill. The hockey is not so good — so hard to evaluate." Kim outclasses her field and it must be hard to stay focused against weaker opponents.

I begin to worry we're just talking about Kim.

"I need to see Kim play at the World Championship. She will be our number one."

This news shocks me. We've never had a number one going into the camp. *That's not fair. She has to earn it.*

"Charline is also doing very well. She is our goalie of the future, and I debated putting her in now."

I don't care how they are doing. *What's happening? Is she cutting me?*

"But for now, you are number two. This will be Kim's year. You will be second. We don't need you to play, only to help Kim."

Number two? How did I go from World Championship MVP to barely on the team by a shoestring?

She also informs me that my roommate, Lori Dupuis, is cut.

I sit down on the floor of my room, staring blankly at the blue walls.

The tears stream down my face. I collapse sideways onto the carpet, weeping.

An hour goes by. *I can do this.* I'll take what I learned from my volleyball teammates, Karen and Stephanie, and I'll be the best number-two goalie they have ever seen. I don't want to. But I *have* to.

I make my way back to Lori's room and gingerly knock on the door.

12

A New Role

APRIL 2001: PREPARING FOR WORLDS

It's been a long travel day and the sun is still bright even though it's nearly seven in the evening. I slump tiredly next to the bus window as we drive two hours from Minneapolis to Rochester, Minnesota, the site of our round robin games at this year's World Championship. Vicky Sunohara is all jokes in her usual spot in the back of the bus while most curl up in their seats for some rest.

My body is holding up, but just barely. At the beginning of training camp two weeks in Toronto, I injured my left hip. The doctors think it might be overuse tendonitis, perhaps bursitis but I don't want the coaches to know how bad it is, so I've been masking it at training.

I can't help but think of the NWHL semifinal game loss to Toronto a few weeks ago. It was meant to be our game, our night. It was on national TV, and it was my birthday. Our team played very well, but despite winning the second game in a two-game series, we lost the deciding overtime in a shootout. It was one of the most difficult defeats I've ever experienced. Knowing I'd be the number two here, I was really putting all my marbles in that performance. I graciously smiled, but inside I was dying. The worst part is several of the Aeros that we lost to are on this bus, and as my teammates they are never shy to get a dig in here and there. It's still too soon for me, too fresh.

I'm not sure what will happen this week as Danièle told me I am back up goalie, but Kim was injured in last night's exhibition game against Team Ontario. She finished the game but looked woozy. I wonder if they've told her anything about being the number-one goalie or maybe they just told me I was going to be the number two to see how I'd react.

I've felt confident in practices feeling like I impressed on the coaches a work ethic that perhaps surprised them.

This year's Team Canada has five new players from last year's World Championship team. On defence, rookies Isabelle Chartrand and Colleen Sostorics took Nathalie Rivard's and Delaney Collins's spots. Dana Antal regained her position on forward after recovering from her broken leg, pushing the now married Amanda Benoit-Wark off the team. Rookie Correne Bredin, from Warburg, Alberta, replaces my roommate Lori Dupuis, but will be called on as both a forward and defenceman, and rookie Gina Kingsbury, from Rouyn-Noranda, Quebec, is called in to replace an injured Hayley Wickenheiser on forward.

Last night at York University, we played against a select team from Ontario. Coached by last year's assistant coaches, Ken Dufton and Karen Hughes, it included all the last cuts from Team Canada. I played half the game with Canada and half with Ontario. The girls on the Select Ontario team are still fighting for a spot on the centralized Olympic team roster, therefore their impression still matters.

Unfortunately, Wick also went down with a knee injury in the game and a forward fell awkwardly on Kim.

I played the first two periods for Team Canada helping us to a 2–1 lead. I then swapped with Kim and joined the team of girls who like me felt slighted.

I wanted to win to prove my worth, just as most of them did. Despite a huge number of shots in the third period, we scored two goals against Kim and won the game 3–2. A team of overlooked girls and recent cuts. Players told they were not fast enough, not strong enough, not smart enough had just upset the best team in the world, and I was part of that vindication.

But will this mean anything?

In the dressing room before the finals of the 2001 World Championship in Minneapolis, Minnesota, I walk past Kim after our on-ice warm-up and ask her how it went.

"Not bad," she says with a smile.

I guess as a goaltender, you never really know what warm-up can mean. Sometimes I've had my best games after a dismal warm-up; other times, I thought things felt awesome in warm-up only for them to derail in the game. Kim is quiet, but confident. *This is good*, I tell myself.

I smile back at Kim and say, "Great — good luck."

I make my way back to my stall, on the opposite side of the room from Kim's. I pass Goyette standing in front of her stall, adjusting her shoulder brace. Too many dislocations have forced her to wear a black contraption that prevents her from lifting her arm. Our team seems relaxed. Hopefully, we got the bugs out in warm-up.

I'm excited for the game, but also want it to be over. Danièle held true to her word, and I am in the back up goalie role for this game. I hate not playing, and it's difficult harnessing the strength to be positive all the time. There's such inner turmoil.

Earlier, we came to the rink in time to see Russia upset Finland in the bronze medal game, for its first ever medal at a World Championship, which bodes well for the future of the game as Canada and the Americans continue to dominate the world stage.

I grab a sip of the Diet Coke I've hidden in my stall. I need the caffeine to get through games that I don't play. It helps me stay focused when adrenaline is not pumping through my body. I know this is the last time I'll be in my equipment this year, and I'm a bit sad. I look down at my skates and wiggle my toes. It makes me smile.

The stalls are made out of a yellow metal wire frame that gives it an industrial look. The colour is for the University of Minnesota Gophers.

I'm proud of myself at how I've dealt publicly with not playing, but it hasn't been easy. Even Danièle told me she was impressed with my attitude and my play. But none of that changes how I feel right now.

Despite my feelings, I do hope we win, and I do hope Kim gets to experience what it's like to have the team pile on her at the end of the game, however I secretly hope she doesn't get a shutout.

The coaches come in and give us their last-minute instructions. Without Hayley Wickenheiser for the tournament, others have been forced to step up. Jen has been dominant defensively and our best player this tournament. She's led the tournament in scoring and has been consistently strong.

Danièle finishes up by announcing the starting lineup: Vicky Sunohara at centre with Jayna Hefford and Cassie Campbell on her wings. Rookie Colleen Sostorics and captain Thérèse Brisson on D. I grab my gloves and helmet and as I head towards the door, I tap everyone on the shin pads. Kim's already at the door, waiting. She gets to go first. I fall into line behind her. I'm the backup.

I cheer and I watch like a fan as Team Canada attempts to beat the Americans on home ice.

After one period, the score is tied 1–1, in large part thanks to Kim's great play. She made a huge breakaway save on Cammi Granato and we were outshot 12–4 in the first. The only goal she allowed was on a breakaway to Carisa Zaban who dipsy-doodled right around Becky Kellar going from right to left to beat St-Pierre high over her blocker on her backhand. Becky has been playing well but that was a tough one.

The Americans showed their prowess, especially on their multiple power plays. They've been centralized since the fall, and it's clear they work well together. Despite their chances, we also score. Our goal was a great power play deflection by Dana Antal off a point shot from Vicky. We are capitalizing on our limited opportunities while the Americans seem frustrated. The tie game works in our favour.

I sit back further in my stall. I feel I'm letting a lot of people down. Minneapolis is only an eight-hour drive from Winnipeg. Numerous people have made the drive from my hometown, including entire school buses and many Manitoba reporters.

I played the first two games of the tournament in Rochester, Minnesota, but the crowds were small. My parents drove down from Winnipeg and my Auntie Margaret-Ann and Uncle Bob, who live close by in Owatonna, Minnesota, joined them. They are big hockey fans and their son Rob played. We used to see more of them when they lived in Winnipeg, and I idolized my older cousins Rob and Debbie, but it was great my aunt and uncle could be here to cheer me on.

After I played Team Canada's first game against Kazakhstan, the second was supposed to be Kim's. Unfortunately, she sliced her foot on a skate in the dressing room and needed a few days for the stitches to heal, so I also started the second game, against Russia.

Several reporters even heralded me as the starter for the remainder of the tournament, but deep down I knew better. Danièle does not seem like the kind of person to go back on her word.

I stand up and walk over to sit next to Jen. She now wears No. 17; it makes her look bigger on the ice than the No. 7 she wore until this point in her career. She asked for No. 17 after Stacy Wilson retired. An homage to her dad's day of birth.

"Good job out there," I say, patting her on her leg. She smiles, but she's not much of a hockey talker. So I change the subject.

"Did you hear about the hanger?"

"No?" She seems intrigued and happy that I'm changing the focus from the game.

"So, this morning, at the end of practice, as we're skating to centre ice for the team cheer, Goyette looks at me and says, 'What's that?'"

"'What's what?' I say, looking down at my chest in the direction of her glare.

"She reaches out and grabs at the tip of a plastic bit protruding from the neck of my jersey, to reveal an *entire* plastic hanger."

"A *hanger* was in your jersey all practice?" she asks laughing, her tone conveying disbelief.

"Yeah, I couldn't believe it — almost as bad as Gina's hat," I say, causing Jen to let out a big roar at my reference to rookie Gina Kingsbury's embarrassing moment in her first game of the championship. Gina's serious and meticulous, often the last player off the ice, or frequently re-watching game tape over and over to uncover the minutiae of the game. However, perhaps due to the nerves of an international game, she forgot that she was wearing a backwards baseball hat and put her helmet on right over top. It wasn't until Coach noticed midway through the first period, her hat's brim poking out the back of her helmet, that Gina, mortified, realized what she'd done.

I want Jen to be the hero today. She knows what I'm going through. She's been an invaluable sounding board all tournament, although I try not to burden her too often. Despite Canada's lacklustre first period, and being on the penalty kill a lot, she's creating chances; perhaps she'll be the spark we need in the second period.

Back out on the ice, we again struggle for the first half of the period, while the Americans continue to be stymied by Kim. Luckily for us, just after the 10-minute mark, Tammy Lee Shewchuk scores. She was a finalist for the Patty Kazmaier award this year as the top NCAA player, losing out to Jen, her linemate and Harvard teammate. Shewchuk is one of the best players in the world from the hash marks down, and she neatly banged home a Kelly Bechard pass giving us the lead going into the dressing room at the end of the second. The line of Bechard, Shewchuk, and Botterill has been dominant all tournament, and it's fitting they scored.

The US has outplayed us, we miss Wick and her intensity, but Kim is helping us maintain the lead with huge saves while on the penalty kill. Cammi Granato had many chances and Jenny Potter, formerly Jenny Schmidgall, nearly put it over the goal line. She is playing only three months after giving birth to her daughter, Madison. Our defencemen have been throwing themselves in front of pucks; the selflessness is remarkable.

We lead 2–1, but the shots are 24–14 in favour of the Americans.

The energy in the dressing room is high between periods. I tap Kim on the pads. "Great job so far," I say with a smile, and head to my stall. Despite everything, we have the lead.

In the third, Kim remains focused and makes some more opportune saves with 10 minutes to play. All the big names, Bye, Granato, King, and Ruggiero, fire more shots. Defenceman Isabelle Chartrand plops beside me on the bench wincing; I think it's her knee, and I doubt she can go back in. Jen's line is double-shifting, their hard work being rewarded by the coaching staff.

With just over three minutes left to play, the faceoff is deep in the American zone, and Jen's one of the best at faceoffs in the world. She draws the puck back to Thérèse Brisson, who unleashes a cannon. Jen heads straight to the net and gets her blade on the blast to redirect it top shelf past Sarah Tueting. I explode to my feet. Jen is jumping up and down on the ice, like roadrunner, her arms pumping to give us a two-goal lead.

It's 3–1, with slightly over three minutes to go.

The Americans press. They are six on five. Bredin takes down King and takes a penalty. Six on four, the Americans finally slip another one by Kim: A.J. Mleczko finishes a pretty passing play to make the score 3–2.

One minute to go. Tueting again heads to the bench, but the ref calls Karyn Bye on a trip against Shewchuk. It's five on five but our team keeps them to the outside. Final faceoff in our zone and Vicky wins it. The final seconds tick off the clock.

The buzzer sounds. We win.

Kim throws her stick high in the air, and I get lost in the excitement. I scramble over the boards in 60 pounds of equipment and rush the pile forming on top of Kim.

On the blue line, arm in arm with my teammates, I stand next to Jen. I feel safe next to her. I find my joy through her. She receives the honour of top forward of the tournament, and Kim receives the top goalie award. I'm reluctantly happy for her. It's hard not to find joy in the exuberant face of a teammate.

Captain Thérèse Brisson accepts the championship plate alongside assistants Cassie Campbell and Vicky Sunohara. Once again, we are World Champions.

André Brin, our media relations coordinator, the same André that worked locally in Winnipeg for the French TV and radio stations, grabs Jen for an interview with TSN. She's had an incredible tournament. I smile enthusiastically during the anthem, holding a giant flag alongside Jen. In spite of this, the feelings are much different this time around.

I wanted to play.

APRIL 2001: EASTER WEEKEND

It's been two weeks since our return from the World Championship and I am sitting in the childhood home of Jayna Hefford in Kingston, Ontario, to celebrate Easter with teammates Ally Fox and Jeanine Sobek and the Heffords. The mementoes from Heff's hockey career that her parents, Larry and Sandra, have proudly displayed surround us in the basement. We're watching the NWHL finals on TV that don't include us. It's not as easy for the Aeros to win against Sainte-Julie as we thought it would be. The first game of the two-game series ended in a tie, and the Aeros are only up 1–0 in this game. It's hard to watch but comforting to have teammates around.

The past two weeks have been a great distraction. Trips to the casino, fun with friends, and forgetting about my lack of playing at the World Championship. But also plenty of time to reflect on what needs to be done to ensure that in 10 months, at the Olympic Games, I can regain my number-one spot in.

I still feel bad for not going to the bar with my team the night we won the World Championship, but I simply couldn't. I celebrated in the dressing room. I held it together and was genuinely pleased and proud of my teammates. I was especially happy for the rookies Gina Kingsbury, Isabelle Chartrand, Colleen Sostorics, and Correne Bredin, who won their first World Championship, and also Dana Antal, who won her first while on the ice. And I was excited for Heaney who won her unbeliev-able seventh straight title.

I was elated for Jen as her performance solidified her as one of the best players in the world. She's had an incredible third year in the NCAA at Harvard. She led the league in scoring and won college hockey's top honour, the Patty Kazmaier award. And at the Worlds, she was named the top forward. All of that should give her a huge amount of confidence going into next year's Olympics.

I was also happy for Kim. She played excellently, and her feeling of joy evoked a lot of memories for me.

But the sting of not playing was too much. I just couldn't go on pretending, so rather than share my sadness on such a joyous occasion, I made my way back to my room. My brother knocked on the door, but I told him to go away. I feel guilty for not celebrating with my family; nonetheless, I just needed to escape from the hockey world and pull the sheets up over my head and go to sleep after a long day.

Back to watching the TV, and the Aeros win the game and hoist the NWHL Championship Cup as we feast on an incredible Easter meal.

The official centralization roster came out yesterday. All 20 players from this year's World Championship team plus 10 additions. Lori

Dupuis is back on the roster, vying for a spot on the Olympic team; however, sadly my friend Samm Holmes from the Thunder didn't make the cut. We trained hard side by side for this opportunity, and now her Olympic dream is over.

Defencemen Fiona Smith, Nathalie Rivard, and Delaney Collins, as well as forwards Amanda Benoit-Wark, Hayley Wickenheiser (who missed Worlds because of injury), and goalie Danielle Dube are also on the list attempting to regain their spots on the team.

Also, young Ontario rookie forwards Cherie Piper, from Scarborough, Gillian Apps, from Unionville, and goalie Charline Labonté will be looking to crack the lineup.

The other announcement was a raise in our carding money — the money given to Olympic athletes by the federal government. It's gone up from $800 per month to $1,100, which makes training as a full-time athlete less of a burden.

Today is our last day of rest. Tomorrow our quest to bring the gold medal back to Canada starts, and I'm determined to show up at camp in three weeks fitter than I've ever been and more mentally prepared to battle every day. I need to be so good that politics and emotions do not play a factor. I played my role in Minnesota, and I'm going to show them I will do whatever it takes to regain the number-one spot and help our team to an Olympic gold medal.

13

The Beginnings of a Team

MAY 2001: TESTING

Testing camp has started in Calgary, kicking off our Olympic tryout. We are 30 women vying for 20 spots. The next few months will be cutthroat, as the coaching staff build a team. Each of us will attempt to prove that we belong and can add value both to its performance and character.

What makes a great team to me isn't the same for everyone. Not only will I have to perform on the ice, I will have to decipher how to mould myself into the coach's image of their ideal team.

At the end of the second of two full days of baseline testing, I stand on the start line for the beep test, also known as the Léger test, basically a shuttle run. I am incredibly tense. Our team has been split in two. Fifteen of us eye the other line 20 metres off in the distance.

We're on the track that surrounds the Olympic speed skating oval. It's cold, but even in my shorts and Cardinal red Stanford t-shirt, I'm already sweating from nerves. My pounding heartbeat muffles the instructions. I hate this test more than I hate any other. I'm more anxious for this than any significant game and I've been dreading it since I did it the last time at camp last October.

Any test to do with strength or coordination, and I can finish in the top groupings; but when it comes to cardio, I am always one of the last. Over the past few years, my training has changed significantly. I've had to go from a power-based throwing athlete to Hockey Canada prescribed workouts. They are generic workouts, not specific for me, but I do them in hope of performing better on these tests.

The first beep sounds.

A British voice on the CD announces, "Level 1." I depart the line and casually jog to the other end. My foot must hit the far line at the next beep. I know it won't be a casual pace for long. Each level is a little faster than the last. I touch the line and turn back towards the start.

I stare straight ahead, trying to avoid looking at our teammates cheering us on. I hate this feeling. It's not that I hate running — I hate being bad at something.

"Level 4." The spacing between beeps begins to quicken.

Our pace increases. The idea is to stay in the test as long as possible. Some great scores will be level 12 or 13 — Geraldine Heaney will likely get 14, she can seemingly go on forever — but my best is 8.5. I know it's bad in comparison, but I've been running nearly every day for the past two months in preparation. I try to stay with the beeps. Stay with the pack.

Level 6. I'm starting to feel fatigued. My face is red and sweat trickles down my face.

I know I look tired because the encouragement from the sidelines is getting louder, specifically, for me. My muscles are tightening, my chest constricting. I'll bet no one else feels this tired. No smiles. This is business. I stare at the line in front.

Level 7. My legs struggle. I'm falling behind. Danielle Goyette makes her way to the end of my lane. She has a test to do shortly, but she knows I need someone. Someone to push me. Every lap I hear her clapping as she crouches down screaming, "One more, Sami!" *Don't quit now.*

I need to catch up. I need to show not only the coaches, but my teammates that I can do this. *Don't lose the group.*

"Stay with Piper," Goyette says loudly, encouraging me to stay stride for stride with rookie Cherie Piper.

I look down. I look beside me at Piper, but I can't focus. As I sprint down the track, I think, *Just make it back to Goyette.*

My posture is failing, my limbs are struggling. I can make it. *Push.*

"Again!" screams Goyette. Another turn, another level. *Sprint. Get there.*

My chest's only intent is to take in more air. Oxygen is tough to find.

Right. Left. Right. The beeps are very fast, I'm sprinting now. I can't hear. I can taste blood in the back of my throat caused by too much lactic acid in the bloodstream.

Lunge. I just barely make the beep when my body gives out. I'm dizzy and disoriented. I collapse, violently gasping for air. Goyette rushes to my side and brings me a garbage can. She gingerly lifts my arm and looks at my watch that reads *Heart Rate: 198*. She puts her arm around me and lifts me up as I lean into her for support.

"I knew you could do it," she says, grabbing a water bottle off the floor for me. "That was 9.2 — that your best?"

"Yeah," I say between gasps.

For the next few days in Calgary, while doing two-a-day workouts, Jen and I search for an apartment. We finally find one that has a lease starting in August for our eight-month stay. The Brampton girls, Lori, Vicky, and Jayna, have decided to find a place together, but I think it'll be best if I'm with Jen. She stays out of the drama and, for the most part, hates talking about hockey. I'll need her in order to find balance and a life outside our team.

It's now back to Toronto for one month of training at home with our trainer Dennis Lindsay in preparation for a three-week camp in Valcartier, Quebec, in the middle of June. This week has been tough, but it's only going to be more challenging moving forward.

JUNE 2001: A LONG WALK HOME

Jen likes bright happy colours and hates the camouflage that's everywhere. She hates the idea of war and having it right in her face is not helping her overall morale.

I'm riding my rented mountain bike on a cycling path just south of the Valcartier military base in Quebec. We train on the military base because our coach Danièle Sauvageau is an ex-RCMP officer, and was able to use her connections to secure funding to house us at CFB Valcartier surrounded by soldiers, guns, and tanks. The military give tours of the armoury, a demo by a paratrooper team, and insight into the inner workings of military strategy and team. Maybe because of my engineering background, I find it all interesting, however, most of my teammates, including Jen, do not.

It is a gorgeous, sunny day. Our group, consisting of Delaney Collins, Amanda "Benny" Benoit-Wark, Tammy Lee Shewchuk, rookie Cherie Piper, and me, is motoring along the 70-kilometre ride. We are at the back of the pack, the last group of cyclists. The only group behind us is the staff members equipped with spare tires and first aid. The mission today is to ride to the Montmorency Falls, break for lunch, and then return home. Each of us takes the difficult turn in the lead of the peloton as we work together to make the ride as painless as possible.

At the falls, our group rests. Lesley Reddon, who is now part of the staff as an assistant to the general manager, was waiting for us with bag lunches.

"Thanks Lester," Piper says enthusiastically.

"How is the ride?"

"It's flippin' hot out there," says Shewchuk, her t-shirt already tucked into her tights, her sports bra exposed. She says it with a smile but is clearly perturbed. Shewchuk is from the English part of Montreal but completely fluent in both languages. I appreciate her demeanor, because you know exactly what you get with her. She has no filter and is candid and honest. At my first women's tournament, the 1991 Canada Games, she was the star of Team Quebec. I traded my Manitoba boots with her in exchange for her Quebec ones, never really thinking our paths would cross again, but she has since been the star at Harvard, breaking numerous school records and leading her team to a University Championship.

We are a little over an hour bike ride from the military base. Benny takes the lead from Delaney, Shewchuk in behind her, Piper is next, and I am at the rear. Delaney slides into the final position behind me.

Delaney didn't make the team last year, despite solid performances in the 4 Nations Cup in Utah in the series against Sweden and in the TSN Challenge. She's exceptionally gifted offensively and makes an accurate first pass out of the zone every time. It will be difficult for her to regain her spot on the Olympic team, as her selection seems dependent on who is the coach. In 1999 she was cut when Danièle was coaching; in 2000 she made the team under Melody Davidson's helm; and then in 2001, when Danièle was back, she was once again left off the roster.

I always appreciate having Delaney around because she loves rehashing my best saves or noteworthy wins. She is fiercely loyal, and one of my most faithful fans.

We ride for nearly 25 kilometres along the paved path in the hot sunshine, each taking our turns in front. As Piper takes the lead, I check my shoulder — no Delaney. I yell through the wind at Piper: "Hold up."

Piper looks back. I point behind us. Delaney is coasting more than 20 metres back.

"Hey guys, slow down," I yell to the rest of the girls.

Delaney gets off her bike. Our group slows down and stops. We turn our bikes around and circle back to her.

"My tire just blew," she mumbles.

Piper gets off her bike and starts walking alongside Delaney.

Shewchuk, Benny, and I ride slowly beside them, our legs pushing on pavement as we did as kids on our BMXs.

Three staff members, with the flat tire repairs, are farther back. They arrived at the falls just as we were leaving. They should be by shortly. Delaney is pushing her bike, as the tire thumps loudly. Finally, the three of us get off our bikes too.

We walk alongside Delaney for 10 minutes, our legs aching. Another 10 minutes go by; the staff still doesn't show. Where could they be?

"Guys, go ahead, you're going to miss dinner," Delaney pleads with us.

"No way, we're not leaving you." Piper is adamant.

We continue walking, sporadically looking behind us for the staff group.

Ten minutes later, Delaney is insistent, embarrassed that we are holding back because of her.

"Guys, go on, there's only five k left, I'll be fine — they should be here shortly."

"Should we go?" asks Shewchuk.

"Maybe we should?" I stammer back, not thinking straight, hungry for dinner. "Delaney, you'll be okay, right?"

She nods. It's a nice day, there are plenty of riders around, and the staff should be here in the next five minutes. What more can we do? We decide to leave.

We pedal the remaining five kilometres in 10 minutes. Piper, Shewchuk, Benny, and I go inside, wash up in the cold military communal showers, change our clothes, and head to the mess hall. Surrounded by hundreds of military, mostly men, we stick out like sore thumbs.

I'm famished.

I grab my tray, and Benny, Piper, Shewchuk, and I find a seat next to Jen. "How was your ride?" I ask. Jen is usually up with one of the faster groups.

"It was so nice to be in the sunshine. Wick was a bit intense, but the waterfall was amazing. Where's Delaney? Wasn't she with you guys?"

"Her tire blew; the staff is fixing it."

I scarf down my food, my body depleted from the ride in the hot sun.

After dinner, I walk with Piper back from the mess hall towards the barracks.

Off in the distance we see Delaney. She is still in her bright-yellow-and-blue cycling jersey, her silver helmet unstrapped, and her face burnt from the sun as she pushes her bike by the seat.

Piper and I run over to her.

Delaney's eyes spill tears. She looks exhausted. She holds her hand up, unable to speak. She's mad.

"The f***king staff never came!" she says, annoyed, pushing her bike right past us.

Piper and I glance at each other. Guilt spreads through my body.

The coaches announced at the start of camp that our team motto for this year will be "We Are Responsible," or the acronym W.A.R. It has much significance, but today I have failed in upholding it. Today I was not responsible for the *we* but simply for the *me*. I failed a teammate.

I feel sick to my stomach as I look at my watch and realize two hours have passed since we left her. I just assumed she was already back. It's easy to get lost in a group of 30 people. She pushed her broken bike all alone. *How could I do that to a teammate? Where was the staff?*

We chase after Delaney, but she wants to be on her own.

I feel awful; I just hope she will forgive me.

JUNE 2001: THE SQUIRREL

The sun is high as we are once again on our mountain bikes for a long ride. Benny leads our group, followed by Piper, me, Shewchuk, and Delaney.

The trees whizz by separated from us only by a patch of grass. The five of us stay to the right as other cyclists pass on the left. The sun is high.

I wear my 7-Eleven pro cycling team jersey that I got on a family trip to Toronto because I can stash snacks in the back pockets. Delaney, who's on a new bike, opted for a sports bra today, just like Benny and Shewchuk. She woke up less mad at us, and we're doing everything we can to make today easy for her. Our group has ridden approximately 60 kilometres of today's 80-kilometre ride. It was supposed to be an individual race, less about sightseeing and more about going as fast as you can, but the five of us figured we'd be faster together.

Days at camp begin at 6:00 a.m. with breakfast in the mess hall and don't end until evening. The days are long, but coach Sauvageau has sprinkled in some fun team building activities to keep it interesting. Every morning we ride our bikes the seven kilometres to the rink. She has brought in Tomas Pacina to work on our individual hockey skills and Lorraine Ostiguy to help with power skating. The afternoons are usually for lifting and off-ice workouts, and the evenings are for martial arts, including yoga. I've been tired nearly every day but know in the end, this base will serve us for the season.

Benny keeps pedalling as we draft behind. She eventually pulls her bike to the left and lets Piper come to the front. Benny slows her cadence as her bike glides to the end of the line. She tucks in behind Shewchuk, her hard work done for now. As Piper emerges in front, my field of view opens. It's so bright, the sun creating a haze on the darkly paved path. I squint through my sunglasses. Up ahead, there appears to be slower riders blocking the path.

I figure Piper will simply avoid them, so I lower my gaze and follow her tire. Suddenly I can see her back brake engaging on the wheel. *Why are we slowing down?* I veer to the left of Piper and slow too.

It's two of our teammates, but I can't tell who. The three girls behind me all veer over for a look too. Four bikes lie on the ground. One is in the middle of the path, the other three lay on the grass beside the path.

As we slowly approach, I recognize Cassie Campbell and Kelly Bechard, and they look hysterical.

Piper asks, "What's happened?"

Kelly can't speak; both her hands are on her knees. Cassie attempts, but her words come out too high pitched to understand. *Are they crying or laughing?*

Why are there only two girls and four bikes? My mind plays through wild scenarios. Piper dismounts while the rest of us straddle our bikes.

"Just breathe," Piper says loudly, encouraging the two, trying not to laugh. She slowly asks again, "What's happened?"

I look down the path and can see the outline of two more girls in the distance. One is standing and one is seated, both in the shade where the grass lines the path. Kelly finally stands erect once she catches her breath.

"A squirrel . . . " is all she can get out before erupting once again in laughter.

"The fur . . . " Cassie tries to continue, but belly laughs overcome her too.

"The squirrel fur what?" I say, and both point to the bike on the road. My gaze catches on the back brake pad of one of the downed bikes.

"Is that . . . ?" I throw my bike down for a closer look. "No way, that's a dead squirrel," I say, looking back at my group. The girls burst out again in laughter.

Out of breath, Kelly recounts, "I was riding behind Vicky, and this squirrel ran out from there." She motions to the trees. "Then I felt fur on my face." Kelly and Cassie are chortling like schoolgirls.

"Vicky murdered a squirrel!" erupts Cassie.

This is not funny, but also really funny at the same time.

"Is that Vicky?" Piper points down the path. More nodding. Piper starts walking towards her and Jayna Hefford.

I look at the bike and feel I should do something. I take off my sweat-filled sunglasses and see blood and guts are everywhere. I try to move the back tire, but it's stuck. Shewchuk, Benny, and Delaney are engrossed with Kelly and Cassie as they replay the absurdity of the situation. We're still at least 30 minutes from home.

I poke at the dead squirrel with my sunglasses. It's really stuck. I look around then walk towards the trees. I need something bigger. I find a suitable stick to poke the squirrel. Nothing. Laughter is everywhere. Can this be fixed without one of us losing our lunch? It's disgusting. I start really thumping on the squirrel. We have to get this bike to work.

One last whack, and finally the blockage is gone.

Shewchuk grabs some leaves, picks up the squirrel, and moves it onto the grass. Benny grabs her water bottle and uses the remaining liquid to spray down the area.

I stand the bike up, spin the tire, and exclaim loudly so Vicky can hear, "All done." I expected the crew to come immediately, but after much deliberation, only Jayna walks towards us.

Within 10 metres, Jayna stops and says from afar, "Vicky says there's no way she's getting on a bike covered in squirrel guts!"

"There's no more squirrel blood or guts on it — we washed it off," I state proudly, and show off our work to Heff.

Heff waves for the girls to come back. Piper coaxes Vicky to walk, but she is hesitant to get too close.

As she approaches, she yells, "No way! There's no way!"

"Vicky, we have to get home, just get on the bike," Heff pleads as the rest of us try to hold back laughter.

An argument ensues between Heff and Vicky. Vicky is not budging.

I'm still holding the squirrel bike by the handlebars. The seat's too low but that's okay. I point at my bike and suggest to Vicky, "Ride that one."

Hesitantly, slowly, her eyes puffy from crying, sad at the destruction of a living being, Vicky heads towards my bike. As she mounts the bike, she turns and says, "Keep that stupid squirrel bike away from me."

I hop on the stupid squirrel bike.

There are giggles and several attempts to console Vicky on the way home but to no avail. As I ride at a respectful distance from Vicky, I have plenty of time to ponder the next few weeks. The rest of the ride is uneventful, but had I not left Delaney behind yesterday, had Danielle Goyette not gone out of her way to cheer me on to my best performance in the beep test, I'm not sure I'd be in this position today. Vicky may never think this situation is funny, but I'm glad I got to be part of it; the rest of us will be laughing about this incident all year. These moments matter. As the coaches build the team from the top-down, we build it internally from the bottom-up. I realize I have unique abilities to stay calm and rational in stressful situations, and if it means I need to ride the squirrel bike to ensure we all get home safely, that's what I'm going to do.

14

Becoming Olympians

In the large boardroom of the Hockey Canada offices at Father David Bauer Arena, I'm eager yet nervous. I'm sitting at a long oak table surrounded by the other 29 players centralized in Calgary trying out for Canada's Olympic hockey team. It's been six weeks since we left the military base. We have our first official on-ice practice tomorrow, but tonight the coaches are laying out the schedules, the guidelines, the criteria for selection, and their expectations for the next seven months of centralization leading up to the Olympic Games.

I left my brother, Luke, back at my new place. He drove from Winnipeg to Calgary with me in our Mazda 323 — the Blue Bomber and his flight from Winnipeg is tomorrow. After graduating he and his fiancée, Gina, joined my dad in the family optometry business.

He took me bed shopping today, and he insisted on buying me a mattress that's now in the middle of my unfurnished room. Rest will be my greatest asset. I can sleep anywhere, anytime; I just need lots of it to perform. My friends joke that sleep is my favourite thing. Sleep and rest will be my key to making this team.

"From the Olympic dream fund," he said with a big brother grin, knowing I could never afford a new mattress on my own. He's always my leading supporter, constantly bragging about his younger sister. When we were little, he coerced his buddies to let me play street hockey. We stayed up late, watching *Hockey Night in Canada* and often snuck into my parents' room after we should have been asleep to watch *Lance et compte*, a French drama based on a local hockey team. We played mini sticks nearly every day, often including too-hard hip checks, which turned into shoving and eventually punches. I was always on the losing end, but I always came back because I idolized my brother. I wanted to play with him, to be good enough to compete with him.

He's taking me and Jen out tonight for one final supper together. I think about how his Olympic dream just fell short. I've seen how close someone can come, know that hard work and effort are not always rewarded, but I don't think he regrets his decision one bit. He tried, and that's what I admire most.

I'm sitting in an oversized plush leather swivel chair. There is only enough room at the table for 15 or so — the rest of the girls have their chairs lining the walls behind us. Head coach Danièle Sauvageau has a slide on the projector outlining the next months' activities. August and September look difficult. Ice times every day, gym workouts every afternoon, and often team-building activities in the evenings. She talks about our high performance culture and how no stone will be left unturned this year.

Can I do enough to prove myself the number-one goalie? Kim St-Pierre, Charline Labonté, and Danielle Dube are the goalies I'll have to outplay. It's hard not to notice the blue walls lined with pictures of past Canadian champion teams. Dozens and dozens. I notice the Trail Smoke Eaters, World Champions in 1960. I met their star Norm Lenardon when we played in Trail, BC, prior to the TSN Challenge last year. He's such a nice man, and we've remained pen pals. Beside them, our trailblazing first women's team, with my friend Susie Yuen, dressed in pink, World Champions in 1990.

"Boot camp," as we dubbed the month together in Valcartier, Quebec, ended on June 29. We were together 23 days in the small confines of the barracks. Exactly the amount of time we will be together in the Olympic Village prior to the gold medal game. I came away from boot camp more confident and more fit, but so did everyone else. I narrowed the gap between my cardio levels and the top players', and I think I proved that I am mentally strong and resilient even in my most tired of times.

Back in the boardroom, assistant coach Mel Davidson is finishing her "player's expectations" presentation when Wally Kozak, our other assistant coach, chimes in.

"Work hard. Focus on the details. Be consistent." I smile. It feels as though Wally is talking directly to me. While I've never had an issue excelling in big games, I've struggled to make every practice matter. I tried to focus on that in Valcartier. I have a new resolve to make every day a chance to get better, to make those around me better. I want to be more consistent. The team needs me to be more consistent.

I'm motivated to get on the ice right now. I can do this. The acetate on the projector shows each monthly breakdown. August and September are going to be tough training months, and in October we travel, play international games, and begin our exhibition game schedule against the local boys' AAA Midget teams.

As Danièle finishes and hands the meeting over to our manager, Gaëtan Robitaille, he explains the team issued meal cards. I look around the room at the 29 girls knowing only 21 (20 plus an alternate goalie) of us will still be together when the puck drops at the Olympics in Salt Lake.

SEPTEMBER 2001: TRAGEDY STRIKES

We have a four-day break from Team Canada and I'm in California for my brother's wedding. Two days ago he married fellow Berkeley optometry alum Gina Mistretta, in Santa Barbara.

For the past month and a half, we've been training twice a day, six days a week with one rest day. The rest day often includes team activities such as a sports psychology session with Dr. Kimberley Amirault, team videos with Ryan Jankowski, or nutrition sessions with Kelly Anne Erdman. There hasn't been much time apart so this break has been nice.

After the wedding I rented a car and drove six hours up the coast to Stanford to visit my former roommate Diana. We had fun, visiting a neighbourhood café, chatting, getting caught up, and feeling like we were in university all over again.

It's 8:00 a.m. and I'm asleep on Diana's couch. She touches my shoulder, gently shaking me.

"Wake up, Sami," she says softly. "We should get going to the airport."

I slowly wake up on her couch to the smell of coffee percolating.

"Can you put on some tea too?"

I grab the remote and flick on her television, trying to find some sports highlights. I change the channel. Same as the last. I change up and change down and all the images are the same. I say nothing, staring at smoke coming from the building on the TV as Diana comes and sits next to me.

"Oh, Dios mio," she says, making the sign of the cross.

The World Trade Center in New York City was hit by a plane.

My parents were supposed to fly out of LAX today. There was a whole wedding full of people flying home after my brother's September 8 marriage.

I grab the phone, and I try to call my parents. Nothing. I try to call my brother. I can't get through. *Are they in the air?*

Worried for everyone, Diana and I sit in disbelief.

A full day goes by and we keep trying to get through. Finally, the following day, I reached my parents. Everyone is okay, but they are stuck in Los Angeles. The American government has shut down all the airports: there's no way to get home. Day after day, we monitor the flights, but they are grounded.

Air travel in Canada resumes a week later, and the rest of Team Canada returns to the ice in Calgary, but not me. I am still stranded in San Francisco. Diana and I go for walks, make some meals, and talk about the year. Anything to pass the time.

We continue to watch CNN, but no planes are leaving. I check in with our coaches, they understand, but I hate to be missing practices.

I try not to sound concerned as I talk to my mom on the phone.

"Maybe we can drive?" she says, as I hear the F-1 bombers flying over the city. "We'll rent a car and should be in San Fran by the end of the day."

I hang up and turn to Diana. "Is it okay if my parents stay here tonight?"

The following day, we take turns driving the 15 hours to the Vancouver airport. We part ways there as they catch a flight to Winnipeg and I catch mine to Calgary, but not before my dad says, "Stone 'em and have fun."

Back in Calgary, I have a few days on the ice to get my bearings before we head out on our first trip to British Columbia for a series against the Swedes.

I find out upon my return, one of the members of Team USA, Kathleen Kauth, tragically lost her father in the World Trade Center. Team USA was at a training camp in Colorado when they heard the news. I feel terrible for Kathleen and selfish for being so concerned about missing a week of training.

·······

The Swedish series provides for several lopsided victories, but mostly serves to unite the team as we travel through small towns on Vancouver Island, promoting women's hockey. We are welcomed into Tofino, Campbell River, Port Alberni, and Victoria with large crowds and long autograph lines.

We have countless long bus and ferry trips. We do so many crosswords that I'm starting to improve. Delaney Collins and I, squished together side by side, tackle a new one every day. We high-five exuberantly when we find a word, and when we are stumped, we hand it over to Pounder or Piper, both genius crossworders. Despite the long travel, I love that we get to experience this country, visiting places I might never otherwise get a chance to see.

A few weeks later and it's the middle of October. Cassie and her boyfriend, Brad Pascall, who works with the men's national team program, have a bunch of us over for Thanksgiving dinner.

While celebrating, news spreads quickly through the group that cuts were made. Defencemen Nathalie Rivard and Fiona Smith, forward Gina Kingsbury, and goalie Danielle Dube have all been cut.

My heart rate quickens, my chest constricts. They must be devastated. After going through so much together, the reality hits that making this team will be even harder than winning an Olympic medal.

On the way home, Jen and I stop at Fiona's. She lives with Isabelle Chartrand and Nancy Drolet. I'm not sure what to say when I see her sadness, but we try to talk about the future. "I'm going to fly to see Rob," Fiona says, speaking of her boyfriend. We've been forced away from loved ones for so long; I can see a glimmer of enthusiasm in her face. These cuts will be hard on the team, but we must find a way quickly to come together.

Not only does my heart ache for my friends, but my grandfather is in the hospital in Winnipeg. He's 90. I ache thinking of him alone in that place. Also, I just found out a few days ago that my Brampton teammate Meaghan Sittler just lost her mom to cancer. Life doesn't stop while I'm here. Some important games are coming up quickly against the Americans and despite all the sadness, I must remember that I'm still fighting for a spot.

OCTOBER 2001: WARM-UPS

I'm sitting in a darkly lit coaches' room in the bowels of the Shark Tank in San Jose. Kim St-Pierre sits beside me. I can tell our head coach is angry.

Danièle sits in front of us. She leans to the side and pulls up a clipboard. Her assistants, Wally and Mel, are sitting on the benches that surround the small room.

"This is unacceptable." She points to the clipboard.

I can't even tell why she's mad. It's a picture of a hockey rink with little Xs and Os scattered throughout one zone — perhaps these are shots from last game? But there are too many goals if that were the case. Kim and I take a closer, more confused look.

We never know what the coaches want. Every day the expectations change, and there's rarely any positive feedback.

"You guys are letting in too many goals in warm-up," Danièle says as if she's teaching us the finer aspects of goaltending. Unfortunately, Dave Jamieson, our goalie coach, isn't here. He's still an elementary school teacher in Oro, Ontario. He'd talk sense into her, but he's not around enough. She raises her voice as she gets into each drill that our team does throughout the game warm-ups.

This has to be a joke. There are countless other things to yell about, and she's choosing warm-up. *Why is this even an issue? Why are they even counting the number of goals scored in warm-up?* She must be upset about our 4–1 loss to the Americans in Salt Lake City a few days ago. With Kim in net, we outshot them 34–25, but they still won 4–1.

Tomorrow's game in San Jose, in front of several of my Stanford friends, will be my game. My first chance to play the Americans this season, and I get to do it in my old stomping grounds. I've been excited about this game for weeks, but Danièle is killing my buzz.

I try not to look at Kim, but Danièle has got my back up. *Why does she even care about this? That's my time.* I just can't let this go. Too much has happened in the last month, I am too emotional, so I counter with an argument.

"Everyone warms up differently. I'm just getting used to the puck, sliding in position, and trying to not get hurt or too tired, can't you see that?"

She's angrier now, and finally reaches the breaking point.

"If this doesn't change, neither one of you will be playing!"

NOVEMBER 2001: A NEW TEAM

After San Jose, we were back in Calgary for a few days and then on the road again. We travel overseas to Vierumäki, the Sports Institute of Finland, for the 3 Nations Cup. The Americans chose not to participate so we play Finland and Sweden twice. Despite another loss against the Americans in San Jose, the warm-up fiasco has brought me and Kim closer together. We don't often talk, we're generally in opposing nets, and we operate in different social circles, but we now have something we can laugh about together.

Sitting at the end of our team's short bench, I am nestled in the corner, watching my team prepare for the second period against Team Sweden. Still irritated at myself for my game against the Americans, I keep reliving each goal in my head. None were bad, but there were still *four* of them. I've never let in that many against the Americans. Our team looked tired, and we gave up 29 shots against and only managed 15 on the American goalie, Sara DeCosta. I wanted to win in San Jose in front of my friends especially because we had already lost to the Americans a few days prior in Salt Lake. After getting yelled at by Danièle for warm-ups, it was my chance to shine, and I played only okay.

Currently, against Sweden, we are up 3–0, and it's probably only going to get worse as the new Swedish starting goalie, 15-year-old Kim

Martin, went down late in the first period with what looked like a knee strain. She's their star; they are going to need her come February for the Olympics.

The rafters are a gorgeous pine colour and I feel like I'm in a giant spa. We are avenging our double loss to the Americans and our team is executing marvellously: no mercy for the Swedes. It's only midway through the game, and it's already 5–0.

Play stops. I look to my left as players untangle from atop the Swedish goalie. No goal; the puck must be under her. The Swedish defence tear our forwards off their goalie, but she doesn't get up. She's down like a sack of potatoes, limbs mistaken for equipment.

The Swedish trainer runs onto the ice to tend to her. Now what? They have no more goalies left.

"Sami, get ready," says Danièle from the far end of the bench. I'm not sure she's serious. Quizzically, I stand up.

"Sami, why aren't you ready?" Danièle now frantically yells.

Bewildered, yet as ready as I'm going to be, I muster, "Coach, I am ready!"

I thought it should be up to the Swedish coaches not ours. Danièle commands me on the ice. Our team therapist, Doug Stacey, grabs my stick and helmet and has it ready for me at his end of the bench. I pull my helmet on. The long sleeve shirt I wore today suddenly seems like a bad idea. I should've gotten my blades sharpened before the game. I can feel my dull skates beneath my feet. I push away from our bench and forget about all that's wrong and stare at the looming net. I skate past the Swedish bench with a sheepish smile. Yellow jerseys tap me on the pads as I skate to their net.

I can't stop the onslaught, but my Swedish defencemen are valiant in their attempt. Between periods, I head to the Swedish dressing room to be with my "teammates." Surrounded by yellow jerseys, the coach presents me with my own Swedish jersey. I pull it over my head and, with a huge smile, head out to defend the net for the third period. We don't make a miraculous comeback, but it is an honour, and I relish the experience and have a new appreciation for what opposition goalies go through playing against our team.

Back from beating the Finns in the finals of the 3 Nations Cup, I sit in my street clothes in my stall at the far end of our dressing room at the Father David Bauer Arena. My teammates and I await our coaches.

I can't help but notice some empty stalls. Correne Bredin is not in her spot, nor is Cherie Piper, Amanda Benoit-Wark, or Gillian Apps. Delaney Collins is not in her usual seat to my right.

Must have been more cuts this morning. I try to stay stoic. Charline Labonté is in her spot, but her eyes are red, sadness on her face.

It's quiet. No one wants to talk in case the coaches come in. Some whisper to their neighbour, but I no longer have a neighbour. My Brampton Thunder jersey hangs above my stall. It's been there since the start of August when we first arrived as a group of 30. The coaches mounted each person's club team jersey above their stall for inspiration. I see Lori Dupuis is still here. I'm happy for her; I hated to see her cut last season.

I stare at the large Team Canada logo embedded in the red carpet in the middle of the dressing room. Thoughts and memories circulate in my head. It's mid-November and it feels like we've already played an entire season. I'm exhausted, and I feel as though my body never has a chance to recuperate. We're supposed to be on the ice in an hour, and I just want to get through it and get home to rest.

Eventually, Danièle Sauvageau walks through the main entrance past the headshots of every girl who has ever played for Team Canada. Mel and Wally aren't far behind. The whispers stop, and all heads turn towards the door where Danièle stands.

Without much emotion, on what has surely been a tough day for the coaching staff, she says, "Congratulations, you are the 2002 Olympic team."

I am torn. I see the empty stalls emblematic of dreams that were crushed this morning. *How should I react?* Delaney is not here. Danièle leaves the room flanked by the two other coaches. Not knowing what else to do, I reach for my equipment and start dressing. The room is filled with mixed emotions.

I am going to the Olympics. I let that sink in a little. *I am actually going to get to play at the Olympics.* I think of my brother and of our dream, started long ago watching the Games on TV. I imagine calling my parents and telling them the exciting news. I let myself smile a little, but then Delaney's empty stall makes sadness swell in my heart.

After a sombre practice, I leave the rink and walk down the stairs and out through the iconic red door that awaits us every day. Sweat still beads on my face despite showering post-practice. My toque conceals my wet hair, trying to protect it from the freezing air. Jen is not far behind me as I approach my car.

As I reach into my sweatpants, my hand routinely slides over the black key I've had for a generation. This car has been with me through all my major moments in life. It's travelled to California and back twice and now finds itself parked here in Calgary, awaiting my arrival as a member of the 2002 Olympic team. The Blue Bomber always waits.

Jen pauses as I unlock the door. As I get into position behind the wheel, everything feels familiar. I start the engine, and I turn to Jen.

"I guess, congrats on making the Olympic team." A big smile emerges on her face. I wasn't there in Calgary for the final announcements in 1998, but I've seen the TV footage. In a much grander event, each player had their own final meeting where they found out about their fate.

"You too. Not quite the same climactic announcement as last time," she says with a grin.

Today just seemed like any other day, but that was far from the case. Today our team became *the* Olympic team.

15

Final Preparations

DECEMBER 2001: HANGING OUT

Sitting at our local pub, I am joined by my friend Gillian Russell for a late afternoon lunch. In front of me on the table is a half-eaten plate of quesadillas and a glass of Diet Coke that's already been filled up twice. I wish I liked beer. Others say you're not a real hockey player if you don't like beer . . . I'm jealous of how they find it so refreshing, but it just makes me grimace. Caffeine is my crutch. From the loudspeaker I faintly hear my favourite band, Great Big Sea. I've seen them at Portage and Main in Winnipeg and saw them live last year in San Francisco with my brother.

We are recently back from our three-game series against the Americans, during which I had my best game to date, despite a 1–0 loss. Relaxed and content, Gillian and I chat about our completely different lives, but find convergent themes. We change back and forth seamlessly between subjects. This is exactly how I want to be spending my first day off in two weeks.

1985: ROLES — SCHOOL RECESS

I am nine years old, and I'm sitting at my desk watching the seconds click away on the clock high above the door. Recess starts soon and I can barely contain myself. Andrew Moffatt conceals the soccer ball at his feet as our teacher goes over last-minute French conjugations. My mind is already on the fields.

I am in grade four at Hastings Immersion. We share a schoolyard with the other Hastings Elementary, the English one, but we rarely see those kids because our recess times don't overlap. We call them the English Muffins, and they call us the French Fries. It's May and this morning's recess game of choice is soccer. We picked teams yesterday and the game has continued. I love sports, and I love being active. We play every game from soccer to football to baseball and basketball. We even make up variations on the games, combining one with another. As always it is just me and the boys, and I intensely want to win.

The school buzzer goes off, and I hurry to the door. I try not to rush on the linoleum-tiled hallway, but my feet want to run. Finally, I burst through the heavy steel doors and into a full sprint towards the middle soccer field.

Running across the paved area where we sometimes play "bunt ball" against the school wall, I pass the jungle gym where a group of girls will congregate. I'm the first to the field, but not far behind are the boys. Some of us are regular players, always present, while others fluctuate in and out.

Each member of the core group has their own superpower, their own natural gift that makes them excel. Craig Smith is the strongest; Michael Guay the fastest; Jeff Ross the most athletic; Andrew Moffatt the most skilled; and I am the most competitive. I'm the only girl, but with a brush cut, shorts, and a t-shirt, I'm just one of the guys.

Every day at recess I play to win, equating it with a World Cup, a Stanley Cup, or an Olympic title. I often play street hockey with these same boys. The game is usually at Craig Smith's because he lives on a cul-de-sac. I am bigger than most of my friends and take the games more seriously than anyone else, but I never let that on. If I lose, I always congratulate the winner and try not to be a poor sport but losing grates on me.

Andrew finally arrives with the ball, but right behind him is another one of my classmates, Gillian Russell. With her Montreal Expos hat pulled over her ears, she asks Andrew if she can play. Our moms are best friends, and we've been friends forever, but she's not one of the guys.

She does gymnastics and girl things. Andrew puts her on his team, which is just as well for me. I want her to go back and join the group of girls on the jungle gym, but Andrew has the ball, therefore he decides. I don't protest; I just want the game to start.

DECEMBER 2001: HANGING OUT (CONTINUED)

Gillian moved into the basement of our place in Calgary about a month ago. She did play several of the sports at school, but also hung out a lot with the girls — she was my bridge to both worlds then, just as she is now. Jen and I have plenty of space, and it's nice to have a friend around who's outside of our small hockey bubble. It allows us to mentally get away from the rink.

Jen's parents are in town this weekend. Her dad is presenting at a sports psychology symposium, thus Jen's out with them today and missing our pub time. I ask Gillian about the guy she's trying to split up with, and she asks about my non-existent love life.

I wish I had someone in my life to share this journey with, but anything I've tried to start in the last year quickly gets derailed by another trip or commitment. Life, right now, is not about boys — it's about doing everything I can each day to win a gold medal. Nevertheless, it is a lonely pursuit, and it's nice to hear about Gillian's adventures and to live vicariously through her.

I grab another bite of my quesadilla, my shoulder still sore from my last game. I've never been a great practice goalie, but now I'm excelling. I led the goalies during our power-skating sessions, even though I thought it strange we had to do all the same skating exercises as the players. Despite not being as technically sound in goalie movements as the other two, my technique is improving daily.

I tell Gillian about confiding in Wally Kozak immediately after Finland, that I was struggling. We got straight to work outlining pre-game routines, going over mental rehearsals, and coming up with a plan of what I needed to improve. Wally is a student of the game, always wanting to learn but most importantly he loves to teach. He believes in teaching the life skills that it takes to win.

I go on to tell Gillian about our recent three games against our main rivals, the Americans. The first game in Ottawa, I backed up

Charline Labonté. Charlie had already been told she'll be the third goalie in Salt Lake.

I desperately wanted to play, but I understood. I tried to put my emotions aside as I knew playing wouldn't be easy for her. Being surrounded by her dream but knowing she wouldn't be playing at the Olympics, she had to battle her own emotions. I tried to support her the best I could, tried to lighten the mood, and tell her at every opportunity that she was doing well.

Charlie is good. So good, in fact, I think her technique is even better than Kim's. She's big but is very agile and extremely quick. She's played a full season of Junior men's hockey in the QMJHL, remarkably appearing in 28 games.

Danièle coached despite being ill, and even though we went ahead 2–0 in the game thanks to two goals by Vicky, we were terrible defensively. Charlie made some huge saves and really kept our team in the game. Shots were 14–4 in the second period, and finally at 9:24 in the third period, after the Americans scored their fifth unanswered goal by Bye from King and Potter, I was sent in.

I felt for Charlie. I tapped her on the pads as I skated past, not knowing what to say, quickly trying to get in my zone. I'd been given an extra 10 minutes to prove myself, and I did what I could. I hate that my chances always come at the expense of others. Despite the onslaught of shots, I smothered anything that came close, trying to slow the game down and provide a spark for the team. Despite the US not scoring again, neither did we, and we lost 5–2 in Ottawa with the final shots being 32-20 for the Americans.

At the end of the game, our girls were frustrated. Tempers escalated and fights ensued with the Americans. Danielle Goyette tried to take out one of their biggest players, defenceman Angela Ruggiero, who then retaliated with a massive hit on Wick. This got our girls fired up. Punches were thrown, but it was the first time I saw our team stand up for each other. Maybe that's exactly what we needed after a 5–2 trouncing.

The second game was the following day and was in Kim's hometown of Montreal. We had more jump and more will to battle for each other, but it wasn't enough. Despite this time outshooting our opponents 29–26, we couldn't come out on top. We lost Game 4 in our year-long series 4–3.

That set me up for the final game of the four-day trip in Hamilton. The game was the closest we played to Toronto all season. Friends and teammates packed Copps Coliseum. Everything that I'd been working on recently seemed to converge, and I played my best game of the season. Pucks that I couldn't see hit me. I read the plays before they happened and did everything I could to help our team win.

Unfortunately, we still lost 1–0 despite being outshot 31–22. Nonetheless, I was ecstatic with my performance. The game was the closest we'd come to winning all season, but in the end, we still lost the fifth game in a row against our main rivals.

Back with Gillian, I wash my quesadilla down with some pop.

"How was the trip back to Toronto? Did the new guy that you like come watch you play there?" Gill asks.

"Yeah, so fun to see him again, but he was wearing a Team USA hat at our meet-up after the game. I know he has friends on that team too, but c'mon, can you believe that?"

"Cross him off the list," she says jokingly.

We chuckle.

"What's up with Jen? Any new boys?"

We gossip as the conversation moves through each of my teammates. I tell her about our small dressing room celebration we had for Wick to celebrate the official adoption of her son Noah. I recount how Becky had her engagement ring stolen during a game from our dressing room. I also share the story of rooming with elder statesman Danielle Goyette on a road trip. How in the middle of the night, blind without my contacts, I came back from the washroom and accidently hopped into bed right beside her. Gillian laughs.

She's been out with the girls enough to know most of them by now and I don't hold back.

There is certainly lots of drama. Thérèse Brisson has been out with a concussion and Cassie Campbell as one of our assistants was promoted to captain and Vicky and Wick became her assistants. Not that Cassie won't make a great captain, but what about Thérèse? Others fight for leadership roles while everyone fights for playing time. Heaney hurt her knee in a game recently and we've often been playing with a depleted lineup. Tensions are heightened because we aren't winning. I want to be supportive, but I've had to become selfish to get through each day.

We had my Thunder teammates Jayna, Vicky, and Lori over for dinner one night. I really miss them — I wish I saw more of them — but I just don't have the energy. They brought their roommate Amanda Benoit. Benny's now an alternate and, despite her sadness, keeps pushing every day in practice. Three of our alternate players have continued to practice: Benny, Piper, and Correne Bredin. With several injuries, at least one of them is playing nearly every game to fill in the gaps, but what a difficult situation for them.

Hanging out with Gillian is different from hanging out with my teammates. With them, it's about trying to find some common ground and create shared experiences. With Gillian, it's easy. She knows me and is my fiercest supporter. Despite never having played hockey, she thinks I'm the best goalie in the world, and I like that.

I use my time with Gillian to mentally prepare for our next stint on the road. Training has been extremely hard lately. Dr. Steve Norris, our sport science performance consultant, has been working with Jason Poole, our trainer, and Dr Suzanne Leclerc, our doctor, to push us to our limits. They're attempting to replicate the playing conditions in Salt Lake City at high altitude so we've been doing our workouts on bikes in hyperbaric chambers, with low oxygen, so that our bodies can adapt to the demands. It's like doing workouts in a sauna. We've also had blood tests every week to ensure we're on pace to perform come February.

It's been a lot, but finally we get to play more games. We travel to Newfoundland to play a four-game series against the Russians in St. John's, Gander, Corner Brook, and Grand Falls, and then it's back to another military base, Saint-Jean-sur-Richelieu, just outside of Montreal, to train prior to Christmas.

The server comes over and asks if we're done. I want dessert. Screw the weigh in for today. Every Monday morning, we must strip down and weigh in on the scale in the trainer's room. He marks our weekly weight on a chart in the dressing room for all to see. I've always loved my body, loved that it's strong, and loved that it has allowed me to be an athlete. However, the pinch tests, the fat tests, and the weigh-ins have really played with my psyche. I try to eat less, but without food,

I'm always tired. Today I don't care — Gillian and I are going to share a brownie sundae.

JANUARY 2002: GOALIE COACH

It's a far push in my gear to get to the spot where Dave Jamieson, Team Canada's goalie coach, is standing. Back from Christmas break, we're at goalie practice at Teen Ranch in Caledon, Ontario.

Kim and Charlie wait their turn in the corner while Dave runs me through the drill. Some days he has extra shooters on the ice, but today it's just him. We've already had a two-hour practice. The rest of the team is at lunch, but we're still on the ice.

I like Dave. He's calm. He pushes me, but also acknowledges my effort. That's what I need in a coach. I don't respond well to ridicule or yelling. I tend to shut down with those types of coaches, but Dave is different. I get to the spot he mapped out for me. I make a hard stop with the inside edge of my left skate and reposition myself square to him. I fall to the ice in a butterfly position, and he shoots a puck low on the ice towards me.

I didn't know how to do a butterfly when I first joined the National Team, now the technique has become second nature after thousands of repetitions. I've learned to be honest with myself. Because of all the different sports I've played, I've had to become accepting of taking input and learning new methods, often looking ridiculous the first time. But the only way I'm going to improve is to focus on my weaknesses.

I block the puck and direct it in the corner. My eyes watch the puck while my right leg already begins the sequence to get back to the post. Goalie gear is cumbersome, and I don't make this look smooth. I push back to the post and begin the sequence again. Again, and again.

1992: REPETITION OF PRACTICE — THROWING

Reaching for my first discus from a pile of five that I've placed beside the cement throwing circle, I grab one and loosely let my arm swing with my fingers cupped gently around the edge. My coach, Al Wirth, stands outside the 20-foot cage while I stand in the middle. Midway through practice, we've evolved from standing throws into half-spins.

Al's been my main throws coach for two years. I'm now 16, and we've already had much success together. I also have Ming Pu Wu, a recent Chinese immigrant, who helps me with javelin. I'm very fortunate to have the two of them who care so deeply about every detail of being an elite athlete. Thanks to them, I've won multiple National Junior Championships and compete internationally for Canada.

Al's fiddling with the minutiae of my technique, but that's what it takes to be a talented discus thrower. The ordinary will become extraordinary. I can already envision representing Canada at the Olympics someday. Al's laid out the plan, described each step, and it's my job to execute.

Track and field is just one of numerous sports in which I compete, but likely my strongest. I also play on our school's volleyball, badminton, and team handball teams, each one teaching me different aspects about myself. Perhaps my favourite is waterpolo where I play alongside my brother. We've won several provincial water polo championships led by one of my all-time favourite coaches, Roger Harrison. His daughter, Jodi, one of my former swimming friends, is also on the team and our team has dominated the local water polo scene for years.

Focusing on keeping my arm high through the middle of the circle, my feet spin, whizzing at high speeds until they come to a grinding halt with a solid block that creates the torque needed to launch the discus. It propels off into the horizon. I don't even look at Al. I could feel my arm was a touch too low.

I walk to the back of the circle and pick up the second of the five discs. I repeat to myself, "Arm high, arm high," and begin the process again. I do this for hours at a time. Throw five discs. Retrieve five discs. Often Al walks beside me as I saunter out to get the latest throws. We talk about what's going well, and the changes I need to make. He knows when to push and when to let me work through a difficult patch.

JANUARY 2002: GOALIE COACH (CONTINUED)

Prior to this season, goalies were always apart from the team. Expected to perform but often having to find our own tools. Having a coach is exhilarating, frustrating, and rewarding all at the same time. Some days, I feel as though Dave is opening a tap and it just pours right through me. My background in individual sports makes me yearn for personal coaching, for the one on one feedback that has been lacking in my hockey career.

I learned how to be a goalie from watching NHLers on TV. I practised their moves on our street and on the ice. Then, for one season when I was 11, I had a coach who printed out chapters from a goaltending manual for me to read. I studied them diligently. I took more books out at the library, bought goalie magazines, and did school reports on famous goaltenders such as Tretiak and Dryden. I learned by mimicking, by watching, and by asking for shooters' input. Finally I have someone I can ask questions, and discuss the intricacies of the position.

Dave replaced our first goalie coach, Andy Nowicki, who was with us at camp in May. Such a nice man — I liked him a lot — but he secured a job with the NHL's Los Angeles Kings. We only get to see Dave for a couple of days once a month because he's still teaching full-time back in Ontario and it isn't the same when he's not around.

Both Kim and Charlie have had lots of technical help with their goaltending growing up in Quebec. That region has produced most of the goalies in the NHL. They both have a classic "French" style that is loosely based on Patrick Roy's revolutionary style of play. They spend a lot of time in the butterfly position, down on the ice, blocking and challenging as much of a shooter's view as possible.

My style is completely different. I'm big and like to rely on my instincts. I stay deeper in the net, and I react to where the players are going to shoot and try to anticipate the play as it unfolds.

I push as hard as I can from the post and try to stop quickly. I'm getting used to my sharper skates. I liked having dull skates to float around the crease, anticipating the play; however, Dave says I need to change. I need to look good for our coaches who aren't goalies. I realize that no matter how good I am, I must fit Danièle's mould. Ultimately, the head coach decides who plays: she holds my future in her hands.

Danièle isn't easy to figure out. She seems tough on the outside. She expects excellence, although she doesn't always know how to relay that message and it comes across as harsh. She rarely talks to me and when she does, she talks about other people. I find her difficult to interact with; I'm always on edge, trying to say the right thing or stay quiet at the right times.

Danièle coached Kim on Team Quebec when Kim was younger, and she selected Kim to be the number-one goalie last year, so I know this is an uphill battle. I'm a little fearful that I'm not being given the same shot as Kim, but I try to suppress those feelings. I need to be so good that she can't help but play me, and I think with Dave's help this is possible.

"You can't teach toughness. You got this, Sami. Only four more times." Sweat is burning my eyes. My hips are in agony. My whole body is sore. I struggle through, fight to get in position and make the save.

With just over a month before we leave for the Olympic Games, I'm peaking at the perfect time. My games against the boys have been solid, practices have been stellar, and my last performance against the Americans was the best of the season. One more month to help the team gain the confidence that we can beat Team USA at the Olympics on their home soil.

We have a three-game series against the Americans coming up to finish off our Olympic preparations in Chicago, Detroit, and then Vancouver. Final preparations to ensure everything comes together in Salt Lake City. With five losses in our first five games against the Americans, we need a win.

JANUARY 2002: SOARING HIGH

It's game day against the Americans in Detroit and I fight to see the puck. There are too many legs. Too many bodies. I lean left, glimpsing the puck as it moves from one defenceman to another. I shuffle to my right. An American forward nudges me; another slashes the back of my legs. I've lost sight of the puck. Lean right. There it is. Ignore the legs, just keep an eye on the puck.

Already down 3-1, we are killing a penalty again and it's only halfway through the second period. We just have to make it through this penalty, and I know we can come back. I see the puck move to a winger on the side boards. I must get there. Still too many people in front. I lean again to find the puck. The American winger shoots for the near post thinking I'm screened, but I see it just in time. I save it but can't control the rebound.

Cheryl Pounder, my defenceman, yells at the top of her lungs, "Cover it!" not knowing the puck is already out of my reach. It careens around the boards but unfortunately doesn't have enough steam to clear the zone. No reprieve. Their defenceman corrals the puck and moves towards the middle shooting lane. She winds up to shoot. I'm at the top of my crease.

The American forwards scramble to obstruct my view, but my defencemen hold them off. The shot is a high wrist shot. Easy save. I stand tall, see it the whole way. I stay square and anticipate the save. We need a break. I'm going to hold on to it.

Then a tied-up American forward lunges at the high-moving puck with her stick and makes contact. I have run out of time to react. The puck bounces down to the ice as I drop, but I'm too slow to stop the puck from squeezing through my pads into the net.

After a second of self-pity, I pop to my feet. Never wallow. I assure myself it's just a lucky goal. Kellar and Pounder are already exhaustedly skating to our bench. Keep battling. The tide will swing our way. I try to stay composed.

My team needs me to look confident. All four of our penalty-killers change. I don't look at the bench but see our next line come on the ice and take their positions. No one comes back to reassure me. No big deal — that's always awkward anyway. Never show the other team they've gotten to you. I watch the replay of the goal on the Jumbotron high up in the rafters at centre ice. *Unlucky*, I say to myself again. If they can score four in a period, we can too.

The play should start, but it doesn't. The ref hesitates. There's a commotion on our bench. I look to see what the ref is looking at. Kim is standing up and our defencemen's door is wide open. My face goes red.

This can't be happening. No, it's a mistake. My heart pounds out of my chest. Kim puts her gloves on and is handed her helmet, her skates already on the ice. I don't even know what to do. I want to crawl in a hole. Everyone in this 17,000-seat arena is staring at me. I'm more humiliated than I've ever been. I don't want to go, but I know it's no longer my choice.

Danièle is pulling me. I begin my skate of shame towards the bench. Kim meets me halfway and looks sad for me. Don't ever show your weakness. I high-five her on her blocker and tell her, "You can do this." I skate the rest of the way to the open door. Robin McDonald, our equipment manager, operates the door. He's the first to tap me on the shoulder. The first four players I see are our defencemen. With a sheepish grin, I break the awkward silence and say, "I'm sorry . . . we can still win this."

I don't even look at Danièle at the far end of the bench. I walk behind the players and make my way to the end of the long bench and take what was supposed to be Kim's spot. I feel all eyes on me. *Keep smiling.* I'm stewing, but trying to hold it together on the outside.

Wally, our defence coach, makes his way down to me. "Don't worry, it's not your fault . . . good battling." I don't know if he means it, but it's nice of him to say.

This was supposed to be my chance to shine. I try to rally the troops from the end of the bench, but we lose 7–4. We have now lost seven straight games.

I feel a combination of anger and sadness, but I can't let my teammates know. With our next game two weeks away, this is no time to wallow. I must regain my form to help my team get back on track. We've lost every game this season to the Americans. We only have one more chance to beat them but post-game, our team psyche is at an all-time low.

Every player who has had the privilege of donning the Team Canada jersey has their own inner turmoil, and there's no reason I need to throw my mess in the pot. I'm tremendously upset at myself for not taking the small window of opportunity that presented itself.

I may have missed my chance, but I'm not going down without a fight. I'm going to do everything I can to make myself and this team better. The last thing this team needs is anyone feeling sorry for themselves and I don't want my feelings to affect the team despite it being difficult to release them from the pit of my stomach.

I know the decision to pull me was a good coaching move, but it's no easy pill to swallow. Having my teammates apologize for their inefficiencies is nice, but the red light doesn't go on behind their heads. I'm the one who must take the blame.

One month left before our departure still leaves me plenty of time to avenge that game. It was only one bad game in a full season. And I'm hoping, two weeks from now, at our final exhibition game in Vancouver against the Americans, I'll get the chance to prove I can be our starting goalie in the Olympic final.

16

In Perfect Position

Alone in front of a crackling fire, an idyllic scene surrounds me at Emerald Lake in Yoho National Park, just outside of Lake Louise, Alberta. Two plaid-cushioned wicker chairs face the fireplace. Our team is sequestered for our final getaway before heading to Salt Lake City. No coaches, no official practices, just the players and some staff. The Olympic Opening Ceremony is only four days away, but that seems like a lifetime from now.

I gaze into the fireplace, feeling the warmth on my face. My roommate, Kelly Bechard, a tall forward from the village of Sedley, Saskatchewan, is out hiking with Jen and some of our other teammates. I opted to stay in, swaddled in our cozy log cabin room, to finish a painting. Despite being outgoing, unbeknownst to most, I am actually an introvert: I gain energy alone in my own company.

The shoulder I had surgery on six years ago while a javelin thrower at Stanford is a little sore today after I felt it pop in my last game; nonetheless, I'm still riding high from my recent two games.

The games were part of a four-game series against the boys to end our games in the Midget AA league. I played the first game, where we were dramatically outshot, but I did my utmost to keep our team in the game. We lost 6–4, but, overall, I was happy with my performance. Kim played Game 2. It was also very high scoring, so I felt I wasn't losing any ground. We were still neck and neck. The following day, Kim started in Game 3 of the series and played extremely well, losing a close one.

I knew she played well, and I could feel my position slipping. I was perturbed at myself for being angry at the result. I couldn't help but think that she had won the coaches over that evening. I was bitter that the team played significantly better for Kim than for me and I went to sleep that evening feeling very low.

Despite the hurt, the next morning I realized there was nothing I could do about Kim's performance. I needed to take my fate into my own hands. The game of goaltending is not about second-guessing what has happened, but rather about focusing on the upcoming event. Maybe the coach's decision is made, but maybe not. I chose to focus on the *maybe not*.

My final game in the series was my best. Bigger, stronger boys outshot us, but we finally came out on top. I put an entire season's worth of effort into that game. My fate depended on a huge game. I was nervous and fearful, but with everything on the line I played stellar. We won 2–0. I played relaxed but with a bit of an *I'm going to prove it to you* attitude.

To conclude the season on the way to Emerald Lake, we played our final game of the season in Canmore, Alberta, against the Podium Team.

I was the Podium Team's goalie facing Team Canada. The Podium Team consists of players who narrowly missed making the Olympic squad. The last cuts. Our three alternates, Piper, Bredin, and Benny, play on the team, and so does my Brampton friend, Samm Holmes. For the final time this season, I get to determine my own fate. I played my heart out for them, faced over 50 shots, and we nearly upset Team Canada.

It was my opportunity to show what the last eight months of hard work have done, and I nailed it. I finished with a bang.

I can see the beauty of Emerald Lake, frozen over, surrounded by snow-capped mountains. Last night, a bunch of us went into the outdoor hot tubs and took in the vastness of the starry sky.

Our team really needs this getaway. Not only are we taking advantage of the altitude to acclimatize our lungs to less oxygen, but we're finally getting to relax. The last couple of weeks, I've sensed several of my teammates at their breaking points. The coaches have been hard on the team. Danièle seems perturbed by our predicament, taking her frustrations out on many, including Kim. While she seldom talks to me, she often yells publicly at her. I'm not sure which side I'd rather be on, but I know it's weighing on Kim.

Jen had a bit of a meltdown last week when she got the brunt of the yelling. Exhaustion combined with fatigue and Danièle being so negative was too much to handle. Like most on our team, Jen simply needs a break. Her facade shows a confident, positive person, but I know the real Jen who hates being yelled at and is incredibly hard on herself. The fresh outdoor air has brought the smile back to her face.

We finished the day yesterday with our team's sports psychologist, Dr. Kimberley Amirault, going over every conceivable distraction and how we would deal with it as a team — everything from bad refereeing to a bomb in the village. Preparation will be key at the Olympics.

Today we have time to ourselves. I made myself a tea and have my painting project propped up above the fireplace. I've brought my acrylics to finish what will become our team poster. I've always loved to paint, and often bring my work on the road as a distraction.

All that's left to do are the finishing touches. I'm depicting a military scene from the TV show *Band of Brothers*. I saw an ad for it in a magazine and thought the grouping of military men pushing towards the same goal represented our team perfectly. Not only did we start this journey together on a military base in Valcartier and spend our Christmas on the base at Saint-Jean-sur-Richelieu in Quebec, but it's also been a year struggling towards a shared goal.

As I stare at the painting, picking out spots that need touch-ups, I wonder if the coaches have made their decision on who will be the starting goalie at the Olympics. I'm sure Dave, our goalie coach, gets a say, as do assistant coaches Mel and Wally, but ultimately, it will be Danièle's choice. *Have I done enough to convince her?*

After my game in Detroit, I hoped to get another chance against the Americans in our final game on January 8 — one more chance to redeem myself. I thought I bounced back well from being pulled, showed my positivity, and really thought I'd get that final game in Vancouver, but I didn't.

Unfortunately, we lost again.

For the first time all series, we were winning in the third period, thanks to an unassisted goal by Jen to give us the 2-1 lead, but fatigued we just couldn't hold on. After an intense workout the night before, we looked beat in the third period. We haven't played a game rested all year and our breakdowns came fast as our legs gave out. Kim let in two in the third on bad defensive giveaways, and we lost. Perhaps that bodes well for me. I tried to stay upbeat, tried to lift my teammates up after our disappointing eighth loss in a row, but everywhere there was tension.

Bob Nicholson, the president of Hockey Canada, flew to the game in Vancouver. He didn't look pleased and we speculated on the flight home that Danièle was going to lose her job. No coach had ever lost that much with the women's program.

Shockingly, when we landed, they cut forward Nancy Drolet. I was angry for Nancy. She had done everything asked of her, put in the work and effort, scored two overtime World Championship winning goals in '97 and '00, and they cut her a month before the Olympic Games.

It sent ripples through our team. We had already celebrated our team announcement in November with a steak dinner paid for by Hockey Canada. We held a press conference and announced to the world that this was Team Canada. We had bonded, and then they cut one of us.

Nancy and I were roommates briefly in 1998. She's emotional, and I'm rational. I need people like her around to gain perspective. All season, Danièle has been hard on her. For some reason, Nancy was singled out more than anyone. She always seemed to take the punishment, knowing that the team needed her as a scapegoat.

The decision to release Nancy seems so wrong, especially when our motto had become about team. Like several of my teammates, I was mad at Danièle; I guess I'm still mad. We talked about the release yesterday at our sport psychology meeting with Kimberley. There remain countless questions, but as a team, we realized that it was not our decision to make. Ultimately, we are accountable to each other and to the 20 other players on this new team.

They replace Nancy with one of our alternates, Cherie Piper. I was happy for Piper that she's going to be an Olympian but was devastated for Nancy. I was also upset for Amanda Benoit-Wark and Correne

Bredin, who like Piper were alternates and played in most of the exhibition games. The naming of Piper to the team must open old wounds they were valiantly covering up for our benefit, but they have been nothing but supportive around us.

We left them behind in Calgary as they packed up their stuff and headed home. This is our first weekend with the actual final Olympic Team.

Geraldine Heaney is back; she's been out since Christmas with an ACL injury. She was only told last weekend by Danièle that she'll be on the team in Salt Lake. Also back, from concussion, is Thérèse Brisson. It was touch and go for her, and Correne played every game in her absence, but with the veteran back, Correne is out.

On the painting, above the scene, I've drawn the acronym W.A.R. — our team motto. "We Are Responsible," not only for ourselves, but also for one another. I scrutinize the poster. *Are the shadows right?*

I haven't been this relaxed in a long time. Forced rest is sometimes the hardest thing for an athlete, but we all need this. Tomorrow it'll be back to the reality of packing for the Olympic Games, but today is about relaxation. Four more sleeps.

FEBRUARY 8, 2002: OPENING CEREMONY — SALT LAKE

Sitting in the very top row of Rice-Eccles Stadium, to my right is the unlit Olympic torch, thrust high into the sky, and to my left are Jen, Becky Kellar, Colleen Sostorics, and Cherie Piper.

We all look the same in our red poor-boy hats but, unlike in Nagano, this time the caps face forward. We have red leather jackets with a white-and-red-striped Canada scarf. The ensemble is finished off by grey pants, black hiking boots, and grey wool socks that were supposed to be pulled up over our pants, but the mission staff protested. This year's look reminds me of an Austrian mountain climber or a throwback to *The Sound of Music*.

The rest of the athletes of Team Canada, representing various sports, squish in around us as other nations begin to fill in the spaces. This year the athletes are seated in the stands, which gives us an amazing view of the spectacle. As we make ourselves comfortable, the final countries do their lap around the stadium. The path is lined with volunteers, all dressed in white, holding lanterns to illuminate the way. The field where the University of Utah Utes football team plays is covered in ice.

The show begins; figure skaters perform on the ice below, but I'm still mentally processing our walk in. What an incredible thrill in front of a packed stadium. Walking four abreast behind our flag bearer, Olympic champion speed skater Catriona Le May Doan, I made sure to share the moment with Jen, but this time I let her have the experience of walking on the outside.

Indigenous Peoples from across North America fill the infield, welcoming the athletes from around the world to their land. Robbie Robertson of The Band is singing.

"Isn't he Canadian?" I ask Jen. She has no clue. I think my auntie Jo's friend dated him. I make a mental note to ask Mom the next time I see her. My parents aren't here tonight but will be at time this game along with my brother and his wife, Gina, who are flying in from Santa Barbara. My friend Diana, from Stanford, is flying in with a friend for the semis.

Dancers dressed as pioneers replace Indigenous men and women. Stagecoaches circle the stadium as the Dixie Chicks belt out the lyrics to "Ready to Run."

The air is getting cooler. Luckily, we've all brought parkas. Becky has brought some snacks from the cafeteria that she shares with Jen and me. We both eagerly snag some of her fruit and granola bars. This is the best concert I've ever attended.

As we eat our snacks, the Utah Symphony Orchestra and the Mormon Tabernacle Choir perform "Call of the Champions." Each person in attendance has been given placards at their seats to hold up during the performance spelling out the giant words, *Light the Fire Within*, the motto of the Salt Lake Games.

Mitt Romney, the president of the Utah organizing committee, and Dr. Jacques Rogge, the new president of the International Olympic Committee, take centre stage to address the crowd. Their figures are too small to see from our vantage point, so I watch on the Jumbotron.

"Because you dreamed and paid the price to make your dreams real," Romney starts. I think of our year's struggles and of the Games that will unfold in the next week and a half. The speeches are followed by President George W. Bush declaring the 19th Olympic Winter Games open.

The cold wind is starting to pick up, but it doesn't take away from our focus on the show. The Olympic flag ceremoniously enters the stadium. A star-studded cast carries it, representing the five continents, arts, the humanities, and sport: John Glenn, Desmond Tutu, Lech Walesa, Steven Spielberg, Jean-Michel Cousteau, Cathy Freeman, Kazuyoshi Funaki, and Jean-Claude Killy. *Am I really in the same stadium as these people?*

Sting performs as Olympic figure skating champion Kristi Yamaguchi synchronizes her jumps and lutzes to his melodies. Quiet overtakes the stadium and darkness ensues. Then a small flicker appears at the far end of the stadium.

"It's the flame!" I nudge Jen's leg. Every Olympic Games that I've ever watched on TV, our family has tried to guess the names of the torch-bearers as they appeared on TV. It was like *Jeopardy* for Olympic junkies. I can't see the faces of the two skating the torch around the infield, but they are announced as Olympic figure skating champions Peggy Fleming and Scott Hamilton. They do one lap of the rink and hand off to two new American Olympic champions. The flame goes around and around the infield, and each time I try to guess who will be next.

The giant cauldron is mere metres away from where we sit. This flame has guided me my entire life. No longer is this just our stage, but this is a world stage. There's a commotion behind us. "That must be the final torchbearer," Jen says, pointing into the shadows, their identity still a mystery.

Two men with the flame approach the base of the stairs immediately below us, and below the cauldron. Out of the shadows, two women emerge. From where we are seated, we can't see them, so we look up at the Jumbotron. Immediately, Jen, Becky, and I look at each other.

"No way," we say in unison.

One of the torchbearers is Olympic skiing champion Picabo Street and the other is current USA women's Olympic hockey captain Cammi Granato. As we look back at the Jumbotron, we watch as our adversary, a smiling Cammi Granato, runs the flame up the long staircase. I'm proud that a female hockey player is carrying the torch, but the memories of Nagano come flooding back. We can't let that happen again. The Americans cannot win this time.

There's more commotion behind us. It looks like there's more than one person waiting. Through the darkness, I spot a Team USA hockey jersey. There was speculation that the captain of the 1980 "Miracle on Ice" Olympic champion men's team, Mike Eruzione, was going to light the cauldron. It looks like him, but there are others.

Cammi and Picabo finally emerge near us at the top of the stairs. Then, from the shadows, not only does Mike Eruzione appear, but he is joined by his entire team. An entire team is going to light the cauldron! In the back of my head, I think that if all goes right here, that might be us someday.

The flame ignites, and my heart swells a little more.

The show closes with LeAnn Rimes singing and an incredible fireworks display. As I watch in amazement, someone taps me on the shoulder from the platform above.

"Sami Jo?" a girl with a wireless microphone asks.

"Yes," I respond, looking to my friends for recognition.

"I've got Sami Jo here," she says into her microphone. "Come with me, please."

Moments later, I have giant earphones on, a microphone in front of my face, and camera lights pointed in my direction.

"And there, I believe, is Sami Jo Small, goaltender for the Canadian team, from Winnipeg. Sami, it's Brian Williams, can you hear me?"

"Yes, I can hear you, Brian," I say, realizing I'm talking to Brian Williams on the live CBC feed to the entire country.

"Was it as spectacular down there as it seemed up here?"

"Oh, it's just amazing down here," I scream over the noise in the background. "And being with the Canadian team, I mean, we are all so pumped. Umm, having Cammi Granato and the 'Miracle on Ice' team light the torch wasn't exactly part of our distraction-control plan." I can hear Brian laughing in my ear, but I continue with a smile, "But hopefully the next time the Games come to Canada in Vancouver and Whistler, that will be us lighting the torch, and we'll give Canada something to be proud of." I'm trying to hold back my emotions, but it's just oozing out of me.

ABOVE: My parents encouraged my brother Luke and I to try many different activities, including skating lessons at the age of two.

LEFT: My first hockey team at the age of five, the Norberry Royals. We skated on the outdoor rink at the club, which is why I'm wearing a hoodie.

I was very fortunate to get to play a lot of different sports growing up including (clockwise): soccer coached by Hussein Salem alongside my friend Adam; volleyball with the AAA High School girls champs at College Jeanne-Sauve; and swimming and waterpolo with my brother.

I played on boys teams growing up because we didn't have girls teams in Winnipeg. I had some great teammates and became the first girl to play in the Manitoba Major Junior Hockey League. I'm pictured here with the AAA Winnipeg Warriors and the AA St Vital Victorias.

I loved the sport of track and field and earned a scholarship to throw discus and javelin at Stanford University.

BELOW: Here I am with our freshman throwing class and my coach Robert Weir.

I played on the Stanford Men's team in the ACHA under the tutelage of coach Ernie Ferrari. I even made upper body goalie equipment for women for my senior project in engineering.

Nagano send off party that my roommate Bobby Blunt threw prior to leaving California for Japan; here I am with my brother, Luke; his future wife Gina; and my former roommates Amanda Van Houtte, Corey Zysman (Karlin), Diana Tellefson, Katrinka Blunt (Jackson), and Bobby Blunt.

Graduating from Product Design in the school of Mechanical Engineering. With my friends Susan Wu, Monique Bradshaw, Corey Zysman (Karlin), Alda Lu, and Diana Tellefson.

With two of my best friends growing up, Adam Salem and Dermot McDonald.

With my friend Gillian Russell at the friends and family function at the Olympics in Torino, Italy.

With my role model and mentor, Susie Yuen at the 2000 World Championships in Mississauga.

My parents, Rod and Pat Small, always willing to brave the cold to watch me play.

Nagano Opening Ceremony with Geraldine Heaney, Becky Kellar, and Jennifer Botterill.

ABOVE: Celebrating my first World Championship victory in Espoo, Finland, with Jennifer Botterill and Becky Kellar.

BELOW: Gold medal with Hayley Wickenheiser.

Playing for the Brampton Thunder.

Playing outdoor hockey with Gord Downie of the Tragically Hip.

Winning the North American Roller Hockey Championship alongside Canadian teammates Judy Diduck, Hayley Wickenheiser, and Manon Rhéaume.

PHOTO BY DAVE SANFORD, COURTESY OF THE HOCKEY HALL OF FAME

LEFT: World Championship, Mississauga, 2000.

BELOW: The stick signed by Kim St-Pierre that I played with in the World Championship finals. In my mind, she was on the ice with me.

Accepting the Directorate Award for top goalie of the tournament for the second year in a row.

2000 World Champions in Mississauga, Ontario.

ABOVE: With Jim Cuddy and Barnie Bentall and my Brampton teammates, Jayna Hefford and Vicky Sunohara.

LEFT: With Wayne Gretzky when he came to our dressing room prior to the All Star Game in 2001.

RIGHT: With friends Dermot McDonald, Jennifer Botterill, and Anders Johansson, alongside Ron Maclean.

LEFT: With Alan Doyle of Great Big Sea, who was being honoured at an Ottawa Senators game.

2001 World Championship in Minnesota — shooting the puck. I always prided myself on being able to handle the puck well.

Playing for Sweden
at the 3 Nations Cup
in 2001.

Pre-Olympic action against the USA in Hamilton, Ontario. Our closest game all
season, losing 1-0.

ABOVE: My parents at the 2002 Olympics in Salt Lake City, Utah.

BELOW: Celebrating an Olympic gold medal with my mom and brother.

Glove save versus Russia at the 2002 Olympic Games.

My brother dressed as Captain Canada in front of the hockey venue in Salt Lake City.

With Hayley Wickenheiser and her son Noah as we await the medal ceremony after our 3-2 victory in the gold medal game at the 2002 Olympics.

LEFT: Celebrating with goalie coach, Dave Jamieson.

BELOW: With Captain Cassie Campbell and Jennifer Botterill at the closing ceremony of the 2002 Olympics.

2002 Olympic Champions.

With Prime Minister Jean Chrétien at a celebration for Olympic medalists on Parliament Hill.

With my Brampton teammates Jayna Hefford, Vicky Sunohara, and Lori Dupuis.

LEFT: Pointing up at my friends and family after winning the 2002 4 Nations Cup in Kitchener, Ontario.

BELOW: My friends Dermot and Anders painted red entering the arena at the 4 Nations Cup in Kitchener, Ontario. My parents are in the front, on the left, in Team Canada jerseys.

My brother, a.k.a. Captain Canada, looks on as I warm up prior to the 2004 World Championship in Halifax.

RIGHT: Ontario training group alongside our trainer Chris Dalcin after winning the 2004 World Championship.

BELOW: National team members and Toronto Aeros Teammates Becky Kellar, Gillian Ferrari, Jennifer Botterill, Cheryl Pounder, and myself, along with our coach, Ken Dufton.

My goalie partners for nearly my entire National Team career, Kim St-Pierre and Charline Labonté. The three of us at Worlds in Halifax, 2004.

The 2005 4 Nations Cup in Finland.

Celebrating an Esso Women's National Championship. Drinking out of the Abby Hoffman Cup.

Nation Champions, 2004. We won back-to-back titles in 2004 and 2005.

My cabin-mates Colleen Sostorics and Caroline Ouellette prepped prior to a cabin race at the 2005 pre-Olympic camp in Prince Edward Island.

Post-triathlon meal with Cherie Piper and Meghan Agosta. We are joined by Cassie Cambell and Katie Weatherston, both recently back from the hospital.

From the rafters, where I cheered on Team Canada at the 2006 Olympics in Torino, Italy.

Champions! Celebrating with Jennifer Botterill, Meghan Agosta, and Cherie Piper.

2006 Olympic Champions. I made sure I got my hand up in time for the photo with my iconic maple leaf glove.

Action shot versus Natalie Darwitz of Team USA, while defenceman Colleen Sostorics looks on. I think my biggest asset as a goalie was that I never gave up on a puck.

Honouring the 1990 Women's team by wearing pink jerseys for our round robin game versus Team USA. Decided to tease our hair like Vicky Sunohara did in 1990. Front row: Meghan Agosta, Jennifer Botterill, Vicky Sunohara, Tessa Bonhomme, and I.

Celebrating the 2007 World Championship on the ice in Winnipeg, Manitoba with Delaney Collins and Jennifer Botterill.

Dropping the puck in Kingston, Ontario at the first official Clarkson Cup in 2009.

Art by Jane Eccles. I bought this painting and donated it to the Norberry Community Centre and the Sami Jo Small Hockey Facility.

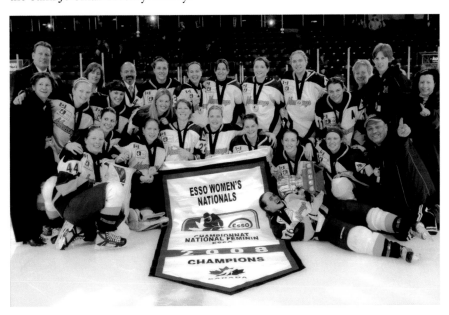

The first year of the CWHL, in 2008, winning the last ever Esso Women's National Championship with the Mississauga Hockey Club.

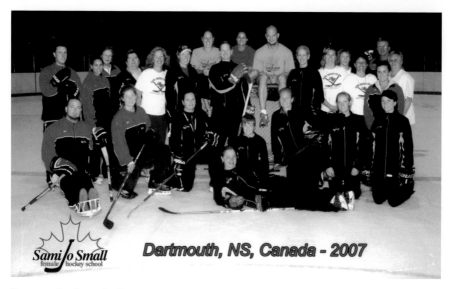

I've run the Sami Jo Small Female Hockey School since 1998 throughout four provinces. I'm standing in the middle of this instructors photo, alongside Billy Bridges, Kathryn McKenzie, Bradi Cochrane, Dermot McDonald, Cherie Piper, Kelly Bechard, and Tara French.

Standing beside a bronze sculpture created by Jonathan Fligel that is housed at the Hockey Hall of Fame.

With my husband Billy Bridges, a five-time Paralympic sledge hockey player.

Cheering on Billy at the Paralympics in Vancouver (2010) alongside my brother Luke, Tara French, and Sarah Love.

I was the maid of honour at Jennifer Botterill's wedding.

The day after my marriage to Billy Bridges in 2011, we had a bride versus groom hockey game that included many of our wedding guests: Luke Small, Jennifer Botterill, Dermot McDonald, Delaney Collins, Kathryn McKenzie, Sarah Love, Tara French, Tyler Stewart (and his daughters), and Jesus Torres (Diana Tellegson's husband), with Katrinka and Bobby Blunt's kids in the front.

"Sami Jo, it's Peter Mansbridge. That must have given you a bit more incentive too, if you didn't need any more than you already have." Wow, Peter Mansbridge, the news anchor on *The National*. I try to stay calm.

"Oh definitely, and I mean it just gives us so much more incentive. We're just so pumped after watching this. I mean, if you can see it in my face just how excited I am — it's awesome!"

"Well, we can," says Peter.

Brian pipes back in. "Sami Jo, now you begin play, I believe, Monday, is it right, against Kazakhstan?"

"Yes, that's right, on the eleventh." It's loud in the stadium, and I'm doing my best to hear their questions through the earphones.

"Talk to me about this team. You have yet to beat the United States in this long series of games leading up, but you tell me that's not necessarily a bad thing?"

"That's right. I mean, we wouldn't choose to be zero and eight right now, but we are. It's a reality. I mean, their chances of winning the ninth game are pretty slim, and that's what we're gunning for, for that Olympic gold-medal game on the twenty-first, and hopefully, we'll have a whole country supporting us, behind us. And like they say, if you cheer loud enough, we'll hear you in Salt Lake."

"Sami, thank you. Congratulations and good luck."

"Thank you so much, and hi to all my friends and family in Winnipeg and across the country."

"That is Sami Jo Small, goaltender for the Canadian women's hockey team, and the team begins play on Monday against Kazakhstan."

The camera lights turn off, but my smile does not dissipate. What does this mean? They chose me from an entire team to speak to the country. This can only be a good omen. The training is done. The exhibition games are done. I'm in peak physical performance and more confident than I've ever been. Let the games begin.

17

Olympic Debut

In shorts and a t-shirt, my cheeks rosy from my off-ice warm-up, I pass through the shower curtain protecting our dressing room from the hallway. Today, at the E Center in West Valley, Utah, I will make my official Olympic debut against Russia. I am nervously confident.

Only Tammy Lee Shewchuk and Geraldine Heaney are currently in the room. Shewchuk's hair is curled, and her makeup's done; she looks better suited for *Glamour* magazine, but she has a saying: "Look good, feel good, play good." She and Heaney kick a mini soccer ball between them, and I avoid breaking up the game on the way to my stall.

"Tammy, is your Coke all ready for the game?" I shout over the music. She's now a brunette instead of her usual blond due to a mistake at the salon before we came.

"Of course," she smiles and nods. Others choose coffee as pre-game stimulus, but Shewchuk drinks her sugary caffeinated drink before the game and between every period.

"How was warm-up? We missed you," says Heaney as I take my seat. I nod and give the thumbs-up. When I'm not playing, which in a three-goalie rotation is often, I usually make my rounds and end up hanging out with these two.

Robin McDonald has tried to replicate our usual set-up of equipment in Calgary, but he doesn't have much space in which to work. There are no individual stalls, only two hooks per player and a bit of a shelf above. Kelly Bechard is my stall-mate to my left, and the bathroom sink is to my right. Robin brought our Team Canada carpet to serve as a centrepiece and adorned the walls with Canadian children's good-luck messages from home.

I sit across from Kim. She already had her Olympic debut two days ago against Kazakhstan. She played well. She wasn't tested much, but when she was, the breakdowns were severe. I know that's what it will most likely be for me today. Often in lopsided games, our players either become complacent or try to do things that they wouldn't get away with against a stronger opponent. The breakdowns tend to lead to scoring chances by the opposition.

The Russians came third at last year's World Championship in Minnesota, winning a medal for the first time, and have a couple of forwards who, if we let them, can rip the puck. I have to be prepared.

I found out I was going to play this game the day before the Kazakhstan game. Danièle told us Kim would play the first game, I'd get the second, and then she'd let us know from there. All season, we've been in the dark, and not much has changed. Sometimes she tells us just before games are about to start. Once she forgot and told us after warm-up. I'm not sure if she's playing head games, if she's undecided, or if she knows and we're just overlooked.

The media has been on both of us every day to know who the number-one goalie will be, but we have no idea. André Brin, our media relations manager, has been trying to steer us clear of the controversy. André has also looked out for me since we met in my early athletic career back in Winnipeg. We have many mutual friends back home in the francophone community and I think he appreciates that I love talking to both the English and French media. However, now it's a bit more difficult when I don't have the answers they need. My stock answer has become "Regardless of who the coaches choose, Kim and I are prepared to support each other . . ." But I do wish I knew.

I grab my skates off the floor and run my finger down the cold steel feeling for any imperfections.

For the last couple of weeks as the coaches prepare us tactically, the goalies have become merely an afterthought, receiving a barrage of shots. Yesterday's practice was different. The team had the day off the ice, but I begged and pleaded for the coaches to allow me skate. I wanted to feel the puck before today's game. Danièle relented, and Charline Labonté graciously joined me on the ice.

Charlie has been amazing. She's easy to get along with, but has a fierce determination. Her work ethic on the ice is unparalleled and I wish I could be more of a sounding board for her, having been in her position; however, I have barely enough emotional capacity to deal with my own situation. At yesterday's practice, it was like the weight of the Olympics was lifted and we laughed, and tried to outdo each other. I haven't had that much fun on the ice in a long time.

1989: JOY — SKATING ON MY OWN

It's mid-January and classes have finished for the day but instead of heading to the bus stop, I'm heading to Norberry Community Centre to skate. I'm 13 years old and I wear my white puffy boys' AAA Warriors hockey jacket with pride as I carry my stick and skates.

Sometimes the community centre doors are open, but not today. There's no one in sight. I tried to convince some of my friends to skate, but no one could, so it's just me.

I love having the ice to myself, adore being the lone skater on a fresh sheet. I check all the rinks for the best ice and decide on the one nearest the club. The white boards look as if they're held up by snowbanks but that's just an illusion. When I was younger, I used to play real games on this ice, and my parents would stand on these snowbanks. We'd go inside between periods, and my teammates would try everything to keep their feet warm, from pepper in their skates to hair dryers, but the cold never bothered me. I could skate out here for hours in freezing temperatures.

Tentatively, I make my way across the ice. No Zamboni today, but the sun has smoothed the surface. It's only -15 Celsius, which is quite different from the -35s of last week. I'm excited that I won't have to double up on neck warmers pulled so high up that only my eyes are exposed. Today, just a toque will do. No prairie wind to slow me down, and the sun makes for ideal skating conditions.

I can see my breath as I hop into the players box. I remove my boots, exposing my sock feet to the elements, but just as quickly I stuff them into my skates, feeling the cold of the plastic toe caps. Despite being a full-time goalie with real goalie skates, I've held on to these player's skates precisely for days like these.

My backpack leans up against the wood planks. I fish around in its depths for my puck. I tie up my skates, trying to minimize the amount of time my hands are outside my mitts. I reach for my red neck warmer and decide to pull it over my head. Best to start warm and de-layer as I warm up.

It's 3:30 p.m. My mom's coming at 5:00 to pick me up. I put on my "garbage" mitts, adorned with coloured marker depictions of the Calgary Olympic logo. I grab my white Titan stick with red lettering. Standing up, I throw my lone puck onto the glistening surface. The ice is all mine.

Stepping down out of the wooden players box I feel the great joy of ice beneath my steel. My skates feel more comfortable than my running shoes. I push towards the puck. I skate, shoot, and stickhandle. I invent games for myself, mimicking what I see on Saturday nights. I pretend there are other players out here with me, sidestepping and dangling as I go. The imaginary goaltender is no match in my make-believe games. I speed up — feel the wind on my face. I slow down to catch my breath and pull down my red neck warmer covered in frost. On this ice, I'm always the star.

FEBRUARY 13, 2002: FIRST OLYMPIC GAME (CONTINUED)

Midway through the 20-minute on-ice warm-up of my Olympic debut, I haven't let a goal in yet. I know I won't be able to prove much to the coaches during the game, but I can show them I heard their message about warming up with a purpose, making my teammates have to be better. I push to make a save, stretch to prevent a goal, and ensure nothing gets past me.

With two minutes left on the clock, I leave the ice. Nothing more to do, and I like to get back to the dressing room early so I have a chance to go to the bathroom before the game. I also want to grab a snack. Today's game starts at 11:00 a.m., so I must stay nourished. I make the long walk back to the dressing room, my equipment already wet from working hard.

As Danièle finishes her pre-game speech, I cinch my glove and blocker on my hands. I tuned her out midway through — most information is irrelevant to me — and started to think about my game. *Stay focused. Stay in the game. Don't do too much. Make good decisions with the puck.*

As soon as she's done announcing the starting lineup, I stand and make my way to the door before everyone else gets up. I avoid sticks and helmets scattered on the dressing room floor. At the doorway, I await Kim. I make sure most of the girls are ready and then begin the long walk through the E Center. We pass many volunteers, and I try to smile or nod at each one. This is their moment too.

As I come up to the tunnel to go to the ice, I feel a sudden wave of calm. Surprisingly, this feels normal. I walk through the dark tunnel into the light of the arena and take my first step on the ice to a thunderous roar of Canadian fans. I don't look up, just down to my net, skating in its direction. My team circles the ice a few times, getting out some last-minute nerves. I scrape my crease, pushing against my skate blades to scuff up the smooth ice. Slowly the team congregates around me. I am on my goal line, elbows on my knees. Everyone has her spot in the semi-circle surrounding me. I look into my players' faces and smile.

What an incredible moment we're about to share together. Danielle Goyette yells out "Three! Two! One!" and in unison we all respond "Canada!"

A few taps of the pads, and the game begins. The action is mostly in the Russian end, but I use every opportunity I can to play the puck and stay in the game. Wick scores off a faceoff early and then Goyette scores to make it 2–0. At the end of the period, I finally look up to see hundreds of waving Canadian flags.

There are not many shots in the second period until Russian sniper Katia Pashkevitch winds up for a slapshot just inside the blue line. The puck ricochets slightly off my defenceman, Thérèse Brisson, and redirects to the top corner. My mind, without thought, trained from a lifetime of moments, instinctively reacts. I stretch my glove as far as it will go and barely snag it out of the air. Phew. Don't want the Russians to think they are in this game.

We are severely outshooting the Russians as the third period draws to a close. Their goaltender, a fatigued Irina Gashennikova, has kept the score closer than it should be. With less than a minute and a half left in my quest for a shutout, the breakdown I have been anticipating all game happens. It took 58.5 minutes of a 60-minute game, but I'm ready.

The Russians are on a two on one. Thérèse is my lone defenceman as her partner, Geraldine Heaney, scurries to get back. The crowd is going bananas. They want a Russian goal. I remind myself, *I've done this a million times. Focus on the puck.* As the Russian player comes within striking distance, all my senses focus on her. I see her load her stick. She's metres away now. She fires the puck low to my right. I kick out my leg, but the shot is difficult to control, the rebound sits just outside my crease. I lunge as the second Russian eyes the puck on her stick. At the last moment, I poke the puck away, preserving the shutout.

FEBRUARY 18, 2002: WHO WILL PLAY?

I'm on our team bus and we are driving towards a friends and family get-together hosted by Hockey Canada. I feel great. This morning's practice, despite being early, went terrifically. I was on fire. Kim didn't skate this morning — she tweaked a groin muscle — but Charlie was still there, and practice went on as usual.

I was disappointed not to play our final round robin game against Sweden, but the rotation continues as predicted. When Dave told me Kim was playing, he emphasized that Danièle didn't want me to tell anyone for fear of it leaking to the media. It's been a hard secret to keep. As we trounced Sweden 11–0, it was tough to sit on the bench, but I was proud of my teammates. Jen scored our first goal in an amazing individual effort, and several others shined. I whooped and hollered at the fantastic plays and took solace knowing I would be playing either the semis or the finals.

I laugh and joke with my seatmate, Jen, as we anticipate seeing our families who have made the trek from Winnipeg. Players occupy their usual areas on the bus. Staff are always in the front, players in the back.

Wick, "the grocery stick," in the middle of the bus. Near her is a great place to be if you need silence. She seldom chit-chats or gossips and always looks like she is replaying the previous game or practice in her head.

Behind Wick are the self-named "Frenchies," glued together by a common language. Jayna, Vicky, Kelly, Lori, and Cassie — the "social girls" — usually occupy the back seats with Heaney and Piper immediately in front of them providing banter; this is where I go if I need a good laugh, want to hear the latest gossip, or need to vent. No one ever balks if you sit with a different crew. I feel welcome everywhere — I just pick my spot based on how I feel that day.

As the bus drifts through Salt Lake City, we pass the Mormon temples. Colleen Sostorics, seated in front of us, beside Dana Antal, finishes her cribbage game in the aisle with Carla Macleod, Becky, and Cheryl Pounder and turns to chat. Her family won't be at the get-together today as they can't leave the farm in Saskatchewan for long and will make it just in time for the semifinal game. This is perhaps where Sos, as we call her, learned her incredible work ethic.

There are many friends and family gathered to greet us as we disembark from the bus. Each of us wades through the swarm of people to find our loved ones. I spot my brother's almost white blond hair. I weave through other reunions to get to my family.

My parents, my brother, Luke, and his wife, Gina, have all come to Salt Lake. We chat about their latest tour stops and what they've seen thus far. They're still excited about when we all got to meet the NHL'ers and have a meal with their families. Through their stories, I am transported into the world of being a tourist at the Olympics.

Luke tells me the antics of "Captain Canada," his alter ego at games. He says it's been great to get to know the rest of the families and that he and Jeff Campbell (Cassie's brother) have bonded over some beverages. My parents are excited to see me, as this is a rarity during a major competition.

I hear about their host family, a local Salt Lake City Mormon family that has taken them into their home. I can tell they were very proud to have watched me play, but I also know it's hard not to watch me play. They just want me to be happy.

My brother asks about the Village, inquires who I've met. He wants all the details and loves hearing the inside stories.

In the middle of a story, Dave catches my eye. He motions for me to come see him. I smile and excuse myself from my family. He guides me outside to the parking lot.

He isn't smiling. Working with him as my goalie coach over the course of the year, I've gotten to know Dave. He seldom masks his emotions. His face worries me.

Slowly he begins. "Danièle has decided to play Kim in tomorrow's semifinal game."

I let the news sink in.

This is good news, right? I begin to smile, and my heart starts to flicker. Based on the rotation, this means the final is for me.

Dave looks awkward, empathetic, and sad all at the same time. Reluctantly, dejectedly, he continues, trying not to take notice of my hope. "And Kim, barring unforeseen circumstances, will also be starting in the finals. If Kim does well, she's the goalie for the rest of the tournament."

I look down. My face begins to heat up. My pulse quickens. My expression perplexed, I let the information settle in.

"What?" I thought maybe I had misheard, but Dave simply shakes his head. I don't think he has the strength to repeat the words, knowing he is breaking my heart.

I turn away. I have nowhere to go. Dave makes his way back into the party.

Why tell me now? Couldn't they wait until we were back in the Village? Why didn't Danièle do it? Why did she make Dave do it?

Anger boils up. Standing alone, I'm not sure what to do. I can see the smiles of friends and families through the glass door. That's the last place I want to be right now.

I can barely hold it together, but my mom always taught us to keep our pain to ourselves. I mask my emotions and walk through the crowd back to my parents. I find my family and jump back in the conversation as if nothing's happened, but it's difficult to focus. *Does Kim know?* I stare at her with her family from the other side of the room. *Does she seem different? Is she happy?* I can't tell.

Finally, it's time to get back on the bus.

I say goodbye to my parents.

"Good luck in the semis! Stone 'em and have fun," my dad says.

I want to cry. *Do they know? Can they see it on my face?* My mind spins.

I climb the steps. My heart is aching. I can't be on this bus; everyone is happy.

"I forgot something inside," I say quietly to Mel, our assistant coach, at the front of the bus.

I get off the bus. I can't lie to my family. I search the scattered crowd and find Luke. Tears well up in my eyes. I can't look him in the face.

"Tell Mom and Dad I'm sorry, I'm not playing tomorrow — but not to worry about me, I'll be fine."

Luke looks shocked. I run back towards the bus before he can hug me. I need to get it together.

I climb back on. I don't take my usual seat beside Jen, opting for a spot closer to Wick, closer to quiet. I sink into my seat by myself and look out the window. Faintly hearing the girls converse about their great visits with their families, I stare at nothing. My eyes burning, feeling like I have been punched in the gut.

18

So Close

I'm sitting at the end of the bench in my corner beside the glass that divides the players from the fans for the start of our semifinal game against Finland. Behind me, our team physician, Dr. Suzanne Leclerc, stands on a milk crate so she is high enough to see over the players. Beside me, two of my defencemen, Cheryl Pounder and Becky Kellar, recount their last shift. They seem satisfied. They should be: we're already winning 2–0.

My helmet and gloves are in the hallway leading to the dressing room, out of the way, but ready. The defence changes with a rhythm consistent with a lead. Each of the three pairings takes their minute shift and then changes, entering through the gate to my left manned by our equipment manager Robin McDonald. Farther down the bench, Doug Stacey, our physiotherapist, opens the gate for the much more chaotic forwards.

I thought the Finns would be more of a threat, but besides goalie Tuula Puputti, playing superbly, we are beating them in every aspect of the game. We are faster, tougher, and smarter. Thérèse Brisson scored our first goal — a point shot through traffic. While she has undoubtedly one of the hardest shots in women's hockey, I don't think Puputti could see the puck through all the players.

Wick followed up with a goal off a nice two on one pass by Isabelle Chartrand, her fifth of the tournament. Her line with Campbell and Goyette has really been clicking. The line seldom talks, even seldom sits next to each other, but they have been our best line in this tournament. Wick's her own toughest critic, constantly scrutinizing game tape and sneaking off to the gym for extra workouts but her intensity is a gift to this team forcing us all to be better. She's so talented, but she's also known to be tough to play alongside, often taking out her frustrations on her linemates. There are always people trying to knock Wick down, but flanked by Goyette and Campbell, she is shining.

The first period is about to end when there's a turnover in our end on a clearing attempt by Brisson. The Finnish player corrals the puck and shoots on net. Finn Sari Fisk gets her stick on the puck, hand-cuffing Kim. The puck is loose. Tiia Reima finds it with an open net staring back at her. Kim tries to recover, lunging with her arms, but it's not in time.

Goal for Finland. 2–1 Canada.

Our bench goes silent. Time runs out on the first period. I stand and take my usual place at the entrance to the hallway. I hold my glove out and high-five my teammates as they walk by. Their silence speaks volumes.

The room doesn't have the same energy it did before the game. My teammates look annoyed. Kim looks mad she let the Finns score. Tough broken-down play, not much she could have done.

Danièle, in her charcoal half-zip sweatshirt and black dress pants, walks in the room with Mel and Wally not far behind. She looks calm, but she slowly stares around the room. Her right eyebrow arches up.

"Ladies, we need to stick to our game plan. The Finns are no match for any of you in this room. Don't let one breakdown ruin that period. We do good things out there . . ." She hesitates. "Let's play our game . . . *our* game . . . for these next twenty minutes. Don't let the Finns back in the game."

We will start the period shorthanded because Hefford apparently got a penalty right at the end of the last — I didn't see it. As Danièle leaves the room, she recites off the starting penalty-killers, "Campbell, Wick, Pounder, and Kellar."

I take my seat in the same spot on the bench. With the change of ends, I'm now among the chaos of the forwards. We kill off the penalty. Back to regular strength. We forecheck hard and then change.

It's a bad line change; the next group isn't out fast enough. The Finns slip in behind everyone. A quick pass up the ice to former Toronto Aero Sari Fisk and they are on a two on one.

Fisk makes a nifty pass to Reima who again is alone in front of our net. Kim slides in a perfect butterfly, but Reima quickly fires the puck high and over her shoulder. The puck is in. I look down the bench at the faces of my bewildered teammates.

2–2 tie.

I can hear Wally behind me talking into his headset to our third assistant coach, Karen Hughes, who sits up in the rafters. I can't hear her response, but I'll bet she's recounting the bad line change to Wally.

I stand and hit my right hand hard against the boards and shout down the bench to no one in particular, "C'mon guys, let's get that one back." I feel helpless. We look tense. The wheels are coming off.

Danièle taps forward Dana Antal on the shoulder. Dana has battled hard to be on this team. She blew out her knee, only to rehabilitate and return a year later to break her leg. From Esterhazy, Saskatchewan, she's an incredibly nice, humble, down-to-earth person. She'll speak her mind when necessary, but in a very careful way to not offend anyone. She's a finesse player who works very hard.

Our fourth line of Antal, Piper, and Caro hop the boards. Their job now is to quell the tide and bring momentum back to our side. Antal wins the faceoff, and once again we put pressure on the Finns. Our youngest line is providing exactly the spark we need.

Wick, Campbell, and Goyette follow them up. They are our top line. "Here we go, guys!" I scream as Wick takes the faceoff in front of our bench. The puck is bouncy, and passes are near misses. We've lost our spark. The Finns are relentless. The puck ends up low in our zone. Reima haphazardly throws the puck in front of our net where we've left two Finns completely open. The pass gets through and onto the stick of Finn Katja Riipa. The pass catches Kim by surprise. Riipa simply redirects the puck on her backhand. Kim sprawls to make the save, but the puck soars high into the back of her net.

The crowd erupts. 3–2 Finland.

This can't be happening. We can't lose to the Finns at the Olympics. We've never lost to Finland. Wally walks down to me.

"Get ready," he says in a serious tone.

I'm not sure whether to spring to action or not. This is not his call, but my heart is exploding in my chest. *Is this my chance?* I look down the bench at Danièle. She is rubbing her chin and hasn't otherwise moved. She looks shocked. *Am I going in?* I try to catch her eye, but she still doesn't turn.

I stand to fetch my gloves, stick, and helmet, just in case. Danièle sees me out of the corner of her eye and finally makes a gesture for me to sit back down. I grab my stuff anyway and sit back in my spot. *I'm ready.* Adrenaline courses through my veins. Wally makes his way to Danièle, and they quietly whisper. Danièle taps Vicky on the shoulder. Her line is up. Wally makes his way back down to me.

"Just be ready," he says, agitated.

The play starts again. Now I'm torn. One more goal and I'll be in for sure. On the other hand, I don't want our team to lose in the semi-finals at the Olympics. My mind is racing. I try to disregard the negative thoughts.

I repeat to myself, *Team wins out.* Team must always win out.

Cheering our good plays, I try to keep our spirits up. We get chances in the second period, but we get nothing past their goalie, Puputti. Time ticks away and eventually the second period ends. We are outshooting the Finns 40–13 but are losing 3–2.

I walk through the entrance to our dressing room. The room is heated; there's yelling and an accusatory tone to every comment.

"Guys, we have to backcheck," a player says shaking her head.

"Who the hell was supposed to have her?" murmurs one of our defenceman as she fills her cup with Gatorade.

Hefford comes over to my stall. "Sami, how do you think I should beat Puputti? I've had so many chances."

Puputti just graduated from University of Minnesota-Duluth under our old coach Shannon Miller. That's why her pads are maroon and yellow, standing out sharply against the blue and white of the Finnish jersey. She's small, but incredibly quick and more than used to North American play.

I ponder the question. "Hmmm, she moves so well laterally," I begin, "but she seems to leave her five-hole exposed. Maybe try that. You're good at hitting that spot." I know this from having practised with Jayna for a long time.

"Shifts are way too long," screams Wick into the centre of the room. Frustrations are high but tempers are even higher. The anger is palpable.

Cassie, standing in her stall, gathers everyone's attention. Always emotional, she commands respect and attention every time she speaks.

"Guys, we've had challenges all year." She's fighting back her tears. "This is how we want it — we want another challenge. Don't give up. You guys are exceptional people and an incredible team, so let's go out and prove that on the ice. Believe in the people around you. Let's play our game!"

Cheers of agreement fill the room. Half the team is standing. The beast has awoken, and we are ready for this third period.

I'm fired up. I want to go out there and win. I want to help my teammates too, but I stare downward. This isn't about me. I take a deep breath and exhale. I put a smile back on my face.

As I take my seat, I see my brother in his red speedo and "Captain Canada" costume complete with a Canada flag cape, running up and down the stairs in the family section leading cheers, willing our team to get back in this game. As soon as our skates hit the ice for the third, our play is different. We are supporting the puck carrier, being creative, and throwing everything at the net. The Finns' luck runs out as Wick takes a feed from Goyette and beats Puputti. Our bench erupts. Her celebration of high-fives lasts right to me at the end of the bench.

3–3 tie.

Next line up. Vicky, Dupuis, and Hefford. Vicky wins the draw forward to a streaking Hefford who goes in alone on Puputti. She fires it five-hole and it squeaks in. I explode to my feet cheering wildly. *That's where I told her to shoot.* The whole bench erupts. Two goals six seconds apart, and we've regained the lead.

4–3 Canada.

Confidence carries us the rest of the period. We've broken the Finns and are relentless for three more goals in the last three minutes of play and we win 7–3.

Relief fills our team as we skate to congratulate Kim in her crease. I wade through the sea of players to tap her on the shoulder. She's smiling with a mixture of relief and disappointment. I make my way to centre ice for the obligatory team handshakes and wonder what will happen next.

Now who will get the final?

FEBRUARY 20, 2002: THE NIGHT BEFORE THE FINAL

It's our last practice as a team. The day before the final game. I push myself, one final look, one final chance to shine; I want to show the coaches I'm ready. Geraldine Heaney already made the announcement she is retiring post-Olympics. We celebrate her during practice. We're loose, carefree, and enjoying our final practice together. Back at the village, we do one last set of bike sprints, one last activation before the final. We've been building up to this moment, training hard all season, however these past couple weeks we have finally been tapering off and it's showing as we look more energetic.

I still have no idea what's going to happen. *Did Kim falter in her game against the Finns? Were the hiccups enough to sway the coaches?* I'm nervous to hear the answer, but confident I've done everything right. I think of all the people in my life who will be watching. My mind wanders. I visualize saves and replay over and over the moment when the final buzzer sounds and we are victorious, and everyone piles on top of me. I let myself think about what I should do with my stick. Should I fall to the ground? I am so confident we will win; I prepare for the eventuality.

With only one practice today, we are left with lots of spare time. I write some postcards to people back home, and then Jen and I go for a walk into the International Zone in the Olympic Village. I feel like I'm experiencing everything for the last time. I'll be different tomorrow and whether our team is successful or not, a new chapter will begin.

After dinner in the Village cafeteria, we head back to our dorms. There's not much in our rooms, but we have shared common space where the team tends to gather. There's a TV and a DVD player, some couches, and plenty of ice for lingering injuries. Ice bags are the most popular accessory. We've pushed our bodies to the limits. Team massage therapist Mavis Wahl's and team physiotherapist Doug Stacey's rooms are down the hall. Outside their rooms there are signup sheets that are completely full. As one player leaves, another enters.

Thérèse Brisson, originally from Dollard-des-Ormeaux, Quebec, is recovering from a concussion that took her out for months. She's back, but at 36 her body still has ailments. Thérèse sits in the common area with a climbing light strapped to her head, her foot in a garbage can filled with ice, an ice pack strapped to her shoulder, and a novel in hand. A tenured university professor, she had to take a year sabbatical to centralize for the Olympic team. She's the brains behind our team.

It's the night before the gold medal, and despite our foyer looking like a triage unit, we have one more game to get through. Thérèse sits as our player representative on Hockey Canada's board of directors. She wrote our first ever players' agreement protecting our rights as athletes. She's been our captain for the last three years, and often spoke out when no one else would. She stood up for us and looked to the future when we were too young to care. She plays for the newly formed Mississauga IceDogs in the NWHL alongside other former National Team members Kathy McCormack, Andria Hunter, and Nathalie Rivard. As a defenceman, she plays hard and is the strongest player on the team, inspiring younger girls to gain strength. Her shot is deadly, but her hip check even more so.

She doesn't look out of place at all, blending in with all the others with ice packs. Vicky opted for a full bathtub filled with ice. She's out of the cold water now, but she's popping Advil as if it's candy. Vicky is always playing with some sort of injury. She's one of the strongest leaders on the team, her love of the game is contagious, but small injuries seem to follow her around. She never takes time off, never shows how much pain she feels.

On the TV, the movie *Traffic* plays — a story about drug trafficking in the United States. A random selection for the night before one of the most important days of our lives, but at this point we've watched most of the DVDs that we brought from home. Someone threw this one in, and I'm captivated.

About an hour into the movie, I'm tapped on the shoulder. It's Vicky telling me Dave is waiting down the hall for me. The drug cartel in the movie vanishes as thoughts about the news I'm waiting for take over my mind.

I look both ways down the dimly lit hall and see our goalie coach. I want to run towards him, but walk instead, trying not to walk too fast or too slow. My mind races, my palms are sweaty. This is the meeting I've been waiting for my entire hockey career.

I'm confident and smile. *How can they play Kim after her game against Finland?* I approach Dave. Our head coach is behind him.

Danièle is looking away. My hearts sinks. Dave looks at my hopeful face knowing that this might be the toughest meeting of his life. He shakes his head, looking like he's going to cry.

"Kim will start tomorrow."

1985: DISAPPOINTMENT — PELLE LINDBERG HEARTBREAK

I grab the sports section away from my dad's already-read pile and place it in front of my cereal bowl. It's 8:00 a.m.; he's getting ready to go to work, and I'm getting ready to go to grade 4. I unfold the paper, so I have enough room to turn the pages. I'm stunned by the photo dominating the front of the sports section: a smashed-up car, the front end clearly gone. It looks horrific. In a square box inset on the photo is a headshot of my favourite NHL goalie, Pelle Lindbergh.

I look to my dad who peers over his newspaper. He's already read this section. My eyes implore *What's happened?* but my mouth is unable to speak.

Picking up the paper with both hands, I bring the horror closer to my eyes. A carton of skim milk waits for pouring onto my Cheerios. I stare at the photo and try not to think the worst, but I can't bring myself to read the article. I recently watched Pelle play this past weekend on *Hockey Night in Canada*. I memorized his saves and used them only yesterday when I was playing mini-stick hockey with my brother on the carpet. I stuck my leg out just like Pelle Lindbergh, I *was* Pelle Lindbergh. I idolize everything about him.

As I read the article, I have a lump in my throat and my face is hot. I swallow hard, trying not to cry. Pelle is being kept on life support until his dad arrives from Sweden to say goodbye. He hit a wall in his Porsche

930 Turbo. I don't want to cry in front of my dad. I can feel his eyes on me, but I stare at the page.

My mom comes from her office, where she's been rustling through papers. She reaches her hand over my shoulder, but I don't turn, feeling as though any sudden movement and the waterworks will begin. She lays down a piece of paper on top of the picture of Pelle.

"I hadn't sent it yet," she says sweetly as she places my own handwriting in front of my cereal.

Pelle's letter. I wrote to Mr. Lindbergh on the weekend. He had played unbelievably, and I told him I hoped he made the All-Star Game.

Now I will never again see Pelle play. I move the letter aside and continue the article, looking for any hope that he'll get better.

Pelle was driving home from a party. He was drunk. *Why was he driving? This can't be right; my hero wouldn't do that.*

I look up at my dad, my nine-year-old eyes puffy, with Pelle's letter in one hand, I sense my world is collapsing.

Dad reaches for my shoulder, his eyes empathetic, but I can feel wetness on my face. I brush his hand away and bolt from the chair. I leave my cereal uneaten and run upstairs to my room. My face in my pillow, I scream in angry tears.

My hero is gone.

FEBRUARY 20, 2002: THE NIGHT BEFORE THE FINAL (CONTINUED)

Dave continues talking, but everything becomes jumbled. I want to run to my room and cry. I think he's trying to build me up, give me some excuses for the decision, but I'm too busy fighting back my tears to hear them. Danièle's still not speaking. Dave's voice becomes amplified, his words piercing into my head.

Tears well up. I don't know what to do. I can't even speak. My throat feels swollen shut, my heart pounds out of my chest, and I can feel my face is red hot.

I want to scream, to get away, but I am frozen. The hallway is dark. I can still hear the movie playing as Dave and Danièle leave me. I'm sweating, trying not to sob. I don't know where to go; Jen, my roommate, has already gone into our room to get ready to go to sleep, but I want to be alone. I open the nearest exit, walk down the six flights of stairs, accelerate into a run. I crash through the doors, the cold air shocking and the darkness comforting. I begin to sob.

I had visualized nearly every situation, but I had never visualized not playing. I couldn't fathom not playing. I still can't. I won't get to make the big saves, I won't get to make a difference, I won't get to have everyone pile on top of me after our victory. My world no longer makes sense.

I dedicated my life to this team. This is my sanctuary, my place where I excel, where I feel most at home. I want to be there for them, I want to be a great teammate, but now I want even more to run away and never come back.

I walk straight ahead, and then run past the gates into the International Zone, but there are too many people here. I try to aim my steps towards the darkness. I run towards the solitude of the Olympic flag. I can barely see through the tears, I run until I can't run anymore, then collapse. The cold night engulfs me. I'm at the farthest end of the Village, an area where each competing country has a flag waving proudly. I stare at the flags. I can barely breathe.

I know how to train my body, I know how to recover from injury, I even know mentally how to recover from the setback of being scored on, but I don't know how to recover from this.

I'm lifeless, shocked, embarrassed. I feel like a failure.

It is well past midnight, and I have nowhere to be, nothing to prepare for. I sit alone in the cold for hours.

I try to build up my courage to take the first steps back, but I can't help replaying the message from Dave. "Kim's going to play." I keep losing focus. Tears pour until I feel empty.

I can see the glow of the dorms in the distance and know that eventually I need to get back there.

1983: ACCEPTANCE — POOL DECK STANDOFF

Sitting on the pool deck before a Manitoba Marlins swim practice, it's cold, and the water will be even colder. My seven-year-old body sits on the blue storage benches lining the deck as long as I can, my green towel draped around me as I stare at my feet.

Dr. Martin is pacing the pool deck watching the clock tick towards 6:30 a.m. He's the coach for the big kids. His clipboard is filled with numbers, split times, and sets. My dad is our coach. I can't even look at him right now, I'm extremely angry at him. It's his fault I'm so cold.

I didn't want to come to practice this morning. I'm not even sure how I got here, but somehow Dad got me out of bed to this standoff on the pool deck. He smiles and laughs with the other swimmers, but not with me. He knows it's best to leave me alone when I'm mad.

I love to swim in competitions. I love racing, winning ribbons, and breaking provincial records. I love looking up at the end of a heat and seeing my time on the score clock and knowing that I went faster than I did before. I love getting the red *Wow, I Improved My Time* ribbons that line my bedroom walls. I love the trophies I get for each event I swim and the day-long meets. I even love practising, but not in the morning.

My brother is getting ready to hop in the pool five lanes over. He swims with the fast kids even though he's only 10. He's very impressive. My brother always wins best swimmer at every meet.

Knowing I have to get in, I fight back tears. I hate this sport right now. This is stupid: my eyes are barely open, I'm irritatingly tired, and my goose-bumped skin is bluish.

My dad turns from the head of our lane back towards me. He doesn't have to say anything, I know I have to get in. The first set is starting. Other swimmers laugh and play near the starting blocks in my lane, already accustomed to the water. I stuff my Marlins towel in my kit bag, exposing my green and yellow swimsuit. I search in the depths of the bag for my cap and goggles. Knowing I'm going to be in trouble soon, I pull on my cap and fiddle with my goggles as I tentatively walk over to the starting blocks.

Don't be a wimp, you can do this. I don't even look at my dad. He shouts to all six of us in the lane the distance of the first set. I look down. The water is so near. Every hair on my body stands up. I take a deep breath. Nothing starts until I jump. Even when everything is telling me not to, *I must jump.* Keep moving forward. Anger propels me, and I dive in to start my first lap.

I am not going to be playing in the gold medal game.

Should I have done something differently?

The role of cheerleader isn't a role I want to play. I hate the thought of it. I don't want to sit on the sidelines of my dream. *After twenty years of training, of pushing my body to the limits, was this my fate?* The thought makes me sick.

I have cried enough — I have nothing left.

I must jump. I get up and start walking.

I make my way back to the Village, one step at a time. I can feel the cold. *How long was I here?*

Walking back through security, I can't even look up. The guards do a double take at my photo on my accreditation, my face is swollen with emotion. Ashamed, I still don't know where to go. The Village is silent. Off in the distance I can see some lights. I follow the glow to the cafeteria. I want to get lost in the crowd. I need to find my purpose.

At this hour, the cafeteria is full of athletes done their competitions. Some are returning from late-night parties celebrating successes, while others lurk in the corners, staring into mid-air, wishing their Olympics had gone differently.

I grab a smoothie and sit down. I find solace seeing other athletes' dejection. Others look the same way I feel. I sit in silence for a long time.

How am I going to do this? This will be my "squirrel bike" to ride. Nobody wants this role, but someone must do it.

Back in my room I tuck myself into bed, trying not to wake Jen. I'm exhausted. Tonight was about me, but somehow tomorrow must be about the team.

19

Olympic Final — Salt Lake City

FEBRUARY 21, 2002: GETTING READY

I awake to the alarm buzzing: it's 8:00 a.m. I don't want to get up. In a fog, I lay on my side under the blue duvet.

I reach out my hand towards the alarm clock on the night table, which is between my bed and Jen's. My fingers search for the right button, but as I push each one, none turns off the sound. I reach my whole body over to the alarm and draw it near. Without glasses, I squint at the device mere centimetres from my face to find the switch. I collapse back into bed and grab my glasses from the night table.

Through the thin walls, I can hear the alarms of my other teammates as I look over at Jen. She's awake now too, and as she opens her eyes, her first movement of the day is a gigantic smile pointed in my direction. I smile back.

It's gold medal day.

But not *my* gold medal day. Fighting my emotions, I turn towards the wall where I've taped up a couple dozen postcards from friends and family, a constant reminder of the most important people in my life. All in one night, anger became sadness, which quickly had to turn into acceptance.

I stand up and make my way to the closet at the end of my bed. I can tell by Jen's actions that she knows. I try to act normal. I don't want this to bring her down and derail her focus.

Making her way to my side of the room, she knows how badly I wanted to play and reaches out, giving me a big hug. I cry a little on her shoulder. She whispers "I'm sorry" in my ear.

Jen and I walk to breakfast almost in silence. We run into several of our teammates. I smile and try to make people laugh to lighten the mood and put everyone at ease. Many of my teammates have no idea who is going to be playing in net today and most don't care.

Breakfast flies by. We walk back to the dorms for our customary pre-game team meeting.

We have surprise guests: gold medal figure skaters Jamie Salé and David Pelletier, recently popularized by a figure skating judging scandal.

They inspire our team by recounting their journey. Despite first being awarded the silver medal, they were proud of how they skated. Their success is a result of their ultimate belief in each other.

I try not to show my emotions. This is hard. We head back to our rooms, and I collapse on my bed for a nap, but I can't sleep.

At the rink, I go through my usual warm-up routine and then join Tammy Lee Shewchuk and Geraldine Heaney for some soccer. Heaney is a phenomenal athlete and has played countless sports over the years including the Irish sport of hurling, where she honed her incredible hand-eye skills. I can see Heaney's confident — she's been here before.

Shewchuk, on the other hand, is talking a mile a minute; nervous energy seeping from her. A gifted goal scorer, she's always been the highest point getter everywhere she's played. As we pass the ball back and forth, I recount their big games, their incredible talents, and try to make her laugh.

Other players start to file back into the dressing room. I make my way to my stall and put my pads on for the final time this season. I feel like breaking down, but the faces of my teammates keep me composed. *They need me to be strong.*

The music beats loudly as Kelly Bechard plays DJ. Jen and Piper seem to be having a dance party, grooving in their stalls. Wick's doing what appears to be yoga, and Vicky, Jayna, and Lori laugh in the corner. Kim's nearly half-dressed, while Thérèse hasn't yet started.

"Pounder, your socks are on backwards," Becky gently says and Pounder proceeds to straighten them out. Ouellette re-tapes her stick for the final time as Goyette cinches down her shoulder strapping. The dressing room is the same as it's always been, which comforts everyone before the biggest game of our lives.

FEBRUARY 21, 2002: THE FINAL BEGINS

Taking a deep breath I find my usual seat at the end of the bench, my cumbersome leg pads touching the metal framework of the rink's boards. My hair tied back in a high ponytail, I'm the only player on the bench without a helmet. I've tucked it immediately to my right, beside all the extra players' sticks lined up in numerical order. Doc puts her milk crate behind me, and Robin, in his white Hockey Canada golf shirt, sets up to my right, in front of the defenceman's door.

It's 11:00 a.m. The puck is about to drop for the 2002 Olympic gold medal game. I look up at the Jumbotron. Vicky lines up against American centreman Julie Chu. Vicky's flanked by linemates Dupuis and Hefford. This is a unique starting lineup for us: usually Wick's line starts every game with her linemates. Perhaps Danièle is not only telling the Americans we will be different but also telling all of us to prepare for anything.

As American referee Stacey Livingston slaps the puck to the ice between the two awaiting rivals, I try to quell the anger bubbling up in my thoughts. I tell myself it's over, there's nothing I can do now to play.

Despite being in the US, the crowd is full of Canadian flags. I know my family is somewhere in the stands; as is my former Stanford roommate Diana. But I don't search the crowd eagerly for them as I normally would. I stare at the ice. This is not my moment. I feel silly sitting here.

Vicky wins the draw forward and we instantly control the play in the American zone. Rested and tapered we're finally flying. My emotions take a back seat to the excitement on the ice. We get the first shots on net.

Our first line changes on the fly; Jen's sent out with Bechard and Shewchuk. We get more pressure in the attacking zone and more shots on net. Their goalie, Sara DeCosta, seems to be the only American without nerves. She looks confident. She was the backup to Sarah Tueting in the final game in Nagano and last year at the Worlds in Minnesota. I now understand what Sara DeCosta must have felt all those years ago. I envy

Sara. This is her chance. She worked hard and gained the respect of head coach Ben Smith.

As the game progresses, DeCosta forces a stoppage in play. Despite desperately wanting to be out there, I do love to watch our team play. As our youngest line takes the ice, there's an energy on the bench that is contagious. I'm excited to see this line play. They are high tempo and always a threat.

Piper takes the faceoff with Antal and Ouellette on her wings. She wins the puck forward and circles around the net nearly uncontested. She's amazingly strong on her skates and plays with an edge. A toughness honed playing a lifetime of boys hockey. Emerging on the other side, and with no one to stop her, Piper tries to jam the puck shortside, between the post and DeCosta's outstretched right toe.

DeCosta beats her to the post to make the save, but the puck rebounds right out in front of the net. DeCosta tries to stay focused on the puck, but she's down on the ice. American defenceman A.J. Mleczko guards the front of the net with her back turned to her goalie, trying to prevent a fast-moving Ouellette from getting to the open puck first. Caro's big and strong, and it takes a heroic effort on the part of Mleczko to keep her from reaching the puck.

Mleczko stands her up, but in the process the American defenceman loses sight of the puck and it hits her skate. The puck redirects back at the net high in the air, travelling in slow motion. DeCosta, on the ice, reaches for it, but it's too far from her grasp. The puck loops end over end and drops behind her into the back of the net.

Goal! 1–0 Canada.

And it's only 1:45 into the game.

Throwing my hands in the air, I yell and nearly knock the Doc off her crate. I turn to Isabelle Chartrand beside me, and we exuberantly hug. Piper celebrates with Ouellette and the others on the ice, and then they make a mad dash for us on the bench. Ouellette leads the celebration followed closely by Antal, Heaney, and Sos. I congratulate each girl with my blocker hand as they go by.

"Yeah, Caro! Yeah, Danes! Yeah, Ger! Yeah, Sos! *Yeah, Piper!*" I catch my breath and sit back down.

Shifts are short. The air in Salt Lake is thin so our coaches have warned us to keep them short, but it's also keeping all four lines in the game. No one is sitting. Danièle, dressed in a very professional-looking grey suit, is making sure everyone gets their turn.

We dominate in every zone. At 6:17 of the first period, American forward Shelley Looney bear hugs Thérèse Brisson and brings her to the ice. The ref's hand shoots in the air: it's a penalty for the USA. Our power play sets up and has some opportunities, but DeCosta is steady. She denies Sunohara and Hefford on some great chances. Campbell nearly puts in a rebound, but at the last possible instant, loses the handle on the puck. We have chances but can't capitalize. Looney gets out to make it even strength but we continue to possess momentum.

I get lost in the play. Our play is terrific, stringing together tape-to-tape passes, and not letting much get through to Kim. I can see the frustration in the American players. They're not playing with the same cohesiveness as we have seen all season. They take a second penalty: this time Courtney Kennedy bumps Wick hard and tries to prevent her from getting to the net, sending her to the ice.

"Let's use this — here we go!" I yell from the bench as Jen's line heads out. Becky Kellar sets up behind our net. Heaney Ger, her defensive partner on the power play, swings low to provide support while Jen swings behind the net with speed and picks up the puck. She flies towards open ice, creating her own space with long powerful, yet seemingly effortless, strides likely inherited from her Olympian speedskating mother. She makes a nifty move just inside their blue line to freeze their defenceman. She sees an opening and fires the puck on the net. My heart jumps, and I start to thrust in the air, but at the last moment, DeCosta gets her shoulder in the way. A narrow miss.

Jen's line takes a seat while Wick's line comes on to continue the power play. The Americans control the puck down low, doing a good job of killing time. Wick sees her opportunity to change, and Jen comes back on the ice. She fights for the puck, and during the skirmish the whistle blows. Karyn Bye, an American forward, is down on the ice, but it didn't look like Jen did anything wrong. The referee's arm is once again in the air.

The ref points at Jen. That's questionable. We should have seen this coming. It's clearly a make-up call for the last American penalty. As Jen skates to the box our team prepares for four on four. The play stays in the neutral zone until Kennedy comes out of the box to give the Americans their first power play.

For the first time this game, the Americans start to click. This is their strength. They have scored most of their goals against us on the power play, and they're poised to do the same again. We've been working all season in practice to combat them shorthanded, but nearly every game they've managed to score.

They always have an open man down low, and their hard, crisp passes are one step ahead of our penalty-killers. The Americans pass the puck around the perimeter until Tara Mounsey decides to unleash a shot from the point. Kim fights to see the puck. She stops it and redirects to a wide-open Cammi Granato parked at the side of the goal mouth. The American captain has a wide-open net. She's scored dozens of goals from that very spot, but this time the puck scoots right between her feet.

That was lucky.

The Americans don't stop. Even when they bobble the puck, they still manage to regain control. Their passing is remarkable. Once again, the puck makes its way around the perimeter to Mounsey. She's right in front of me. I could reach out and touch her if I wanted. She winds up. There are a ton of players in front.

"Find it, Kim," I whisper to myself, dodging and ducking as if I'm playing. Kim's screened. It hits her and rebounds straight out in front to Jenny Potter.

Potter has some of the best hands and best control on the American team. She has a wide-open net. She fires the puck, but it narrowly misses the outside post and sails wide.

Another close call.

We aren't stopping them; luckily, they're stopping themselves. Finally, Kim covers the puck and halts play. A new line of penalty-killers heads out for the faceoff.

Wick, Campbell, Pounder, and Kellar prepare as the linesman drops the puck. Wick falls to the ice on top of the puck. The Americans spear their sticks at her hand and rib cage, but can't dislodge it. Another whistle. Stacey Livingston, the head referee, is pointing at Wick and motioning her to the penalty box.

"That's absurd!" I shake my head.

Covering the puck with your hand can be a penalty, but it's at the ref's discretion and rarely is it called while one team is on the penalty kill. Wick joins Jen in the box. This is unreal. This is how we got beat in Detroit.

Hefford joins Pounder and Kellar who stay on the ice. Only 10 seconds until Jen is out.

On the bench, we watch with anticipation, cheering in unison as the Americans fire the puck wide. Jen comes back on the ice, we clear the puck down the ice.

Once back to five on five, we start playing defensively, not as aggressive as before. At 17:01, the referee's arm shoots straight up. Another penalty on us. This time it looked legit as Brisson took an American player hard into the boards. Three straight penalties against us, and once again we must kill off a five on four.

There's no time to panic. The Americans control the play around the outside. Kim sees a loose puck at the side of the net. It looks too far for her. She falls to her knees to try to smother the puck but can't reach it.

"No, Kim," I murmur.

Potter gets to it first, and Kim is caught behind the net. She scrambles back to the front as Potter finds an open Granato. Kim's way out of position but miraculously she recovers in time for Granato to shovel the puck into her pads. Great save and Kim gets a stoppage.

Livingston's arm is in the air again. *What? Another penalty?* Another questionable call. Sunohara gets nabbed for cross-checking. She was playing aggressively, but normally on the penalty kill you can get away with that. Not today.

Another two-man disadvantage. Once again, we manage to keep them to the outside. Campbell's our first forward out, then Hefford. All our defence are getting time on the ice. The Americans get some shots through, but not many; our penalty-killers are doing a great job blocking shots. It looks tiring for Kim. While she's not getting many shots, she must follow the play in her ready position, prepared for anything.

Finally, just as our second penalty expires and Vicky comes back on the ice, the period draws to a close. I stand in my usual spot and high-five everyone as they leave the bench. The smiles are big. That was a tough period, but we're ahead. The players who were penalty killing have red faces and are breathing heavily. Other players don't even look like they broke a sweat — they probably haven't seen the ice for a while.

"What the h*ll is the ref doing?" yells a player in the corner of the room.

"This is bullsh*t, this ref is clearly on their side," yells another player.

I make my way to my stall and tap Kim on her pads as I walk by. "Great job, keep it up." I say, smiling as she takes a sip from her water bottle.

Echoes of frustration continue to fill the room. Some directed at the refs, some directed at teammates for taking penalties, others towards the coach for lack of playing time.

To my left, Dana Antal stands up. The chatter subsides. Dana rarely stands to talk in the dressing room. A quiet player, her hard work is her example. She stands long enough for all eyes to turn to her.

"Emerald Lake," she says as the voice of reason, calm and logical, as she glances around the room. She pauses. "Remember in Emerald Lake . . . it wasn't about the coaches, wasn't about what they were or weren't doing, wasn't about the politics . . . it was about us. It was about enjoying each other's company and remembering the journey."

The room erupts with cheers. "Yeah, about us." She's right — we have to do this together.

I get up on the pretense of wanting some Gatorade, but really, I just want to be busy. I pass by Piper. "Amazing play," I say enthusiastically.

"Thanks, buddy," she says as she looks up at me with a big wide grin. She genuinely seems to appreciate the comment. Her response buoys me, and my equipment suddenly doesn't seem so heavy. I pass Jen, who seems disappointed. Maybe with her missed chances or maybe the penalty she was given, but she's been invaluable, using her smarts to generate chances and create energy with every shift.

"Jen, keep firing the puck! That last one was so close," I say, empathetically demonstrating with my hands just how close it was. She smiles back.

20

Rewards of the Hardest Day

FEBRUARY 21, 2002: SECOND PERIOD

Jen takes the faceoff to start the second period. I glance up at the Jumbotron and see a great overhead picture of it with the Olympic logo marking centre ice.

The Americans gain the puck and enter our zone. Wick trips up Krissy Wendell. The whistle blows, and referee Stacey Livingston points at Kellar. It wasn't even her, but she skates to the box. Time for another penalty kill.

As the Americans break out, Campbell collides with American Julie Chu, sending her to the ice. Looked like a huge hit, but no call. Kim makes a great save on Wendell, but Team USA's power play continues to get chances.

Finally, at 2:16 of the second, Tara Mounsey takes a shot from the point. Lori Dupuis slides, trying to block the shot, but it gets through. Granato redirects the puck, and Katie King deflects it over Kim. She had no chance. Power play goal.

The game is tied. 1–1.

At least we get to play five on five again. It doesn't feel as deflating knowing that we seem to have the edge while even-strength. Danièle sends out the young guns, Piper, Antal, and Ouellette, who try to regain the momentum. Jen's line is up next. The play continues to go back and forth, the crowd on the edge of their seats.

Jen's wingers, Shewchuk and Bechard, change as Goyette and Campbell take their spots.

Goyette hasn't seen as much ice time as her linemates have been given the grunt work of penalty killing. However, Goyette is flying. Her efficient, powerful stride, propels her down the ice. She takes a pass from Campbell while entering the American zone, creating a one on one against defender Sue Merz. Using Campbell as a decoy, Goyette pulls Merz to the right and then cuts back to the left shooting against the grain at DeCosta.

As a goalie, I know these kinds of shots are hard. It's difficult to get set while still moving to maintain the proper angle. DeCosta stays with the puck and makes a great save with her left pad but can't maintain control of her rebound. A sprawled Merz crashes into her own goalie taking her out of the play and creating a wide-open net. Fortunately for the Americans, the puck harmlessly rebounds right past Campbell and the mass of players driving the net.

In the interim, Jen has changed after her breakout pass, sending Wick onto the ice.

"Go to the net," I hear Wally yell.

Wick is behind the play but close enough to salivate at the gaping net. There's a mess of bodies in front, but Wick at full speed gets to the puck first at the top of the circles and rips a shot high into the small opening.

Goal for Canada! The game's now 2–1.

Wick's beaming. She outskates her linemates, her stick high in the air. Heaney and Sostorics corral her at the blue line. As the players train their way down the bench for high-fives, I'm excited for Wick, but even more excited for Goyette.

Goyette has always been a great teammate to me. Last year in Minnesota when I didn't get to play the final, she sat next to me and encouraged me to keep working hard. At our next-to-last exhibition game last month, she was singled out in the dressing room by Cassie for poor play — in front of the entire team. I felt bad for her, but she took it in stride.

"Way to go, Go-yet-tee," I yell as she swings past. She doesn't have her hand in the air — too many shoulder dislocations — but she gives us her elbow, which I gently tap and she smiles.

There's still a lot of game to play. Forty seconds later, Stacey Livingston's arm juts into the air again. Ouellette has sent Chu to the ice just inside our blue line. The hit didn't look like much, but it's another penalty against us. Piper slams her stick on the ice, Ouellette argues the call, shaking her head in disbelief. There's a loud boo for the ref from the crowd. They just want to see five on five hockey.

Here we go again. Wally confers with Danièle behind me. I'll give her credit, she's not getting angry or frustrated.

As the clock starts again, we get lucky. Livingston ignores a massive hit by Sostorics and blatantly misses a too-many-men call against us. I suppose we *should* have six penalties called on us by now, just not the six she has called.

Wick and Campbell are followed by Antal and Bechard on the penalty kill. We manage to clear the puck several times, cutting into their power play time.

Tricia Dunn skates hard down the wing uncontested from her zone. At the top of the circle, she winds up for a slapshot. The puck comes off the heel of her stick and rises quicker than expected. It hits Kim in the shoulder, but I can tell it hasn't hit equipment. She covers the puck long enough for a whistle, but she's hurt and goes down on all fours.

My heart starts palpitating. *Will she need me to go in?* I start getting myself mentally ready. I slow my breathing down while I stare patiently in Kim's direction.

Slowly she stands up. I can see her contorted grimace. Just a stinger, she'll be all right. My heart sinks.

The American centreman wins the faceoff in our zone and instantly they have control. Wendell passes down to Angela Ruggiero who has slid down from the point, apparently unnoticed.

Kim dives headfirst to prevent a goal, but it's too late. Ruggiero shoots the puck into the open net. Wendell's hands thrust high in the air in celebration. Miraculously, the puck careens off the far post rebounding to Tricia Dunn, alone in front of the net. She swats at the puck, but Kim thwarts her attempt, clearing it away. There is a collective sigh from our bench.

We get away with another one as Vicky upends an American player driving to the net, but referee Livingston knows she has missed it and makes up for her mistake seconds later by calling a penalty on our defenceman Isabelle Chartrand. We kill it off again.

Afterwards, Jen gets in Ruggiero's way on a backcheck, and Ruggiero falls to the ice. Looks like incidental contact, but Jen's sent to the penalty box.

There have been eight straight penalties against us.

I will the Americans to not score while Jen's in the box. She'd feel guilty. She never gets penalties.

The penalty kill is doing its job, not letting the Americans set up. With less than 30 seconds to go in Jen's penalty, Campbell stands up Wendell at the red line and once again Livingston's arm is in the air. *This can't be.*

As she drops her arm, she points at Wendell. I'm confused. Wendell had the puck, and you can't get a penalty when you have the puck. Maybe the ref has realized the injustice she's created. As Campbell stands to fetch her stick, she claps her hands sarcastically in Livingston's direction and skates towards the players box for a change.

As Jen's penalty ends, we find ourselves on the power play for the first time since the start of the game. Antal creates several chances but is denied. A mental lapse defensively right at the end of our power play gives American Darwitz an opportunity at the other end. Tensions are high as Tricia Dunn throws Ouellette into our net. No penalties are called.

Kennedy and Ouellette get mixed up two minutes later at centre ice, and Livingston sends them both off. Maybe she's trying to regain control of the game. There's less than two minutes left in the second period.

Antal's rewarded for her last shift and sent out for the four on four with Piper. She's winning races all over the ice and providing a spark for all of us. With less than 30 seconds left in the period, Wick gets the puck stripped from her, trying to escape our zone. Darwitz fires the puck and Kim makes the save. Although I think the puck may have been sailing wide, it looks good, and Kim keeps her glove there an extra second longer than needed just so the Americans know she made the save. I hate when she showboats, but Kim thrives on it.

Vicky and Hefford head out on the ice with Brisson and Kellar for the defensive zone draw. Vicky gives Hefford a look as they skate towards the dot and instantly Hefford knows what she must do. Vicky looks back at Brisson and Kellar and shouts instructions. She readies herself for the draw and wins it back.

Brisson then passes over to a supporting Kellar waiting in the corner. She takes a couple of strides up ice with the puck and looks up.

Hefford has taken off right from the drop of the puck up the right wing. Her speed has taken the American defenders by surprise. Kellar sees she's open and sends a long high pass up to Hefford bolting through the neutral zone. The puck ricochets off both American defencemen, Mleczko and Ruggiero, though not enough to be stopped entirely. Hefford has cut behind their defence perfectly in time to corral the pass. She catches the bouncing puck in her left hand while in full stride at the blue line and throws the puck down in front of her. Only one more stride until she's right on top of DeCosta.

DeCosta, seeing that Hefford doesn't have full control of the puck, seizes her chance to poke it away. She dives in her direction, but the puck bounces. Hefford swipes at it on her backhand at the same time as DeCosta's stick makes contact. Heff wins the battle and the puck flips over the sprawled American goaltender with only three seconds left in the period.

Goal! 3–1 Canada.

Our bench erupts, and Vicky tackles Hefford to the ice. Brisson and Kellar pile on top. The celebrations seem to last forever as Canadian flags wave throughout the arena.

A quick faceoff, and the period ends.

Back in the dressing room, the team is thrilled, emotions are high, and discussions revolve around referees.

Players yell, "let's do this," and "we got this," in all directions and at no one in particular. Water bottles are thrown around the room to thirsty players. We seem loose and energized. Killing off all those penalties might be the fuel we need to get through this game.

Cassie, our captain, stands up. With tears in her eyes, she yells like an NFL football coach, "The Americans have our flag on their dressing room floor and are using it as a doormat to walk across every time they step on the ice."

We are outraged and ready to do anything.

Twenty minutes to go.

FEBRUARY 21, 2002: THIRD PERIOD

Wick takes the opening faceoff against their top line of Potter, Bye, and King as our bench settles into the period. Unfortunately, our aggression disappears, and Kim is forced to make great save after great save.

Jolted back into action, the Americans look for the goal to ignite their comeback. Fortunately for us, Hefford's speed down the wing is too much for 16-year-old American defenceman Lyndsay Wall to handle, and she pushes Hefford to the ice. Penalty for USA. I breathe a little easier.

On the power play we can't get anything working and tempers continue to flare. A minute into our power play, and again Stacey Livingston is on our case. Kellar is too aggressive away from the puck and gets tangled with Natalie Darwitz, and it's enough to put another Canadian in the penalty box. Even up call.

The crowd chants *USA! USA!*

It's four on four, but the Americans can't seem to set up. The seconds tick away as Kellar steps back on the ice. Penalties done. Back to even strength. The five on five play doesn't last long; Sostorics is called for angling out Chu into the boards.

It's the 10th penalty against us continuing our parade to the penalty box. That's more than a period's worth of play at less than full strength. With 15 minutes left in this game, Danièle sends out Vicky and Dupuis with Pounder and Kellar. Because Kellar plays both the penalty kill and the power play, she's logged a lot of ice time today.

As the Americans regroup in the neutral zone, Bechard and Wick are sent out. Entering our zone, an errant American pass draws Kim out to the faceoff dot to play the puck. She's been playing the puck a lot today and thus far has made some good decisions.

As I ponder whether Kim should risk playing the puck that far out of her net while we're on the penalty kill, she corrals the puck, and leans on her stick to apply torque, and unbelievably her stick snaps in half.

Disbelief. The puck doesn't go far, and Kim's stuck in no man's land with no stick.

The incident takes everyone by surprise, and the shocked Americans don't pounce on the loose puck. Kim scrambles to get back in her net as Chartrand hands her a player's stick. We manage to get the puck out to the neutral zone, but only for an instant.

The Americans salivate seeing the tiny player's stick in Kim's hands. Potter flies wide around the net with the puck, looking for an open teammate. It's awkward when a goalie has a player's stick — it throws their balance off. I dread to think what they will do, but Bechard manages to steal the puck and clear it back into the neutral zone, eventually creating a whistle as the Americans re-enter offside.

I grab Kim's stick beside me, handing it to Campbell who delivers it to her. The linesman throws the broken stick in my direction. Looking at it, I can't believe it shattered. I throw the pieces down the hallway.

Sostoric's penalty expires with only 13 minutes left. Despite the lopsided penalties, we're still outshooting the Americans 25–23.

Play continues back and forth, but as Dupuis skates on a backcheck, she trips up American Laurie Baker. Livingston's arm is once again in the air like the Statue of Liberty. It's annoying, she just can't let us play. Incredibly, she takes both players to the box, Dupuis for hooking, and Baker for holding. At least we're not shorthanded.

We look strong four on four. Jen and Shewchuk start us off with a great forecheck. Piper and Ouellette continue the momentum with some more good chances. Wick gets a breakaway pass from Kellar, but the linesman calls it offside. Didn't look offside to me, but the refs don't seem to see what I see today.

Back to even strength and Goyette once again creates an opportunity, nearly tucking the puck in a gaping net.

Only five minutes left. We're so close I can feel it.

I start to think about how I'm going to exit my area after we win. It'll be pandemonium. *Do I hop the boards?* It's always risky to jump the boards in 60 pounds of gear with adrenaline pumping through my veins. I don't want to make the highlights by falling flat on my face. *Or do I go through the door to my left?*

Back to reality as Livingston's arm, almost comically, rises in the air again. There's 4:20 left in the game, and we have another penalty, our 12th. This time it's Bechard for a trip on Granato in front of the net.

The Americans delay the faceoff, and Wick, ready at the faceoff dot, pleads with the ref to drop the puck or call a delay of game. Campbell, Wick, Pounder, and Kellar attempt to accomplish the unenviable feat of preventing the American power play from capitalizing on their good fortune.

Our penalty-killers have been on the ice nearly the whole game. The Americans take control right off the hop. They pass the puck around the perimeter, egging us to move out of formation.

Mounsey finds Bye across the blue line for a one-timer from the point.

Kim is deep in her net, but I know she can make this save. Heaney waits in front to fend off any American players. I see the trajectory of the puck, headed straight towards Kim's outstretched pad, but at the last possible instant, the puck hits something and bounces over Kim's pad into the net. The American crowd erupts, and the red light flashes behind Kim.

Tough to tell how it went in, but with only 3:33 left it's now a one-goal game: 3–2 Canada.

Bechard makes her skate of shame back from the penalty box. It was bound to happen eventually — she shouldn't feel bad. I stand and use my blocker to hit against the outside of the boards and in my most calming and confident voice, I shout, "We can do this, guys," trying to reassure myself as much as my teammates.

Danièle sends Vicky's line out. They are often our most reliable. It will be their job to quell the comeback and regain our confidence.

With only 1:44 left, Jen's line is back out. What confidence that shows in Jen's defensive abilities. With Shewchuk and Antal, her line has created some great offensive chances, but more importantly, they have been steady in the defensive zone. They hem the Americans in their zone but unfortunately go offside in the process and as Shewchuk clears the zone, she inadvertently touches the puck. The lineman declares it intentional and moves the faceoff deep into our zone.

Ben Smith calls a time out and Sara DeCosta skates to the bench for an extra attacker.

Standing to see what our coaches' plan is, the entire team circles Mel and Wally who go over our strategy for six on five. They have overseen odd-man situations all year. Danièle has her lineup card out, silently scanning the players. Everyone squeezes in for a view as Pounder has her arms around Kellar and Piper.

"Girls, this is it," says Wally as we leave the huddle. The American bench looks scattered. Ben Smith gives last-minute directions to the six who will be on the ice.

The potential is palpable.

Out skates Vicky with wingers Hefford and Wick and defencemen Sostorics and Pounder to take the draw in front of Kim. The entire team is now on its feet. Vicky takes the draw and wins it back to Wick who sends it down the ice. No icing as the ref motions Bye touched the puck as it flew past.

The Americans regroup in their zone and break out. Granato brings the puck into our zone. We do everything we can to keep her to the outside, away from Kim. Granato circles the net looking for an open man, but Vicky miraculously poke-checks the puck away to an awaiting Wick who once again sends the puck down the ice. Every Canadian on the ice changes and Jen, Shewchuk, and Antal fly over the boards.

Looking for a stretch pass, the Americans ice the puck.

The faceoff is deep in the American end with only 27 seconds left to play in the game. DeCosta returns to her net and Danièle leaves Jen on the ice as the centreman and sends Wick and Antal to be her wingers, along with defencemen Brisson and Kellar.

Wick switches with Jen to take the draw, but Potter manages to win it. Jen's quick on their defence, and even though they manage to get the puck out of their zone, the Americans, without full possession, dump the puck into our end.

Only 15 seconds left. DeCosta skates to the bench, and as the Americans forecheck they once again have six players for their final effort.

Becky tries to rim the errant puck around the boards to an awaiting Jen, but she has two players on her, and it is poked back in the corner to Potter. The entire crowd is on their feet. The Americans are scrambling.

We are in defensive position. Potter makes a pass from the corner out to her waiting winger on the sideboards, but Jen anticipates it and intercepts the puck. She spins and clears the puck out of the zone as the seconds tick away.

The final buzzer sounds.

3–2 Canada.

We've won. We are Olympic champions.

FEBRUARY 21, 2002: GOLD MEDAL

Euphoria propels me over the boards, following the exodus of the bench towards Kim. I skate past the yard sale of gloves and sticks scattered all over the ice and jump heavily on top of the pile. I instantly slide off. I'm screaming. I stand up and jump again. The noise is deafening. Slowly the pile collapses and players begin to stand. Everyone's hugging each other.

"We did it!" I scream.

Our staff joins us on the ice, including Dave Jamieson, our goalie coach, and Charlie, who watched from high in the rafters. We strip off our helmets. The dejected Americans wait impatiently for us at centre ice for the traditional postgame handshake. With exuberance, I follow behind Shewchuk as we slowly make our way to centre ice.

I say *good game* to each player, but the Americans' sadness breaks my heart. We were them four years ago.

The Swedes, who had beaten the Finns in the bronze medal game, join us on the ice. We shake their hands and make our way to the blue line for the medal ceremony.

Standing next to Kim, I hug her, saying, "That was incredible. You played amazing!" While I desperately wanted to be in her position, I know what she went through. The nagging injuries and the constant scrutiny.

"That was close, but we were amazing," a humble and smiling Kim says back to me as she adjusts her ponytail. Ouellette, Kim's best friend on the team, joins us as we await the gold medals. The ceremony isn't ready yet.

I skate down the line and tell each person what a great job she did. With incredible pride, I give a huge hug to Jen. I think about how we all helped each other get to this moment. Every single player on this team had their own inner demons to quell and mountains to climb, but we ended here together on this blue line.

I think of the players that aren't here. I think of my stall mate Delaney and my old roommate Nancy Drolet, amongst others. The anguish they must still feel. I think of all the girls and women that fought for this opportunity for us. All the veterans of the sport who will never get to feel this moment. We stand on their shoulders this afternoon.

I think of my friends back home, of Gillian, Dermot, Adam, Jamie, Susie, Kathryn, Stacey, Karen, and Stephanie, who taught me to love sport and pushed me every day to compete and be the best I could be.

I think of my friends from Stanford, including Diana, Susan, Corey, Monique, Katrinka, Bobby, and Gina, who taught me that I am more than just a hockey player, more than just an athlete, and despite our different backgrounds we can always learn from one another and share in each other's success. The last person on the blue line is Wick. She's holding her two-year-old son, Noah, in her arms, a calming presence for her. I stand beside them.

"Wick, you were amazing today." Glancing at Noah I say, "What did you think of Mommy?"

"Mommy," he says back to me, just excited to finally be in her arms.

Swelling with pride, I watch Canadian IOC member Dick Pound put a gold medal on the first person in line, captain Cassie Campbell. Watching with anticipation he makes his way towards us.

My mind turns to my Brampton Thunder teammates and the many players who could easily have been in this situation.

I think of the Stanford men's hockey team who not only let me play, but also expected nothing but my best effort. And all my minor hockey coaches and teammates that not only stuck up for me, they accepted a girl on their team and pushed me to succeed.

I remember my life as a multi-sport athlete and all the sports teams I played on growing up, all the amazing coaches and teammates who helped shape who I am. All the fun and opportunities I've been fortunate to have through sport.

They place a medal around Jen's neck, her smile is contagious as she accepts a bouquet of yellow flowers while waving to the crowd.

I think of my brother and how this was our dream together. How we watched every Olympic Opening and Closing Ceremony together. Of how we played mini sticks in our basement, dreaming of moments like this. How he taught me to have resilience and drive, and always pushed me to be better.

I think of my extended family and know each of them, spread throughout North America, would be proud.

Lastly, I think of my parents. They had to put up with other people's fears of girls playing male-dominated sports. They had to stand and fight for me to play the game I love so much. They put up with my highs and lows, supporting me in every way they could. They encouraged my dreams and painstakingly lived every goal, every win, every loss, and each major milestone by my side.

Finally, it's my turn. I'm beaming. I lean down. I shake Mr. Pound's hand and thank him. I stare in disbelief at the medal.

I am an Olympic champion.

PART 3

21

A Summer to Move On

MARCH 2002: POST-OLYMPICS

It's three weeks after the Closing Ceremony of the Olympic Games. Sitting alone at the top of Mount Rigi in Switzerland. I gaze far into the countryside; the view is breathtaking. I'm on this adventure to play more hockey, but today is a day just for me.

My Olympic experience changed me. I am more intensely aware of sadness, more empathetic to others, and more aware of the necessity to create my own happiness.

It was a slow, long leisurely hike through towns on the way up, but my legs are tired. According to the sign, I'm at 5,379 feet, but I feel like I'm on top of the world.

Up here, it doesn't matter if I am an Olympic champion. Here, I'm free to find myself after a year of trying to impress others as I attempt to turn sadness into optimism.

Darren Boyko, a friend of mine in Toronto, from the Hockey Hall of Fame, hooked me up to play in Switzerland. He was in Salt Lake City with the International Ice Hockey Federation, collecting artifacts for the Hall. After our gold medal final, he asked if I'd be interested in playing for his friend, Gion Veraguth, in Zug, Switzerland, and I jumped at the opportunity. *Why not*, I said to myself. *If I have new adventures, I won't have time to dwell on the past.*

During the second-period intermission of the men's Canada versus USA final, while the rest of the stands were cheering, a little inebriated from two straight days of partying with my teammates, I signed my first hockey contract.

No money, but my flights and daily expenses would be covered. That sold me. *What did I have to get back to?* My Brampton team has Stacy Kellough as well as my friend Marie-France Morin as a backup goalie already signed for their National Championship. The entire year was about the final Olympic game on February 21 and I hadn't really planned for what would happen after.

I've already played two games with the Zug-Seewen Ice Hockey Club. My teammates have housed me, showed me around Switzerland, and included me in their activities. Panci, Ruth, Christina, Sandra, Doris, Steffi, Marion, Karen, Gion, and many more brought me into their homes and helped me see life beyond the Olympics. New stories, new experiences, and the amazing opportunity to travel.

Despite the pain of not playing the final, I still love the game.

I stare into the valley. The famous Matterhorn can be seen in the distance. The solitude feels nice. I am exceptionally small in this giant place. I never thought feeling alone would give me so much hope. I'm excited for the next few months of adventures. From here I'm off to Austria, then back to Calgary for a few weeks to hang out with Gillian and do some skiing (which is not allowed when training with the National Team), and then I will pack up my belongings to drive my car to Winnipeg. I can't wait to get back to Winnipeg and celebrate (and commiserate) with my friends and family. I haven't seen most of them in well over a year.

After that I'm off to Australia thanks to an incredible gift from Air Canada of a free flight anywhere in the world. I'm going to visit my Stanford friend Monique Bradshaw, who now lives in Sydney.

This summer promises to be one filled with nomadic adventures, meeting new people, hanging out with old friends, and reconnecting to life.

MAY 2002: NEW ROOTS

I'm sitting in the living room of the house I just bought in Winnipeg. The purchase closed yesterday. Jen, Dermot, and Adam are here too. They are sitting in fold-out lawn chairs circling the small living room. I bought a house with the bonus that Molson Brewers, thanks to their CEO, Dan O'Neill who had unwavering belief in us as a team, gave us for bringing the gold back to Canada. I used the $20,000 reward as a down payment on this $80,000 house. Never in Toronto would I have been able to afford a house, so I decided to invest here, in my home province. I'm in Winnipeg for nearly five months a year from the end of the hockey season in the spring to the start of the next one in the fall. I could stay with my parents, but it's nice to have my own place. Last summer I rented with Dermot and our friend and fellow thrower Suzanne Dandenault. I figure this is a good investment. Dermot's going to rent it, but I'll keep a room in the basement for summer training and any visits home.

"Did you really get to play with the Tragically Hip at the Olympics?" asks Dermot.

"Yeah, it was because of Jayna. She's from Kingston like them and knows the guys. She brought a few of us to Gord Downie's house last year to play outdoor shinny with him. Gord's a goalie too and we chatted technique and equipment and I got to know him. When they played our wrap-up party in the Olympic Village Jayna asked me to come on stage with her to introduce the band. It was amazing! The whole team then got to sing and dance in the background of their set."

"Your brother must be so jealous."

A blue, sticker-covered chest acts as a makeshift coffee table and on it sit three Slurpees from 7-Eleven, a loaf of bread, and a jar of peanut butter. There's no other furniture, but a fan whirls above our heads in an attempt to cool us from the near 30 Celsius mid-May weather.

"The cottage was so great," Jen says recounting her weekend at her parents' place near Kenora, Ontario. It's her happy place. She still has another year left at Harvard, but for the summer she can relax. As she continues telling us about her weekend of R & R, Dermot and Adam pass a rugby ball that I bought in Australia back and forth, often bouncing it off the bare walls.

"You guys should all come up next weekend."

"Yeah, that'd be awesome," I say in response.

"Do you ever just stop and think, *Wow I'm a gold medallist?*" Adam asks casually to neither one of us in particular.

"Do you ever just walk around naked with your medal?" Dermot weirdly asks, still throwing the ball.

"Uh . . . no," Jen says back, looking over at Adam as he just shakes his head.

"I would," says Dermot confidently, as the rugby ball ricochets off the swirling fan into the kitchen. Neither of the boys wants to get up, so Adam grabs the loaf of bread and throws it back to Dermot as a make-shift ball. I grab another sip of my Slurpee.

"How was Australia?" Jen asks.

"So good," I say. "It was great to see Monique. I went to galleries, zoos, vineyards, and saw the Blue Mountains."

"Of course, you went to the galleries and probably museums too?" Jen says mockingly, knowing our ideas of vacationing are vastly different.

"I went to the beaches *too*, even surfed a couple of times. And I stopped in Toronto on the way home. I had the AGM for Hockey Canada."

"Oh, that probably wasn't as fun as Australia," Jen says.

At the AGM, I'm our team representative on the board of directors, having recently taken over this role from Thérèse Brisson. She established a voice for us at a board filled predominantly with men, and it's my job to ensure that it continues to be heard. It's a voted position, and this role makes me feel like I'm still a leader on this team.

"It wasn't bad. It was fun to hear everyone's story of where they were when they watched the final," I say, grabbing another sip while contemplating.

Travelling is becoming addictive; yet I love these moments too. Sitting around with friends, just hanging out. Even though not playing in the final has changed me, I love that it hasn't changed anyone else. I try to focus on new moments, new memories, and appreciating each day.

As I'm reminiscing, suddenly bread is flying everywhere. Dermot has thrown the entire loaf into the fan and crumbs rain down on us like bits of snow.

JUNE 2002: MEETING THE PRIME MINISTER

Once again, I'm on another flight, this time to Ottawa to finally get to see the rest of my Olympic teammates again. I haven't seen most of them since the end of the Olympics, nearly four months ago.

Our entire team was invited, along with all the other Olympic medallists, to meet Prime Minister Jean Chrétien. Between festivities, we head for a celebratory lunch.

So much has happened in the last few months, it's almost overwhelming to try to catch up with everyone. A select few were recently with me at the inaugural Good As Gold golf tournament in Muskoka, Ontario. This charity tournament has chosen our team to support with its fundraising efforts.

Sitting with Jen, Piper, Becky, and Colleen "Sos" Sostorics, we scarf down burgers.

"Did you know they named a street after Sos in Kennedy and a rink after Antal in Esterhazy?" says Becky referring to their hometowns in Saskatchewan.

"Did you know Becky got to fly in a fighter plane?" says Sos, a bit embarrassed.

"Did you see Cass on TV?" says Piper, noting Cassie's debut with *Hockey Night in Canada*.

Jayna comes over and taps me on the shoulder, and I spin around to say hi. I haven't seen her since our final team party back in Calgary just days after winning. I stand to give her a hug.

"How are you, you superstar?" I say to her, thinking about her incredible game-winning goal.

"How has the summer been? How was Australia?" she asks.

As we get caught up, I can tell she wants to get something off her chest.

"Ummm . . . Ally just called. She says you need to call the coach right away," Jayna finally blurts out.

"Ahhh, you're in trouble," Piper jokes, chuckling.

Jayna isn't amused and says I should call our Brampton Thunder team's coach immediately.

I can't imagine there'd be much to chat about in June with the season still months away, but I dial our coach's number.

"Hi Terry. It's Sami Jo. Ally said I should call — what's up?"

I thought there'd be small talk.

"I read in the newspaper you wanted to play in Vancouver next year." Nancy Drolet now plays with the Griffins, the new addition to the NWHL, as do Americans Cammi Granato and Shelley Looney.

"No, Terry, I've never even talked to anyone in Vancouver. I still want to play in Brampton." This must be why he needed me to call. A simple misunderstanding.

"But Vancouver would be closer to your home."

"Vancouver is still a thirty-hour drive from Winnipeg," I say. *Is he trying to convince me to go?*

"Well, we assumed you wanted to play there, so we've decided to go in a different direction and have signed two other goalies."

"What? I don't want to play in Vancouver. Terry, it's only June — why didn't you call me?"

Silence on the other end until, awkwardly, as if he's reading off a sheet of paper. "We've signed one of the top American goalies, Erika Silva. She flew up during the Championship Cup for a meeting. We really like her. And we have someone else to back her up."

"But Terry . . . "

"We really like her and she's going to be our goalie."

There's not much more I can say. I hang up the phone. I'm confused and shocked.

"Sami, what's up?" Piper asks. My entire table had been silent for the conversation.

"I think I just got cut," I say, shaking my head.

"From Brampton? What the hell? Let me call Kenny, you could be an Aero," Piper says, smiling and referring to the Toronto Aeros' head coach, Ken Dufton.

That sounds wrong to me. I don't want to be an Aero; I want to be on the Thunder. All my close friends play for Brampton. Our new house, with Lori, Jayna, and Ally, is in Brampton. Our Brampton team constantly fought for league supremacy with our cross-town rivals. I couldn't possibly be an Aero.

I head over to the table where Vicky, Lori, and Jayna are seated. They seem shocked.

Jayna confirms that Brampton had indeed signed two other goalies. I'm angry, but even angrier for my former goalie partner and roommate

Stacy Kellough. She had taken Brampton to the finals last year, losing in overtime to Toronto. She's a very talented goaltender. She doesn't deserve this. *Why did they get rid of her too?*

Is this what it feels like to be traded in professional sports? I'm reeling. I feel betrayed by my team, but I can't see myself in another uniform.

After lunch, I follow my Team Canada teammates on stage. I smile for the cameras. I take my picture with Prime Minister Chrétien, but my mind is elsewhere.

Standing around waiting for our next cue, Piper hands her phone to me. "It's Kenny, he sounds excited."

Ken had been an assistant coach with the National Team for our World Championship in 1999. He has put more girls on the National Team than any other coach.

"We'd be interested in having you on the Aeros; however, you'd split games with our current goaltender, Kendra Fisher."

Do I even want to play for Toronto?

I'm no longer on the Brampton Thunder. I've got to wrap my head around that.

"Thanks, Ken, I really appreciate you finding me a spot. I'm just not sure I want to play for the best team. You guys are already so good. Perhaps I should go to Durham or Oakville?"

"It's your choice, Sami, but there's a spot here if you want it. Just remember, with us, you'll get girls that are committed, that have the same goals you do."

On my flight to Winnipeg, I finally accept that Brampton no longer wants me and decide I'll call Ken as soon as I get off the plane. Like a schoolgirl with a new crush, I outline the letters in my diary:

Sami Jo Small, Toronto Aeros.

Still looks strange.

JULY 2002: BACKPACKING IN EUROPE

Back to my home base of Winnipeg, I see my family, hang out at my house with Dermot, and then I head off to Europe. I've always wanted to backpack through Europe, and now seems like as good a time as any. No commitments, no schedule to keep.

It was my childhood friend Anders Johansson's idea. He recently graduated university. We grew up on the same street and, although he's a year younger, have many friends in common, including Dermot, Kathryn, Stacey, and my longtime neighbours, the Sigurdsons. For him this will be a great adventure before he starts teaching in the fall; I'm fortunate I can tag along.

Perusing the *To Do* section of my travel journal, I sit on the metal waiting benches of the Brussels, Belgium, train station. The station was packed, but now that it's almost midnight, I can count the number of people on one hand. The last train left a few hours ago, and the next one doesn't leave until morning.

I should call home and check my voicemail. Anders is seated across from me, reading a paperback. His feet are propped up on his giant hikers backpack, and he seems content with the fantasy story he's reading.

I glance around the train station looking for a pay phone. Spotting one, I wander through the empty benches towards the far wall.

I dial my calling card number into the phone. There is a strange man rolled up in a ball, sleeping in the corner. Maybe, like us, he missed his train or maybe he's homeless — at this point it doesn't matter. Once I hear the operator, I dial my cell phone number in Canada to check my voicemail.

As I listen to my messages, I hear my mom's voice and write down her name to call back. Then Dermot's. His message is actually audible. "Call me." Normally he leaves random messages that stretch on about the minutiae of his day. I continue with the next messages. My mom again, and then Dermot again. *Weird.* They sound robotic yet with an urgency in their voices.

I hang up and start the whole calling card process again. I habitually dial my parents' number. It's only 6:00 p.m. in Winnipeg when Mom answers the phone. She sounds relieved, but I can tell she is excited to hear from me.

I tell her of our latest adventures.

We've been through England, Sweden (where we connected with some of Anders's family) and Denmark. With each new city, new adventures. I dragged him to the local museums and historical sites, and he dragged me to the pubs and the shows.

From Denmark, we took the train to visit my Swiss teammates. We stayed with my team's general manager, Gion Veraguth, and his partner, Babel. They hosted a barbeque for us, and it was great to see the girls from my Swiss team again.

Mimicking my last European trip in March, we then took the train to Austria. We were hosted by a friend I had made at the Olympics, a Nordic combined athlete, Willi Denifl. Willi was a local celebrity as a ski jumping Olympian. His family lived above their bakery in the Tyrol province. His family was incredibly welcoming, filling us up for every meal.

From Austria we used our Eurail passes to train back through Switzerland to Lausanne, to visit the Olympic Museum. We then hopped over to Brussels and up to the Netherlands to visit one of my Swiss teammates, Marion Pepels. She's the captain of the Dutch National Ice Hockey Team, and we stayed with her in Maastricht. She showed us the countryside and drove us to Amsterdam. I tell my mom about the chocolate sprinkles we had on our toast in the morning. Mom is being unusually quiet, so I just stop talking. There's a long pause.

"I just don't know how to tell you this." Her voice stumbles. My heart rate quickens. *What's happened?* Europe fades away and I stare at the keypad not wanting to anticipate the worst.

"Adam passed away yesterday."

I can't respond. I want to cry. Adam, whom I've known my whole life. Adam, who could run for miles and miles. Adam, who made me fall in love with running and taught me to push to be better every day. Adam — one of my best friends.

No answers. My mom doesn't know the reason. I am alone at a pay phone. The call ends. I slowly put back the receiver. I want to be anywhere but here. I fight back tears, my throat closing in on itself.

I look back across the train station at Anders. He knows Adam too. Adam grew up on the next road over from ours. How am I going to tell him? I try to hold it together, but I can't. I turn back to the phone. Through my tears, I start to dial Dermot's number.

22

Rededication

Nervous for my first practice with the Aeros, I push open the red dressing room door at the York University Ice Palace. There's faint chatter, and some eyes turn in my direction. I instinctively smile to try to make others feel more comfortable. I make my way to an empty stall and sit. The room is cold, dark, and dingy. I nod to my new teammates, but I still want to be on the Brampton Thunder, not here.

This rink is far from Brampton, so I needed to find a new place. I moved in first with my parents' friends, the Shakespeares. They lived right beside the new Team Canada training location in Scarborough, the Fitness Institute where we work out with our new fitness coach, Chris Dalcin.

I searched the area for apartments and last week moved into the basement apartment of a Sri Lankan family's home. Because the Blue Bomber is still in Winnipeg, I rollerblade to the grocery store and can walk to the gym; but I must find rides to the rink. Today Coach Ken Dufton picked me up.

This dressing room feels different. I look around and spot my Team Canada teammates Cheryl Pounder and Becky Kellar, but they're deep in conversation at the far end of the room, and there's no space to squish in near them. Unfortunately, Cherie Piper's away at Dartmouth along with Gillian Apps who was also centralized with us leading up to Salt Lake. I find an open spot, dress quickly, and make my way to the ice. The rink is frigid. While I wait next to the glass for the Zamboni to finish, Geraldine Heaney comes out.

"So, you're finally an Aero," she says with a sly grin. No longer the Beatrice Aeros, the sponsorship ended, the team is back to simply the Toronto Aeros.

My face red with embarrassment, I look out onto the blank sheet of ice. "I guess so," I say, longing to be somewhere else.

"You're one of us now," Heaney says, tapping me on the pads. *One of us. Am I really?*

Girls laugh and play around during the first few laps, but once Ken, in his gardening gloves, whistles for the first drill to start, the playfulness stops. Intensity is high. The girls go hard, no mercy on teammates. This feels like a Team Canada practice.

As practice progresses, I see their tenacity and talent, and work harder to keep up. I think of my friend Adam often. I think of his spirit in the final metres of a race when he always found the next gear. I want to harness that ability to battle until the end.

In Brampton, the drills were seldom geared to goalies and we were frequently bored. I often thought about the validity of a drill and my intensity would drop. But there's no time for such thoughts. Ken has coached this team for nearly 15 years. Every practice is meticulously prepared and executed, and he has developed more players post college than any other coach. Like Wally Kozak, he approaches hockey in a wholistic way, teaching the life skills needed to win. Most importantly, he was a goalie, therefore he ensures every drill includes us.

"Get to that rebound," Ken barks.

"Pick it up, girls!" he says skating beside a player entering into the zone. I compete to stop every puck. I want my teammates to believe in me, to like me.

"Nice saves," Amanda Benoit-Wark says as we skate towards the boards. I reach my goalie partner, Kendra, and tap her on the pads.

My face is red and sweat beads on my face as one drill ends and I await the next one to begin. This is my new normal.

Once again, I'm playing with Team Canada at the 4 Nations Cup. There's less than 10 minutes in the third period of the finals against the Americans. The Kitchener Memorial Auditorium is packed, and the crowd chants, "Go, Canada, go!"

We've been the better team today, but we only lead 2–1. My palms are sweaty as I watch the play in the other end. Erin Whitten is playing well in net for Team USA and keeping this a close game.

I need this opportunity to prove to the coaches I can still play in critical games. The first Team Canada tryout camp of the new Olympic quadrennial cycle was in Toronto in October and included 40 athletes vying to be a part of the next cycle. It was a tough camp. Long training days and lots of hockey but it went well, and the coaches let me know that I came out as the number-one ranked goalie.

As the game continues, we have possession of the puck in the American zone. Cheryl Pounder tries for a cross ice pass. She's executed the same pass countless times. Pounder is reliable and conservative and rarely makes errors. She's not risky, but uncharacteristically flubs the puck. American forward Katie King pounces on it. She springs for a breakaway, clear of any Canadian defender.

I've played against King many times. She's a power forward with skilled hands. The puck is in front of her stride as she crosses the blue line. I know she likes to muscle it five-hole. I prepare for the eventuality, dropping in a butterfly. King reacts to my early decision, changes tactics, and fires it high, blocker side.

Fortunately, the puck goes sailing past the net and careens off the boards. Narrow escape. Play continues. We've lost our momentum. Time is not counting down fast enough. The crowd is nervous. *Sami, stay with it, the team needs you.* Leg save, blocker save. We beat them 7–0 a few days ago, so I know we have more to give.

I didn't expect to shellac the Americans in the round robin. It was Kim's game and our first match-up since Salt Lake. I expected the Americans to be out for revenge, but they were lacklustre. Erika Silva, the goalie that replaced me in Brampton, played in the American net and made some big saves, but their team had no chemistry. With only nine players returning from the Salt Lake City team, they played differently, lacking cohesion.

King is back on the ice. Once again, she steals the puck and comes barrelling down on a breakaway. She went high last time. She's bound to go low this time. Pounder is on her right shoulder, trying to force her to make a move. King has no choice but to go to her left, but I am there. She sees me and desperately fires the puck high. I have the side covered, but the puck, like water through sand, finds the tiniest of openings and squeaks between my post and me. Despair floods my body. The puck is in. Pounder looks upset as she skates away. I hate to see my defence sad. My team needs me to be composed. *No big deal. Just another goal,* I say to convince myself. The crowd is deadpan.

The score is now tied 2–2 with eight minutes to go. The ref signals for a TV time out.

As I huddle with my teammates again around our players bench, I take a few breaths and get some much-needed rest. I look over at Vicky and nod. Being teammates with Vicky, Jayna, and Lori is reassuring. Even though we are no longer teammates in Brampton, we all had the incredible honour of being inducted into the Brampton Sports Hall of Fame last week.

I look up at the crowd and see my friends near centre ice about halfway up. They are in a group that includes my parents, Dermot, Anders, and Kathryn as well as friends from Toronto, Craig Coughlan and Ted Dean. The crew is staying at my place in Scarborough, having an amazing time without me. Dermot has painted his torso and face red. I mean, completely painted half his body, including eyelids, red. I see him, hands high in the air, a red lamp shade from my living room on his head, cheering madly, valiantly trying to get the crowd of 7,000 people back in the game.

I chuckle to myself thinking of the day my friends showed up in Kitchener for the game against Finland. It wasn't my game, and I didn't know they'd be there. My helmet already on the bench, I skated out behind Kim for our team cheer before the opening faceoff. A few strides in, I heard my name shouted loudly in unison behind me.

"Saaaaammmmm—eeeeee!"

I swung around, surprised to see my friends. Excited, I waved and smiled, but didn't stop skating. I failed to see the red carpet that had been laid on the ice for the national anthem singer, and I stepped right on the rubber mat with my skates. I slipped and took a hard fall to the ice. The entire arena erupted in clapping with the loudest cheers coming from my friends.

Back in the moment, the ref signals for play to resume. *Play calm. Stay focused.* The play restarts, and Erin Whitten continues to make save after save as I counter.

Only a minute left in the play, and the game is still tied 2–2.

Overtime seems inevitable. As we press in their zone, veteran defenceman A.J. Mleczko sees an open American player through the neutral zone. She fires it from just inside her blue line, but it hits her own player's skate and ricochets to an awaiting Danielle Goyette. She then immediately sends the puck over to Hayley Wickenheiser, who goes in all alone on Whitten. Whitten lunges, but Wick walks right around her, sliding the puck into the open net. My arms thrust into the air, the crowd roars. Caroline Ouellette adds an empty net goal, and we've won.

My team rushes off the bench to celebrate with me. I jump up and down with Pounder. "Sami, we did it!" she screams as I absorb the satisfaction.

Gloves are scattered on the ice, players still hugging, and I turn to find my friends and family. Dermot's red torso is not hard to find. I enthusiastically point in their direction letting them know just how much I share this victory with them.

JANUARY 2003: OFF-ICE TRAINING

Today's workout is going to be tough. I unfold the sheet of paper again. The weights have gone up and the reps have gone down. I like lifting heavy, but I know that inevitably I'm going to be sore.

Team Canada's January camp finished last week and now it's back to building strength. This month is the last push before the World Championship in China at the end of the March. Pressing play on my Walkman I see *CHINA*, which I've written on a piece of tape as motivation, and I begin warming up on the stationary bike.

As the 10-minute mark passes, Chris Dalcin, my fitness trainer, casually approaches my bike.

"How do your legs feel?" he asks, knowing that we had a long Aeros practice last night. I consciously assess my legs as they slow to a halt.

"I guess they are okay," I say dismounting, reaching for my water bottle. "Practice wasn't too bad last night for the goalies."

I linger and strike up a conversation about our last game against Brampton. Chris was at the game, and between the two of us, we could chat hockey all day. Alas, Chris has learned my delay tactics, and he makes me follow him towards the dumbbells and focuses me on the first circuit.

Usually there are at least a couple of Team Canada hopefuls working out together but today it's just me.

Chris picks up two 50-pound dumbbells and hands them to me. They already feel heavy. I walk towards the track and take a deep breath and start to lunge forward. I alternate legs, making my way to the end of the short track. My legs burn and I'm having a tough time keeping my grip. As I rise on the left leg for the final time, I throw the weights down. I take 30 seconds' rest. I look back down the track at Chris, and he nods. It's time to go again.

This time I lunge in his direction. I grit my teeth. A groan escapes me on the final lunge, and I let the weights fall to the floor.

"Did you see the last Cowboys game of the season?" Chris asks excitedly, trying to distract me from my pain. I shake my head while catching my breath and writing in my log book. Unlike most hockey players, a lifetime in track and field has made me a meticulous documenter of my workouts. I walk in a circle with my hands on my head.

"And . . . *go!*" Chris exclaims mid-sentence. I walk towards the dumbbells still sitting in the middle of the track as he tells me about an amazing touchdown play.

"Last set," he says, and I begrudgingly pick up the weights.

MARCH 2003: GOING TO BEIJING

In our Team Canada dressing room in Calgary I've showered and changed. I'm waiting for the staff to come in. We are at the pre–World Championship training camp, getting ready for the Worlds in Beijing, China. Today I felt excellent on the ice, tracking the puck well, working hard. It's been a great season with the Aeros — we finished in top spot, and I found my groove. I'm in better shape than I've ever been, and it's translating to the ice.

Our head coach, Karen Hughes, has been very positive with me all year, but especially during this camp. I'm getting the feeling she might start me in the final, but I don't want to read too much into her actions. I want to keep my intensity high. The Americans and two other teams have already arrived in Beijing. But with SARS scaring the world there have been rumours about delays.

Unfortunately, we haven't seen our doctor in a few days. Dr. Christine Young was at Scarborough General when the first cases of SARS came to Toronto. She's put herself in a voluntary quarantine here in Calgary. She's one of my favourite staff members, very good at her job but also hilarious. At one of our games she dressed in some extra gear and skated the warm-up with us. As an adult rec player she looked like one of the "experience a dream" kids who skate with us during warm-up but says it was one of her highlights, despite later getting in trouble.

The dressing room is sombre as we wait for the staff.

Karen Hughes walks in the dressing room first, followed closely by Mike Pelino, who's come to us from the NHL; my coach, Ken Dufton; and team manager Julie Healy. They are joined by Hockey Canada president Bob Nicholson.

I tighten my hands together trying to hold the hope in.

The staff sit down while Bob stands alone at the front of the room. "First off, congratulations to each of you for being here," he rambles.

Just get to it, I want to scream.

"Unfortunately, we are going to delay your flights to Beijing. Practice will continue until we know more." He continues to speak but I zone out, focused on the word *delay.* There's still hope.

Bob carries on as my thoughts turn to Beijing. This whole year has been focused on China. I've heard countless intriguing stories from my friend Susie Yuen, who has been there coaching Team China. I've been reading book after book about Chinese life, and my brother even made our team a scrapbook guide to the capital.

At practice the next day, I can tell my teammates lack hope. The news is dominated by SARS. We are still practising twice a day, but we need rest. My hips hurt from overuse; I'm recently back from a trip to Pittsburgh where I visited a hip specialist. Post-season, I have to decide whether to have surgery or opt to re-hab. In pain, my motivation is dwindling. Our team is falling apart. Half of the players want to go, and half don't. There's animosity in the dressing room and tension is building. We need answers.

Two days later, and we still have no answers. The World Championship are set to start soon. I'm doing my best to put my all into practice every day but as hope fades, that task becomes more difficult. I want to prove how hard I've worked this year; prove how much I've sacrificed.

Finally, four days after the delay, Bob comes into the dressing room to deliver the news.

"You will not be going. The World Championship is cancelled."

1985: SETBACKS — SKATEBOARDING

I am rolling around the kitchen on my new *Back to the Future* themed skateboard. At 10 years of age, it is the coolest thing I've ever owned. My brother and I got them yesterday. In my shorts and bare feet, my new skateboard takes me from one end of the open-concept kitchen to the other. I can't leave the kitchen because beyond this small vinyl surface is the carpeted living room.

My mom is cleaning up after dinner in our makeshift home.

Our family is on spring break in Palm Desert, California, just outside Los Angeles. This is my Auntie Jo and Uncle Larry's place. I was named after Jo, my mom's sister, and she shares my body type. My size and my strength were never an issue for me because she always wore it with elegance and grace. Seven years my mom's senior and very different from my mom, they have grown into best friends. My aunt and uncle introduced my mom and dad. My cousins Jay and Jill are much older than Luke and me, but they are always entertaining to be around. Jay is a big-time swimmer, competing for Canada on many occasions, and my brother idolizes him.

We often go visit their whole family at their summer cottage in Minden, Ontario, which is also next door to my Aunt Susan and Uncle Ernie's. There Luke and I play for hours on the beach with their kids Jeff and Lindsay.

Upon arrival in California, my parents took us to the stadium where, less than a year ago, the Los Angeles Olympics took place. I have never seen a stadium so immense.

"Get out of the kitchen!" Mom glares in my direction. But I make one more pass, the fastest of them all. I'm getting good, my balance is getting stronger and my focus narrows. I swerve to avoid my mom, but I misjudge the proximity of the dishwasher to the floor. The gap looked wide enough to squeeze my board under, but unfortunately not for my board *and* my feet.

Sometimes we are halted on our greatest pursuits. The big toe on my leading foot took the brunt of the impact. I come to an agonizing halt, my foot stuck under the dishwasher, and my toenail completely torn off.

APRIL 2003: NEW FOCUS

Despite no World Championship, hockey still continues. We won our quarter-final NWHL playoff series against Mississauga, but that's the furthest thing from my mind right now as I have a blind date tonight.

His name is Allen. He works with my Aeros teammates Stephanie Boyd and Karen Nystrom. I'm nervous. In my basement apartment, I've tried on five different outfits and have been preparing since the end of our game. I'm trying not to get my hopes up, but I can't help it. He sounds so nice on the phone. I'm supposed to meet him at the restaurant at seven.

Because of our win, we're off to the NWHL Championship tournament and will play my former team, the Brampton Thunder, in the semifinal game. Ken likes to play it fair when it comes to the goalie rotation (which can be annoying, but I get it), and because I played Brampton in the provincial finals in February, it'll most likely be Kendra's turn for this big game.

As I wait at the bar, I watch my former Stanford classmate, Tiger Woods, at the Masters Tournament on TV. Maybe this was a bad idea. I'm too nervous. Maybe he's not coming.

"Sami?"

I turn. This person couldn't possibly be the guy I'm waiting for. He's too good-looking. Clean cut, square jaw, and fit. I smile like a schoolgirl and try to act cool.

Five dates in, and I've forgotten about the rest of the world.

I have even forgotten that we beat Brampton today, and that I played. Not sure why Ken went with me — maybe for my own personal redemption — but I felt bad for Kendra; it was supposed to be her game. At least now she'll have a final to play. What a thrill, and what a relief to beat Brampton in my final game of the season. But what keeps running through my mind is Allen. He's transformed me into mush in less than two weeks.

It's the NWHL Championship Final against Calgary in front of a packed Brampton Powerade Centre. We're good, but Calgary is extraordinarily strong. They prove to be too much. Kendra does her best, but we can't score.

No League Championship for us this year, no World Championship, but I am not as upset as I would have been in the past.

I'm playing at the top of my game on one of the best teams in the country. I have some great teammates and coaches who push me every day to be better, and ultimately, with Allen in my life, I've found new meaning, a new purpose, and a new sense of balance.

•••••••

It's a month later and my car rolls along Highway 11 between Kapuskasing and Hearst, Ontario, for my "Share the Dream" tour. My friend Dermot has joined me on this tour I've created, speaking at schools in small towns along the way, staying with locals, and making enough money for gas to get to the next town. We even spoke at my coach Dave Jamieson's school in Oro, Ontario. What's great about Dermot is that he's always up for any adventure. He didn't even hesitate when I said we'd be driving nearly 24 hours over 10 days and staying with random people along the way.

Much has happened this past year, yet we are still just two friends telling stories and finding new memories. I share the story of my grandpa's funeral in January, how my dad gave the eulogy. I tell him all about Allen, and he talks all about his new girlfriend, Kim. We reminisce about Adam and tell funny stories of the three of us doing school projects (they'd make me do the work) and long bike rides.

We remember images of our friend Adam running. He never gave up. He was a feisty competitor who never wanted to get beat. He sprinted when there was nothing left in the tank and had an inner confidence — if he got beat, he came back stronger the next race.

During the trip we find out Vancouver has secured the bid to host the 2010 Winter Olympics on home soil. *A new resolve.*

I'm proud of myself, my dedication, and my play. Change isn't easy, and I often skated into it unwillingly, but despite difficult times, good things have come, and I know great things await.

23

Two Seasons of Hockey

MARCH 2004: NATIONALS — SHERWOOD PARK

By the following March, Allen and I had been together almost a full year. Nearly an entire hockey season has flown by.

Facing off in the finals of the Esso Women's Nationals in Sherwood Park, Alberta, we play against the Calgary Oval X-Treme. The game has begun slowly, almost hesitantly, by both teams, but gradually, with a National Championship on the line, intensity ramps up.

Calgary controls most of the play, but I relish the opportunity. I feel light, I feel quick. They are outplaying us, but it's fun. Their team is loaded with talent, including Hayley Wickenheiser, Cassie Campbell, and Danielle Goyette, who play together on the same line. Their second line includes Olympians Dana Antal and Kelly Bechard along with my friend Samm Holmes who moved to Calgary after disappointingly being left off the National Team roster. On their back end, they have Olympian Colleen Sostorics, and Correne Bredin with World Championship experience. It's a challenge every time a new line steps on the ice.

I make save after save until, finally, Calgary scores near the end of the first period on a rebound goal from Wick. No derailment, no end of the world, just the acknowledgement of a good goal, and my mind returns to the play.

Cassie Turner and Kim Malcher are stalwarts on defence for us. Both recent cuts from Team Canada's program, they want to prove they belong. Cheryl Pounder and Becky Kellar are always steady together, often in their own world on the bench. Kellar missed the last few months with a shoulder injury, but she seems to be back in great shape with a new burst of energy. In addition, Gillian "Gilly" Ferrari and Kelly Sage provide muscle on the back end.

Gilly is one of my training partners and she once again made the National Team this year after the team was forced out of the 2003 Worlds in Beijing because of SARS. She's solid and a real goaltender's defenceman. Always a jokester off the ice, she's a tyrant to anyone who tries to enter my crease. My defence are my saviours, picking up loose rebounds and ensuring that Calgary doesn't get too many chances. I try to play the puck up to them as often as I can, helping to save their energy for more important tasks.

Our team is led by captain Geraldine Heaney. She retired from the National Team last year, but she stuck with the Aeros for one more season. I went to her wedding last fall. This is her swan song and her chance to finally play forward. Our biggest addition is Jennifer Botterill, a recent Harvard graduate. I convinced her to come play for the Aeros under Ken Dufton. I'm thrilled she joined our team as she not only makes those around her better on the ice, but is also a great influence for me off the ice. We have a strong team with good depth, but Calgary has the superstars. Thus far in the NWHL season, we have four losses, one win, and one tie against them, but in the round robin of this tournament we held the advantage with a 6–5 win in which my goalie partner, Kendra Fisher, secured the victory.

Ken rolls the lines, and the score remains 1–0 for Calgary throughout the game. It's our unheralded third line that includes Heaney on forward that finally, in the third period, puts the puck in the net. Centreman Jenn Butsch, an American from Vermont who has moved her life to Toronto to play for our team, deflects the puck off a point shot from Gilly past Calgary goalie, Amanda Tapp.

The game is tied 1–1.

Despite chances, I manage to hold Calgary at bay. Their team, though full of talent, doesn't seem to be clicking. Tomas Pacina, the Calgary coach, is Wick's partner and father to her son, Noah. Wick started the season in Finland on a men's pro team. After a full season last year, she returned to the Oval just after Christmas this year to be with her family. As Pacina tries to manage Wick's talent within the team dynamic, he attempts new line combinations, but without success. The game comes to a finish and it remains 1–1.

Desire propels us into overtime. Annie Desrosiers, from Saint-Antoine-sur-Richelieu, Quebec, perhaps one of the best players in the world not playing at the international level, starts on the first line with Jen and Heather Logan, the captain of Canada's Under-22 team.

They keep the play in Calgary's end. I watch like a fan as we out-manoeuvre their defence. Our second line of Sommer West, Lara Perks, and American Jessica Tabb keeps the pressure on. Despite a long tournament, we are flying, players putting in their maximal effort. Ken rolls through all three lines, including our 10th forward, Amanda Benoit-Wark, until we're at the top of the lineup again. Quick shifts mean one chance and you're off.

Heaney hits the ice again with her linemates, Butsch and Boyd. Technically this is our third line, but they play smart. Heaney's still the most intelligent player on the ice. She chases down a Calgary player in the neutral zone and pops the puck free.

Turner finds the loose puck and propels it from just inside our zone towards Boyd — who also came over from the Thunder — waiting at centre ice. Stephanie Boyd tips the puck to an open Butsch who takes her man down as she redirects the puck to a streaking Heaney, crossing the blue line on the right wing with one player left to beat. She fakes to the right and lures Calgary's defenceman to lunge. Heaney niftily cups the puck back to her left and skates free for a breakaway.

My brain starts to celebrate even before Heaney lifts the puck up over Amanda Tapp's shoulder. Heaney has already announced this will be her final year, her final game.

"Yeaaaaaaaaaaaaaaaaaaaaaaaaaaah, Ger!" I scream as I rush down the ice. Jen is the first person I reach, and we join our teammates celebrating with Heaney.

We are national champions.

My first call is to Allen. "Did you watch the game?" I say, barely able to contain my excitement.

The evening's celebration lasts well into the night, and Heaney announces to us that she's pregnant. What an incredible way to finish a career. I savour every moment with this incredible team.

APRIL 2004: WORLD CHAMPIONSHIP — HALIFAX

A month later, with Team Canada, I win my fourth straight World Championship title. At the post-Championship party I nestle my face into Allen's shoulder as we dance in the middle of the dance floor at an Irish pub in Halifax, Nova Scotia.

Team Canada are World Champions, but sorrow is my only feeling. I try to push it down, but grief consumes me. Amid the jubilant victory celebration of my teammates, our friends, family, and supporters, I let some tears fall on Allen's shirt.

I did what I was supposed to do. When I found out I wasn't playing the final, I didn't take anything away from the team. I smiled, I laughed, and I cheered — I even celebrated with my teammates on the blue line and for hours in the dressing room, but now in Allen's arms, I can no longer be anyone but myself.

Allen's parents flew to Halifax from Brampton to be here for me. They sit with my parents at a corner table just behind the dance floor. My mom is hurting too. I know she hates to see me this way.

My brother has flown in from Santa Barbara, California, the opposite corner of North America, where he now lives with his wife, Gina. He and my friends Dermot and Anders make the rounds of the pub, sharing a little in each table's celebrations, still dressed in their Canada attire.

1991: I HATE TO LOSE — MY MOM

Driving home from a school volleyball game with my mom, I'm 15 years old. We lost the game and I don't feel like talking. Staring out the window, I watch the world go by.

"How was school?" Mom asks.

"Fine," I say looking at people in the other cars. *Do they know I just lost?* I watch the trees pass as our teal Mazda 323 rolls along St Michael Road at exactly the speed limit.

I'm still stewing about our loss. My mom makes one final effort. "You played well."

I'm unresponsive, knowing I missed some key opportunities. I continue to stare out the window.

In another life, my mom probably would have been an athlete, but sports were just hobbies for kids in her household. A swimmer, a water-skier, and anything else she was allowed to be as a girl, she excelled, but eventually life got in the way, school took over, and sports were not pastimes for young ladies.

She has a meticulous attention to detail — I get that from her. She runs our household now and is the only reason my brother and I partici-pate in so many activities. Organized to a tee, she keeps the peace, is the taxi service, helps us with homework, acts as the chef, and is unfortunately the one who must deal with me after every loss.

Our car turns onto Tyrone Bay and rounds the corner. I'm disap-pointed in my performance on the court. I hate to lose. It doesn't occur to me what my mood does to the people around me. Our car pulls up the driveway and parks in the garage.

Grabbing my backpack I walk in the house, past my dad and my brother in the living room and straight into my bed room. I need silence.

APRIL 2004: WORLD CHAMPIONSHIP — HALIFAX (CONTINUED)

Right up until 11 o'clock last night I thought I'd play the World Championship Final. Surely if I hadn't heard by then, I'd get the nod. There wasn't any doubt in my mind that the coaching staff, similar to last year's — including head coach Karen Hughes and assistants Ken Dufton and former NHL defenceman Doug Lidster — would go with me.

I had a solid selection camp at the Thanksgiving Festival in October in Dartmouth, Nova Scotia. A victory at the 4 Nations Cup in Skövde later in November and a recent National Championship victory with Toronto Aeros.

A new format to the World Championship had us square off against the Americans in the round robin. There were nine teams instead of the usual eight: SARS last season meant that no team got relegated to the lower division. In our round robin game against the Americans our team didn't look good. We gave the puck away a lot on their aggressive forecheck, and in the end, their 3–1 win broke our 37–0 streak of games won in a row at the World Championship.

Kim looked uncharacteristically shaky. She played deep in her net, unconfident. She had her chance and I thought for sure it'd be my turn. I got the nod for the semis against Sweden but when it comes to choosing goalies for a gold medal game, it's often down to a coach's gut instinct.

The finals were played in front of a packed Halifax Metro Centre. The crowd was loud and raucous. Kim played great in the finals. Delaney scored along with Wick. Jen led the tournament in scoring and was named MVP. Captain Cassie Campbell, flanked by assistants Vicky Sunohara and Hayley Wickenheiser, accepted the first ever IIHF World Championship trophy (replacing the previously awarded plates).

As the party continues, I slip out the back door and head to my hotel room. I crawl into bed and pull the covers up to my chin. My brother knocks at the door and I tell him to go away. The party will go on without me. Sleep is my only sanctuary.

·······

After the Worlds, back in Toronto, we still have our NWHL finals to play. In women's hockey, we have two championships: a National Championship and a League Championship with almost the exact same teams. It's confusing.

Ken is true to his word and Kendra Fisher plays. Despite her valiant effort, we lose to Brampton in the semifinals and must watch them lose in a thrilling 6–5 shootout to Calgary in the NWHL Cup Finals.

MARCH 2005: NATIONALS — SARNIA

A year later, my Toronto Aeros are in the same exciting predicament of being in the final game at the Esso Women's National Championship, this year hosted in Sarnia, Ontario. However, we are a completely new team, and I have different reasons to want to win this game.

Sitting in the dressing room between the first and second periods, we're down 1–0 to our cross-town rivals the Brampton Thunder.

This season, I've ramped up my training to be stronger, fitter, and quicker. I work out in the gym five days a week and am on the ice nearly eight times a week. Chris has come up with new and innovative ways to make me a better goalie. From elastic band plyometrics to mental toughness training while fatigued, we work together on pushing my limits.

Allen and I also moved in together this year, providing a sense of stability I've never had. It's helpful that Canadian elite athletes received a pay raise last year, and the Athlete Assistance Program known as "carding" is now at $1,500 a month.

Despite everything, two weeks ago, I found out I will be the third goalie for this year's 2005 World Championship in Sweden. Charline Labonté will be in my spot. I'll be travelling, but not playing.

The Aeros, still in our white, red, and black jerseys, have nine new names on our roster. Our general manager, Maria Quinto, a mainstay in the Aeros organization and a vital cog to our success, is still with us, but we have a new coach, Vern Ladouceur, Ken's assistant from last year. Ken left us to help develop the Aeros Junior team. Gone is our captain and seventime World Champion, Geraldine Heaney, at home with her newborn. Gone is two-time Olympian Becky Kellar, who we found out afterwards was also pregnant in our National Championship game last year and the World Championship in Halifax. Back from giving birth, she now suits up alongside Thérèse Brisson with the Oakville Ice much closer to home.

Gone is my training partner Gilly, the funniest person I've ever played with. She went to the dreaded Brampton Thunder, joining Vicky, Lori, and Jayna, hoping it would help her solidify her spot on the National Team. Also gone is Annie Desrosiers, who was one of our best players at last year's Nationals. She moved to Toronto for love; it didn't pan out, so she moved back home to Montreal. In addition, Stephanie Boyd retired after 15 years of playing in this league.

We're not as good as we once were, and we're often disjointed. Our stars have been replaced by new, unknown recent college graduates: Allison Edgar, Bradi Cochrane, Danielle Ashley, Karen Rickard, Lauren McAuliffe, and Susan Hobson. Two of our best players are hurt. Jessica Tabb, who this year made the US National Team program, ruined her knee a few weeks ago, and Lara Perks, a member of the Canadian National Team program, has been relegated to her dark bedroom most of the year suffering from a severe concussion. For this tournament, with our depleted lineup, we were forced to call up players from our Junior Aeros team: youngsters Haley Irwin and Hayley McMeekin.

I squeeze by the food table set up in the middle of the room and grab one of the water bottles our assistant equipment manager Marty Schwartzberg has filled up for us. Marty's been with the team since its inception and despite a developmental disability can recount to me every goal I've ever let in as well as name the artist of any song he's ever heard. I gingerly push Kendra's pad to one side and take my seat next to her. She smiles and pats me on the thigh with the mitts I lent her. She's welcomed me into the organization and she's always been supportive.

Across from me, Jen chats with her linemates Sommer West and Lauren McAuliffe, their hands drawing up imaginary plays in the air. Lauren played with Jen at Harvard, and Sommer and Jen have such great chemistry. They are our dominant line, and we rely on them to score most of our goals. I glance over at Cheryl Pounder to my right as she stands to command the room.

Pounder took over the captaincy from Heaney after her retirement. Her equipment never looks like it's been put on straight: tape is wrapped haphazardly around her shin pads, her socks have holes, and her dress clothes are exploding from her stall into neighbouring stalls. But she works incredibly hard and has everyone's respect. Pounder was named MVP of the tournament last night. She gestures to Danielle Ashley to dim the music.

"Guys, this is Brampton," Pounder says emphasizing the hatred of the word *Brampton*, sweat still beading on her forehead. "In our zone, we need to support better. Forwards, we need you lower in the zone, especially when Heff and Vicks are on the ice. And get more pucks through."

Coach Vern walks in.

"Shoot more and, just like Pounder said, support more. No one outside this dressing room thought you'd be here. Heck, I'm not sure I believed it throughout this season. It's been tough, even the round robin was tough [we lost to both Brampton and Calgary], but you are resilient. This third period, play with that chip on your shoulders and leave everything on the ice. Never give up."

Danielle Ashley starts up the tunes, and the Celtic hit "Heave Away" blares loudly. It's always our last song as we head to the ice. The score-board reads in bright lights 1–0 in favour of Brampton with one period to play. As I watch the refs check the nets one last time before the opening faceoff, the ice glistens. I feel calm. I know my parents are glued to their TV screen in our living room. I stand in my crease on the goal line and tap my posts. My gloves are wet from nearly two hours of play, the leather on the palms now slippery. I cinch them on tighter and await the faceoff to salvage our season.

I save shot after shot. Today I can see the play two moves ahead. Midway through the period, the referee calls Butsch, our unsung hero from last season, for a penalty. Brampton's power play, one of the best in the nation, rarely misses a chance like this. I watch Jen prepare for a faceoff in our end and shout at my team.

"Make sure you get it out."

The faceoff is a scramble, the puck ends up behind my net; Pounder's feet are quicker than a pigeon's running across hot pavement, and she corrals the puck and fires it down the ice.

As the puck clears the zone, I take a moment to breathe, and then cautiously reposition myself for their attack. Brampton's defenceman, the shifty Kerry Weiland from Team USA, carries the puck up to their blue line as her forwards swing in a set power play breakout pattern. Heather Logan — our semifinal hero, scoring on Montreal Axion's Charline Labonté to win the game and propel us in the finals — attempts to thwart what looks like a predetermined play. I've never seen Heather play this well. Like my other Aero teammates in the Team Canada player pool, West, Malcher, and Turner, she was told last week that she will not be centralizing for the 2006 Olympics in Torino, Italy.

Logan reads the play perfectly, intercepts Weiland's errant pass, and pushes the puck forward, sending herself in all alone on a breakaway.

Brampton's goalie, Lisa Moreland, is surprised by the turnover. The puck's still hopping on Logan's stick; she doesn't have full control. Moreland lunges, but the puck now looks to be attached by Velcro. She sweeps the puck around an outstretched goalie stick and tucks it just inside the post. Her hands thrust in the air; her smile is bigger than her cage. We just scored on the penalty kill against one of the strongest power plays in the nation. My shocked teammates mob Logan.

We battle through the rest of the penalty, killing it off. The period unfolds as expected, building for potential overtime. With just under three minutes left in the third, one of our rookie defencemen, Bradi Cochrane, a recent graduate of Niagara University, is crushed behind our net. Bradi played for the Aeros prior to her college career, playing as a teenager with some of the biggest names in women's hockey. Bradi is down and a tussle ensues. Haley Irwin, our call-up, steps in. Only 16 years of age and already a presence on the ice, she shoves Jayna Hefford who, shock on her face, shoves Irwin right back. The ref grabs both and sends them to the box. Not a bad trade-off as Irwin takes one of the best players in the world off the ice.

Twenty seconds later, our defenceman, Danielle Ashley, steps a little too hard into Coley Dosser of Brampton and sends the small player flying. Often in a tied game, referees will put their whistles away, especially if there is a National Championship on the line, but not this time. A ballsy call puts Brampton on a power play with just over two minutes left to decide the champions.

I reach down towards my toes, wanting to feel my hamstrings activate. Jen sets up for the faceoff to my right. Not only a prolific goal scorer, Jen is perhaps one of the best defensive forwards in the game. I always feel confident when she's on the ice. Jen's had a tough year recovering from a concussion in the summer. She collided with Edmonton Oilers star Raffi Torres at centre ice during a shinny game and the concussion put her out for three months. At first tentative, she's now back to the player she once was. West joins her on forward, with Malcher and Pounder on defence to kill the penalty. The play starts up, and bodies fly everywhere, but I focus on the three-inch diameter piece of rubber that darts around my crease.

Finally, West crushes a Brampton player behind my net and separates her from the puck, squeezing it free. She finds the puck and sends it the entire length of the ice.

Time slows down as I try to focus my energy for their final push. Slightly over a minute left in the game and nearly as long in our penalty. I take a deep breath.

Gillian Ferrari, now a member of the Brampton Thunder, rushes towards their end to grab the puck off the boards 200 feet from me.

West's in hot pursuit with Jen following close behind. Any delay they can cause Ferrari gets us closer to overtime.

As Ferrari swings to pick up the puck, looking to reverse it to her other Brampton defenceman, West is already close and has caught her by surprise. She pushes Ferrari into the boards, forcing her to reverse the puck earlier than anticipated to her defence partner; that partner, though, is nowhere in sight.

Sommer turns to the loose puck and spots Jen barrelling into the zone. Polar opposites in personality, these two work incredibly well together. Jen's appeared unnoticed by the Thunder. There isn't much space to thread the puck to her through the defenceman who has reappeared to defend her net, but West's pass lands right on the mark. Jen one-timers the puck top shelf over a stunned Lisa Moreland's shoulder. An arena in disbelief erupts.

2–1 for the Toronto Aeros.

We have scored a second shorthanded goal.

No one could have predicted this outcome. As my team jubilantly celebrates at our bench, I am alone to let the epilogue soak in. One more faceoff, one more final effort by Brampton, and one more buzzer.

We did it. I exhale — not the sudden jubilation of last year, but a relieved breath combined with a sense of satisfaction.

Hoisting the Abby Hoffman Cup. We are National Champions. Again.

MARCH 2005: NWHL CUP

Two weeks after our Esso Women's National Championship victory and I am back in familiar territory standing in my net watching the play unfold in the far zone.

However, this time it's overtime of the 2005 NWHL Cup and this time our opponents are Charline Labonté's Montreal Axion.

The game is tied 4–4.

Montreal is a team stacked with stars and future stars, led by Team USA's defenceman Angela Ruggiero who also suited up this year in the ECHL, a men's pro league, for a game alongside her brother with the Tulsa Oilers.

This was not supposed to be my game, but the team needs me now. Perspiration drips off my cage as I wait at the top of my crease, my elbows on my thighs. The crowd wants a goal. Hosted in Brampton, they don't care who scores, as they don't have much of an allegiance; they just want to scream.

Vern Ladouceur, our coach, has followed most of Ken Dufton's coaching habits, including playing the goalies fairly. Therefore, because I played the Esso Nationals, this was Kendra Fisher's game. She's a tall goaltender with a fantastic ability to read the play. She has such talent that she's played for Canada's Under-22 team and her easy going demeanor makes her a valued goalie partner.

Montreal, out for revenge from their loss in the National semifinals to us, started the game on fire. As I sat in the first spectator seat beside our bench, I watched former teammate Annie Desrosiers score, shooting right through our defenceman on the first shift of the game. They didn't stop. Vern looked down at me, but I never looked back. Suddenly it was 3–0, and we had played less than 10 minutes of the first period.

"Sami, you're in."

I scrambled to my feet and tried to find my gloves and stick on the bench as Kendra skated off the ice. I hate seeing another goalie's face when they're pulled.

"I'm so sorry," I say, tapping Kendra on the blocker as I make my way into the net, adrenaline instantly getting me into the game.

We claw and scrape our way back, led by Jen and Sommer West. They are our best players on the ice, never giving up hope. West scores two quick ones in the second period followed by a goal from our young 16-year-old player Haley Irwin to make the game 3–3. We have Jessica Tabb back from a knee injury playing alongside Heather Logan and Irwin, but unfortunately defenceman Cassie Turner is hurt, and we're playing with just five defencemen.

The third period sees both teams exchange goals, with West scoring her third of the game, sending us into overtime.

As the play resumes with eight minutes left in a 20-minute overtime period, the puck makes its way behind their net. I try to keep my emotions in check. My equipment feels wet and heavy. This game has been long, made even longer by TV time outs, and I haven't eaten much today.

West and her winger Lauren McAuliffe fight for the puck behind Labonté. McAuliffe falls to the ground as West gets pinned by Canadian Olympic defenceman Isabelle Chartrand. Still in the corner, West kicks the puck free to Jen. She cycles the puck up the boards, creating some space. Halfway up the boards, at the hash marks, Jen glances at the net and immediately sends the puck towards it.

Sommer West has such an incredible knack for finding space on the ice. Her attitude was the knock against her when she was younger, but under Ken Dufton she's matured into a leader. She has fought off Chartrand for stick space in front, and the puck ricochets off her awaiting stick high over the shoulder of a stunned Labonté for her unbelievable fourth goal of the game.

Once again, we have done the unthinkable, led by unlikely heroes. We pile on top of each other, and Pounder grabs me, crying, in a tight embrace.

"We did it Sami, we f***king did it!" she says as we hoist the NWHL Cup and savour being National and League Champions.

24

Olympic Preparations

MAY 2005: BOOK CAMP — PEI

Two weeks of Team Canada's May camp, and fatigue has not once left my body. I'm driving a minivan full of my teammates the 30 minutes back to dinner from our training centre at the University of Prince Edward Island (UPEI). The rental car smell is mixed with the stench of eight women who've been sweating all day. Our accommodations are on the other side of the island on Brackley Beach, at Shaw's Hotel & Cottages. The van is quiet but for a local radio station that I have on low. Darkness descends. Everyone is beat.

The coaches are pushing us to exhaustion, but for good reason. For the first time ever, last year, we lost the World Championship. They were held just after the NWHL Cup in the beginning of April in Linkoping, Sweden, and we lost in a shootout to the Americans. I was the third goalie, hanging out mostly with the other players not playing: rookies Tessa Bonhomme and Meghan Agosta, and my training partner from back home, Gillian Ferrari.

Unfortunately for me, both Charlie and Kim played extraordinarily well and incredibly didn't let in a goal the entire tournament. Kim played the Championship game, and we fell 1–0 in a shootout. The loss hurt our team; Canada's first ever silver at Worlds. Nearly every day here in PEI we are reminded of where we want to be.

The van passengers include my two cabin mates, Colleen "Sos" Sostorics and Caroline "Caro" Ouellette. Sos sits beside me in the passenger seat, staring straight ahead. Growing up on a farm in Kennedy, Saskatchewan, she learned her toughness from years playing boys' hockey, but despite her strength, she takes a lot of punishment. She was also a star in rugby, but concussions have plagued her career and her moods. Currently symptom-free, as long as she has a coffee in the morning, she can tolerate others. However, at present, like all of us, she's tired and sombre.

Caro is one of the six squished in the back. She's from Montreal. With the French girls, she's outgoing, a true leader; in English she tends to be quieter, more reserved. I try to speak in French as much as I can with her. She understands everything in English, just seems shy to speak the words. Her language skills have improved immensely since she enrolled in college in the States. She has finished her third year at Minnesota-Duluth, after already completing her course to become a police officer in Montreal. Despite her playing in the NCAA, her parents are still at nearly every Montreal Axion game, her mom gregarious and outgoing, her dad always wanting to talk hockey.

I turn the last corner and drive down the gravel driveway. I slow down and keep an eye out for the Shaw's golden retriever as we approach the cabins.

I stop in front of the first one and drop off long-time veteran Danielle Goyette with rookies Katie Weatherston and Ashley Riggs. Both from Ontario, Weatherston's from Thunder Bay and Riggs is from Pickering. Similar players, they are both small, quick, and possess exceptional hands, which means they are most likely battling for the same spot on the team. I know their cabin is dysfunctional — two rookies put with our oldest player creates tension — but today I don't have the energy to step in and resolve their disputes. They are quiet as they walk far apart from each other.

After my last drop-off, I pull up to cabin number 21 and park our van out front. Caro and Sos get out in silence, and Sos and I head to our shared room. Caro throws her stuff in her room and makes her way to the kitchen; it's her turn to cook dinner.

Our day started this morning at 7:00 with a cold run along the beach. Dressed in tracksuits and toques, our feet heavy in the red sand, the sun came up and our run ended. We then finished the workout with another 30 minutes on the beach.

After that, we headed to rink. Knowing that I need to show the coaches my desire to be better, I stayed on the ice this morning after everyone got off, as I have done for the last week and a half. Dave Jamieson, our goalie coach, is not here in PEI until next week, but as I did goalie drills alone on the solitary ice for an additional 20 minutes after the two-hour practice, I saw head coach Melody Davidson, back at the helm, watching intently from the stands.

After another 20 minutes on the bike to cool down, I finished my last bite of a ham and cheese sandwich from last night. I quickly grabbed my stick, skates, glove, and blocker and went to a 30-minute shooting session on synthetic ice followed by an hour of off-ice stickhandling down on the paved arena floor.

At 2:00 p.m., our group of 14 players switched off with the other group for another hour and a half of weightlifting. At this point in the day, I was so fatigued, I was simply going through the motions.

I melt into the sofa and Sos puts her feet up on an oversized comfy chair, but our day is not over: still one more aqua aerobics workout back at UPEI tonight after dinner.

"Food's ready," says Caro from the kitchen. Caro has made us a stir-fry tonight. I'm not sure I can muster enough energy to get up off this couch. As I stare out the giant window, I know tonight will be a battle of mind over matter trying to conquer fatigue.

Caro walks into the living room with two plates in her hand and sets one down in front of me.

"I figured I'd help you out." She grins. As we dig into our meals, life starts to slowly fill the room as Sos talks about a drill from practice.

"She always messes it up," Caro says about one of our teammates who is notorious as a drill killer. We laugh, and I momentarily forget about the pain in nearly all my joints.

"Old Hags killed it on Saturday," says Sos, referring to a four on four hockey game in which the coaches divided the teams by age. "Sure beat up on the young punks."

"Showed them," I say back to Sos. Tired, exhausted, we still find joy in each other's company. As I savour my last morsel, the sun sets outside our bay window.

JUNE 2005: BIKE RIDES

As the first of our four bike rides is about to begin, I walk towards my bike while I clip my helmet strap. Only six days remain on our three-and-a-half-week boot camp in PEI. Just four long bike rides and a triathlon. Our fitness trainer, Jason Poole, goes over last-minute instructions for this ride.

"Eight riders per team. Today's is not a race. You'll start with five minutes between groups. It will be seventy-five kilometres, and a chance to get used to your bikes and the trails. Stay with your group. There will be a rest stop with snacks in about thirty minutes. Make sure you stay with your group."

I put my headphones on and tuck my iPod Shuffle into my cycling jersey's back pocket. Putting my water bottle in its holder, I psyche myself up, and climb on my bike. My group is now eight abreast for a photo op.

I smile. My last smile for a long time.

The ride begins on pavement as we head towards the historic Anne of Green Gables house. The sun is high over the ocean.

As we turn onto the highway, we form a drafting line. Only two minutes into the ride, I realize something is wrong with my bike. I fall into line in last position and look down at my gears. I'm an engineer; I should be able to fix this. I scan for potential failures. *Why is there only one chain ring?*

As our group starts to climb the first gradient, I'm pushing hard, harder than everyone else it seems, and slowly falling farther and farther off the back. *My cardio is not this bad.*

My group slows to a near halt at the top of the hill as they realize how far I've dropped behind. I'm starting to hate that Jason said, "Make sure you stay with your group." I'm emotionally frustrated. As soon as I catch up, they start again. Ten kilometres into the ride, I'm fully drenched in sweat, and my face is beat red. No one else even looks like she has broken a sweat. *How did I end up with this bike?* Another hill, and once again, without enough gears, I struggle slowly to the top.

Vicky Sunohara swings back to ride with me.

"What's wrong, Jami?" Vicky calls me that from years ago, rhyming Jami with Sami, when we all mixed up our first letters in our name with our last name. I became Jami So Small. I've trained with Vicky; she knows I'm better than this.

I can barely talk.

This is only the first 10 kilometres and I still have 350 to go over the next four days. I fight back tears.

"Vicks, I don't know" is all I can muster through confused gasps.

I can see Vicky is worried as she easily pedals beside me. She's no longer my teammate on the Thunder, but she's still a good friend. Vicky could be a first line centreman, or a fourth line player and her demeanour remains the same. She's always there for her teammates and always willing to do whatever it takes to win. She makes those around her not only better hockey players but also better people. She's always the first to take a problem on her shoulders, but there seems to be no solution to my dilemma.

She says, "Everyone hits the wall at some point, Sami. Don't worry; your wall is simply at the beginning."

I chuckle.

"Put your hand on my bike. Let me help you."

Reaching out, I grab the back of Vicky's seat as she labours the rest of the few kilometres beside me.

Anger consumes me as we roll into the parking lot of PEI's most famous fictional resident. Pulling up with Vicky, we see the mass of bikes belonging to my teammates who are already inside eating. Vicky heads in. I throw my bike to the ground and pace for a bit.

A bike technician spots me in the distance and starts to walk in my direction. He's here in case of flat tires.

"What the heck is wrong with my bike?"

Confused, he comes closer and picks up my bike. "Why did you pick this one?" he asks innocently.

Seething inside, I hold it together. "You told me to take that one."

Little did I know that instead of the nice 21-speed hybrid bikes most of the girls were cruising on, I got stuck with a "Mary Poppins" three-speed, which would have been more appropriate for riding down the back lane with a basket or a slow jaunt around town instead of serious training with the National Team.

Walking over to his truck, he takes out a new hybrid bike like the rest. I take it for a spin around the parking lot. It feels glorious; the difference is staggering.

I leave the technician to deal with my other bike and walk inside to grab a sandwich.

"About time," yells Cassie, laughing in jest with her crew. Ten minutes ago, I would have lost it on her too, but I know with my new hybrid bike, I'll be better.

At the end of the ride, we stay at a campground, nestling into our mummy sleeping bags in tents lent to us by the armed forces.

We awake early Tuesday for our second ride in two days. Today's is 125 kilometres. In the saddle of my new bike, I experience a tempest of emotions on the Confederation Trail, from excitement to exhaustion to anger. For seven and a half hours along the dusty gravel roads, zigzagging through the trees along the former rail line, the same 20-song mix of music plays over and over on my MP3 player. At the end, my body feels like it has been through a washing machine.

The following day, we line up for the start of our third ride. Jason Poole begins, "Today's ride is a cabin race. It will be seventy-five kilometres, and you will be with your cabin mates." Sos is already on my right and Caro on my left. They are very capable on the bike, and I need to be fast for them. We knew this was going to happen today, so we went to the local Walmart last night and secretly bought matching shirts. They read *Tough Cookies* on the front, with a big number 21 that I drew in marker, on the back for our cabin. I feel a sense of pride that no one else has matching uniforms.

We keep a fast, gruelling pace the entire race; they let me draft for much of the ride.

"C'mon, Sami, keep up," comes out of their mouths several times during the race, urging me to pedal faster, my heart rate skyrocketing.

Crossing the finish line, I collapse in a heap on the side of the road. Regaining my breath, I hear Lesley Reddon, our assistant team manager, tell us we came in fourth place.

Caro, Sos, and I celebrate the accomplishment. Nine teams comprised of some of the top athletes in this country, and we are fourth. As we make our way to build our campsite for the night, I say, "You know I hated you guys today, but without you, I'd never have gone that fast."

We set up our tent and head over to the team campfire. Hayley Wickenheiser and Gillian Ferrari have been clam digging down on the shore. Their cabin, along with Gillian Apps, came in first.

"They are so sandy," Gilly says as she plops a clam in her mouth out of the boiling pot.

Cheryl Pounder's eye is swollen to twice its normal size. "I swear this bee followed me for miles." Her hands gesture as if they are the bee. "I tried swatting it, but I kept swerving, and eventually it got inside my sunglasses and stung me right there." She points to her puffy eye.

Only Pounder.

The pain from the day is forgotten as we laugh and tease each other telling exaggerated tales from the trail ride around the fire.

We turn hot dogs into spider dogs and cook apples, bananas, and pineapples over the flames as the entire team gathers around the campfire.

As night falls, my legs sore and my energy depleted, I write some comments in the journal I've tucked in my backpack.

The following day, we make our way, once again, to the start line. "Today's ride will be an individual race. Seventy-five kilometres on the trails. No teams — just you and the gravel road," Jason announces.

I look around and catch Cherie Piper's eye. She pulls her bike closer to mine. I knowingly nod. Delaney scoots her bike closer; as do rookies Meghan Agosta, Katie Weatherston, and Ashley Riggs. I'm not sure this is what the coaches envisioned, but these next four hours are going to be tough, and I'd rather have help.

We start the race with adrenaline coursing through our veins, but that quickly dissipates. Great Big Sea and the Barenaked Ladies roll through their greatest hits on my iPod, as I take my turns at the front of the pack, excited when my turn to push is over. Boredom, exhaustion, and delirium consume me for the next few hours, and I rely on my teammates to keep me going. The final 20 minutes of our ride is the first time I contemplate our incredible accomplishment: three hundred and fifty kilometres on dirt trails over four days.

There's a mass of my teammates gathered around the finish line cheering our crew as we cross. Mel and her assistants, Margot Page and Tim Bothwell, hand each of us a red *Hockey Canada* emblazoned t-shirt, with *Made in PEI* crested on the back. Grateful but still on my bike, I need to use the t-shirt to wipe the perspiration from my forehead. As I dismount and walk alongside Piper back to the hotel, we hear unreal stories from our other teammates. Pounder suffered two flat tires and Cassie blew a tire mere kilometres from the finish line, stashed her bike in the trees, doubled on the back of Gillian Apps's bike, and then hitch-hiked in some random person's car back to the hotel.

The start of camp feels like forever ago, but nearing the finish signifies the beginnings of a new team.

JUNE 2005: TRIATHLON

Beyond exhausted, more than anything I want to go home. I miss Allen, I miss thinking for myself, and I miss not feeling constantly sore.

One more day of hard work. Our final battle of camp will be a triathlon race as a cabin. When the triathlon was announced, I was excited because finally we were doing some cardio that suited me. My competitive swimming experience from childhood is going to be my redeeming quality.

We've done some aqua aerobics here in Charlottetown and played fun games of water polo, and I'm amazed at how many of my teammates can barely swim.

Sos and Caro went back and forth last night trying to decide who would do the 30 kilometre bike ride and who would do the 10 kilometre run. Neither really wanted to run, but eventually Caro said she'd do the arduous leg of running.

I look out of place in my cap and goggles among the other swimmers as Mel blows a whistle to start the 1500-metre swim. Each swimmer has their own lane. Beside me is Gillian "Appsy" Apps. She is an enforcer on the ice, leading the team in penalty minutes; on the other hand, off the ice, she's extremely nice, gregarious and a joker. She's very intelligent and often serves as the glue between various groups on the team.

Appsy's cabin, with Wick and Gilly, is the pre-race favourite. All three are great at cardio. Beside Appsy is Jen who, like Apps, is also a strong swimmer. Next to them is Becky. Having given birth to her son less than a year ago, she is the first woman to come back after childbirth to make the National Team. Amazingly, last year, she played pregnant winning a National and World Championships. Her six-month old son, Owen, is staying with her here in PEI. A friend of Mel's takes care of Owen during the day. Not only does Becky have to do everything we do, she then must go home at the end of a long day and take care of her infant. I wish I could visit Becky and Owen more, wish I could be more a part of her life, but this camp is so exhausting, it's hard to be there for myself, let alone anyone else. Next to Becky is Kim and then Kelly Bechard. The three of them look to be decent swimmers.

Already 10 laps in, and I've managed to get an entire length on Appsy. Sos and Caro are at one end of the pool, urging me on. I haven't swum this far in a long time, maybe since I was 10, but the water still feels natural. I feel light and confident. I can see Jen and Becky as I turn my head to breathe. They still look strong, but they're losing ground to Appsy.

I find my rhythm. Only 10 laps to go, and I can see Appsy's six-foot frame, her arms splashing in front of me. This entire camp, I've never passed anyone. I wasn't a good enough runner, and I certainly wasn't good enough on the bike, but here, for the first time, I can sense it. Adrenaline surges, and I lap Appsy, racing right until the finish. Tired, I still fight for every stroke.

My technique, learned a long time ago in Mini-Marlins, is falling apart, but I fight to keep it together. "S stroke," my dad used to yell, meaning to move my hand in an S pattern under the water. I hear his voice. "Reach with your hand!" My arms reach despite their fatigue. I will my legs to stay on task. The final hundred metres I sprint, feeling like I'm 10 years old at the Pan Am Pool in Winnipeg. I touch the wall in just under 30 minutes to a resounding cheer from all my teammates and reach up to touch a smiling Sos.

"Awesome, Sami!" she yells, and takes off towards her bike. I want to leap high in the air like Olympic champion Mark Tewksbury, but I am too tired.

I gather enough strength to pull myself out of the pool. Appsy is still swimming. Everyone is still swimming as I fetch my towel. I'm done, both physically and mentally.

A few minutes later, Appsy touches the wall to send Wick off on her pursuit of Sos on the bike course. Jen finishes shortly after with Becky, Kim, and Kelly not far behind. I congratulate them all as they slide their bodies out of the pool.

There are three groups still in the water who weren't lucky enough to have a competent swimmer in their cabin. I walk over to the final three lanes where everyone has gathered. Carla MacLeod, the only rookie on last year's World Championship team, still has 10 laps to go, but at least she looks like she can swim, albeit in a rudimentary style. Next to her, Charlie is only half done. She seems to be willing her body to learn to swim as she thrashes down the lane, fatigued. Last, Piper floats on her back, kicking, pulling with one arm. Two shoulder dislocations; this just looks painful. She still has 20 laps to go.

Finally, Carla finishes and tags Goyette, sending her out on the course in seventh place. At this point Mel suggests to the other two swimmers that they have suffered enough and can be done too. She sends their cabins' cyclists off and counsels the girls to get out of the water. It's been an hour of near drowning.

Along with Jen, we make our way to the cycling–running exchange outside the front doors of the UPEI recreation centre.

Wick first appears on the path — she's made up ground and has passed Sos on the course. But Wick has always been a strong cyclist. She crosses the line and tags Gilly who begins her run. A few minutes later, Sos appears in the parking lot, frazzled, and spent.

I give one last pat on the shoulder to Caro and tell her, "It'll all be over soon — you've already done us proud just by agreeing to run." Sos tags her and she takes off on her long, lanky legs.

As I grab Sos's bike, she reaches her arms in the air and yells, "I'm friggin' done!"

Pounder has made up ground on the bike for her team and is now in third place. She arrives tagging her cabin mate Gina Kingsbury.

Fifteen minutes pass. Bikes are loaded onto trucks and word comes from downstairs that Charlie and Piper are finally finished the swim.

"They kept swimming?" I look quizzically at Jen. It's been nearly two hours, and I'm dumbfounded and impressed that they finished.

Next down the driveway is Goyette. She's Carla's teammate. She went from seventh to fourth. Either she's really fast or something is wrong.

"There's been an accident!" she's screaming as she approaches. She grinds her bike to a halt and tags rookie Ashley Riggs, whose blond ponytail swings as she bounds away down the trail.

"C'est Pounder, elle a eu un accident!" Goyette yells. All eyes turn to Pounder standing beside me on the pavement.

Confused, Goyette restarts, "I mean . . . I guess someone's down on the road. At the intersection downtown. Vicky's with her. I don't know who it is. The ambulance is there, and there's blood everywhere."

Horrified, Jen runs to get Mel inside with the swimmers. Mel confers with the medical staff members who quickly hop in a van to the local hospital.

What happened and who actually fell?

Five of nine teams have finished the bike leg.

Cassie appears on her bike in the distance. With a full head of steam she comes barrelling towards us at the finish line. She's pedalling hard and clearly frantic. Tessa Bonhomme is waiting for her tag to start her run.

Cassie's not slowing down. Tessa steps to the side, reaches out to tag her, and takes off running. Cassie's going too fast and can't get her outstretched hand back on the handlebars in time. The curb is too close. She pulls on her brakes, but her tires can't hold, and she crashes to the pavement. She and her bike skid across 10 metres of raw pavement and come to a halt.

Goyette and I rush to her.

"Bredo is hurt!" Cassie screams through frantic sobs, referring to Correne Bredin.

The right side of Cassie's leg has exposed flesh.

"Someone get to the hospital!" Cassie is panicked.

"Cass, someone's already gone. She'll be all right," says Goyette as I try to dislodge Cassie from her bike. On her leg there's a patch the size of a watermelon, oozing.

"I'm fine, I'm fine," she says, trying to push us away. "It's Bredo — she's in a ditch."

Suddenly Bredin's six foot frame rounds the corner. We are confused.

Bredo's handlebars are twisted and her brake pads are noticeably grinding her wheel. Mud covers her sweaty face. Bredin normally has such an easy going, pleasant demeanor. Smart, funny, and nerdy, she's often making jokes at her own expense. A graduate of Dartmouth College, she'll likely go on to become a PhD but right now she looks frazzled. All medical efforts turn to Bredo as she tags Sarah Vaillancourt. From Sherbrook, Quebec, Sarah recently finished her freshman year at Harvard. She's an exceptionally skilled forward with phenomenal stick handling ability. Sarah's maybe the fastest runner on the team, and she'll surely make up ground. Seven teams have now finished biking.

We look around. There's still no Vicky (Charlie's team, seventh out of the water) and still no Katie Weatherston (Becky's team, fourth out of the water). *I hope Katie's okay.*

Meghan Agosta and Dana Antal, the last runners waiting, are urged to start running. This triathlon is turning into a disaster.

"Bredo and I clipped tires about five kilometres back, and she ended up in a ditch. I said I'd come and get help," explains a pale-looking Cassie as we walk Bredin inside and downstairs to the dressing room.

"Sit down, Cass," Kelly says. She unwillingly obliges. We leave Bredin, who has some bumps and scrapes but nothing major, and tend to Cassie. Goyette holds her hand as Mel takes her heart rate. Jen comes back into the dressing room with the arena's medical supplies.

Cassie's heart rate is low and faint, and she's getting paler. Mel is clearly concerned. Appsy rushes to get blankets, and I try my best to pick the gravel out of her hip.

"We need to get Cass to the hospital," Mel leans over and gently whispers to me. Trying to quickly finish my fix-it job, I cover her wound with a gauze pad. Cassie is barely aware as Goyette escorts her upstairs to a waiting minivan to take her to the hospital.

We all follow, knowing the runners should be back soon. Too much time passes. We stare off into the horizon, willing our teammates to be done and for this ordeal to be over.

"I'm going to see what's wrong." Wick grabs her bike and takes off down the path. Ten minutes later, she reappears with her teammate Gilly beside her. We cheer as Gilly crosses the line. A few minutes later, Gina comes running down the path in second place and only seconds later Caro, representing cabin 21, appears through the bush.

I put my arm around Sos, and we proudly scream for Caro, arms held high in the air. Caro looks fatigued. She leans across the line and comes to a staggering halt. We rush over and embrace her.

"That was not ten kilometres . . . I think more like thirteen," Caro says, panting. A month ago, I didn't really know these two girls, but now they've helped me through the hardest month of my life.

After a much-earned shower, we all make our way to supper at a local restaurant. Cassie is back from the hospital, still in her shorts, still pale, one full IV drip in her arm, her leg bandaged. Bredo has gashes on her face. Pounder's eyes are still puffy from being stung by a bee.

Katie Weatherston is also here. She looks horrendous, but she's okay. She landed on her head going through an intersection in downtown Charlottetown. Luckily she was wearing a helmet because she has road rash across one side of her face, stitches, two fat lips, a gash on her chin, and three broken teeth.

Thirty-one days done. We are a broken bunch, but we made it through the month. Exhaustion doesn't mean the same thing to me anymore. I now know I can keep going when every last cell in my body wants me to quit. I know that my teammates need me as much as I need them. We are on this journey as a team, and ultimately, we are stronger together.

25

Support Network

JULY 2005: SACRIFICING FOR A DREAM

Back from captain Cassie Campbell's beautiful wedding in Calgary, I'm trying to tie up loose ends in the GTA, knowing I won't be home again for eight months. I've written post-dated rent cheques, took my car in for maintenance, and am trying to spend lots of time with Allen. We start centralized training in three weeks, on August 1 in Calgary.

Feeling guilty about leaving Allen, it's been tough to communicate lately, and I'm not sure he fully understands. How could he. He experienced first-hand my devastation of not playing the final in Halifax, of being the third goalie at last year's Worlds, and I called nearly every day from PEI, complaining about how hard the training was.

He's trying his best to be supportive, but I know it's not easy on him. Being the partner of a backup goalie is unquestionably difficult. We just moved in together last summer, and now I'm leaving for the year.

I'm going over some medical forms for Hockey Canada when I hear the front door open.

"Hieeeee," I say enthusiastically, in a loud voice for Allen to hear.

"Hi." I can tell by his voice that it's been a long day at work. All I want to do is run and give him a giant hug, but I don't. I go back to my notes and continue filling in the forms, giving him the space he needs.

Our lives are very different. He's off to work early, sits in front of a computer all day, and returns home miserable. I work out, hang out with friends, and play hockey. I know this isn't fair, but I want him to be excited when he comes in the door. After a few minutes of hearing him putter around in the kitchen, I say in my most compassionate voice, "There's dinner in the fridge, if you want it."

Allen emerges from the kitchen, a beer in hand, and plops himself down on the other side of our L-shaped couch.

"How was your day?" I say, knowing it's probably too soon to ask.

"Fine." He reaches for the remote.

"Hey, you should just move to Calgary with me. Screw your job, you can get one there," I say, as charming as possible.

He glares over at me and after a long pause says, "You know I can't do that."

I do know that; he has a secure job and benefits here. I'm being selfish.

The next three weeks become more and more difficult. As the first day of centralization draws near, packing becomes more depressing. I say goodbye to our house and Allen and I gather my life into the Blue Bomber and drive 23 hours to Winnipeg. The conversation is light, but there's a constant tension in the car. Distance is already starting to separate our dreams.

In Winnipeg, Allen gets on a plane back to Toronto, and after running my hockey school, I continue the drive to Calgary alone.

As the skyline of Calgary looms large in the distance, I'm excited to show the coaches where I am both physically and mentally, but part of me wishes I'd never left Allen behind.

Jen found us a nice little place to rent right near the rink. I miss my home already, but I know I chose this dream. Of all the people rooting for me, I just wish Allen was here to hold my hand.

SEPTEMBER 2005: A NEW FAMILY MEMBER

I'm sitting in my hotel room in the town of Hämeenlinna, Finland, just north of Helsinki, for the 2005 4 Nations Cup Championship. We're staying at what we've dubbed the "Tuberculosis Inn" — a former Tuberculosis sanatorium.

"It's a girl!" my brother shouts into the phone. I can hear his wife Gina in the background as a tear slowly forms in the corner of my eye.

"It's a girl!" I shout back, waving my hand in the air trying to get Kim's attention. I'm on my hotel bed, and she has her headset on and is sitting at the desk.

"Felicitations, Luke!" Kim calls out towards the phone with genuine enthusiasm.

Mel told me last week this was going to be my tournament. She was putting the pressure square on my shoulders to perform. No matter what, I knew going in that I was going to get to play the USA twice during the week. A sizable responsibility made even more significant by the fact that the coaches were leaving five of our veteran players at home, including our captain Cassie Campbell, our assistant captain Vicky Sunohara, and our oldest player and brilliant playmaker Danielle Goyette.

"We named her Annika," my brother quietly says.

"Like the golfer?"

"No, like in *Pippi Longstocking*. Annika is Pippi's best friend."

I want to hold Annika, and be there with my brother.

"How's Gina?" I inquire.

"She's a star." I can hear his voice quivering, and I picture him looking at his wife and his firstborn.

A few seconds of silence.

"You got a shutout?" he says. Suddenly I'm snapped back to reality. I can hear the excitement in his voice.

"Yeah, it was a good game," I say, still thinking of Annika. In our new black helmets to match this year's uniforms, we beat the Americans for the first time since our World Championship loss in Linköping, Sweden, last year. It was a round robin game, but still a critical win. It was my first game against the USA in nearly two years, and not only did I want to prove something to the coaching staff, I wanted to prove something to myself. I was nervous and anxious, but I embraced the feeling of a big game and used that excitement to my advantage.

"I suppose the shutout was for Annika." I smile to myself. "They are not the same team without Granato, but I still had to make some key saves."

The Americans just released Cammi Granato from their Olympic team. It was a very strange cut by coach Ben Smith. Granato had been the face of USA hockey since 1990 and their team captain since I've been around. She's always a threat on the ice. When I think of the Americans, I can still see Granato setting up down low on the power play, waiting to snipe the puck past me.

"Do you think you'll get the final?"

"Yeah, they already told me I would."

"Sami, she's amazing." I can hear the pride in my brother's voice.

I finish the call with Luke, beaming, wondering what Annika looks like and when I'll get to meet her.

·······

Two days later, we take on the Americans for the 4 Nations Cup Championship.

This one's for Annika, I tell myself. The game is exciting, both teams have plenty of chances, but we pull out a victory thanks to a goal by Dana Antal late in the third period to win 2–1.

Despite it being late, I call Allen to share the good news.

I am elated about the win, and even though the Olympics are still five months away, I'm playing the best hockey of my career, and this tournament could not have gone better.

SEPTEMBER 2005: COACH'S REPORT

As I wait for my meeting with Mel, I'm nervous. *Are these cuts?* My stomach churns with dread.

The door clicks, and Kelly Bechard emerges from her meeting with Mel. The entire team has one today. Kelly looks sullen, her face red, wearing a fake smile as she rushes past. I take a deep breath and feel like a schoolgirl walking into the principal's office.

Following Mel, I see assistant coaches, Tim Bothwell and Margot Page, analyzing video from last practice with mentor coach Wally Kozak. Margot was on the National Team in '90, '92, and '94. She's been coaching the U-22 team and is the head coach at Niagara University. Tim was a defenceman in the NHL with the Rangers, Blues, and Whalers over a 10 year career, and has been coaching the Calgary Oval X-Treme team for the past two seasons.

"Hi Wally," I say a little over exuberantly. It's nice to see a friendly face. He's also the head scout for Hockey Canada, coordinating with regional scouts across the country. He scouts girls from young ages and tracks their development. Now with a scouting network from coast to coast, there will likely never again be a story like mine, going from unknown to the National Team.

Mel seats herself behind a desk that nearly fills the room. The lighting is dim. I take a seat in one of the two chairs that face her. Pictures of Mel's other world line the wall to my left — pictures of her with her friends and family, as a real human being.

These meetings seem to be taking a toll on Mel. She looks tired.

Fidgeting, I wait for the opening of the meeting, loathing the silence. It's been three weeks since the victories at the 4 Nations Cup in Finland and practices have been going favourably. I feel confident but my palms sweat.

Mel looks down at her notes as I try not to let my heart rate control my thoughts. *Answer smartly and stay positive.* Mel flips the page in her notebook to reveal a brand new page. I see her scribble *Sami Jo Small* at the top.

"So, what's up?" she asks.

I urge myself to think of something intelligent. *What does she mean? Does she mean hockey-wise or life?* "Ummm . . ."

And suddenly, I blurt out, "I like having Denis around. He's great, and I'm learning new techniques."

Denis Sproxton comes to us from the WHL's Medicine Hat Tigers. It's gratifying to have a goalie consistently around when Dave Jamieson can't be here because of his teaching commitments back home. I took a lot out on Dave after Salt Lake, blaming him for the decision not to play me. He's an extraordinary person and suffered my wrath for too long. I struggled to find trust again, despite him being only the messenger. It took me a couple years, but Dave persisted and I think we're back to where we once were.

I've had some heart-to-hearts with Denis, and he's helped me mentally as well as physically. He's honest with me.

"Sami, you have to *look* like you're trying as much as you are. Goaltending is as much about convincing your own coaches as it is about stopping the puck."

I don't tell Mel any of this insider information.

Mel stares back at me. Is she smiling or frowning? I can't ever tell.

I hold my ground.

"You played very well in Finland," she says without feeling. "I didn't expect that."

My genuine smile quickly turns forced.

"But just so you know, I'm nervous when I watch you play," she says with a sheepish grin, as if she's confiding the secrets of a conspiracy to me.

How do I answer that? I try not to take offence at the slight.

"You don't look good making a save, but you make it," she says as if we are buddies, like long-lost friends ribbing each other. "Your rebound control has been above par, for you, and I guess I just have to develop confidence in what I see."

A compliment or a dig? I'm not sure. My style is one of calmness and conservation of movement, but clearly, I have to change something.

My heart races and my face gets hot. This woman holds the keys to my dream, and I'm not sure I've made any headway with her. Her face is showing me confidence, but her words hurt. I think this is good. I think she's giving me a positive message, but I'm not sure.

"Let's see in the Midget boys tournament," she says, giving me the ultimatum. "Each goalie will get one game, and the best performance will get the final. We need the goalies to steal a game. It's up to you to show me."

SEPTEMBER 2005: MIDGET BOYS TOURNAMENT

The Midget boys are stronger than us, they shoot harder and skate faster than we do, but our team combats this with smarts. The boys are asked not to hit, but that doesn't mean we aren't physical with them. It can be a difficult situation for the boys, but unlike in 2002 when we made our first foray into the Midget AAA league in Alberta, women's hockey is now more mainstream.

Most of the boys have seen other girls play; maybe they have sisters, classmates, or moms who play. The boys are generally respectful and quite proud to be part of our journey. They play tough because their friends and girlfriends are in the crowd. They often show off and the last thing a 17-year-old boy wants to do is be embarrassed in front of his friends. Some of these boys will likely go on to become NHL players, but right now they're just adolescents.

I want to show Mel I can do this. I love the challenge of a big game, all the pressure square on my shoulders.

My game today is our team's third, and it's against the Calgary Royals. Our first two games were tight, but we lost both. Today is our third game in less than 36 hours, and my teammates are understandably exhausted.

I know they will need a huge performance. I think of my brother and his new baby girl, Annika. I think of the sacrifices Allen has made, the sacrifices everyone in my life has made, and I try to harness all that positivity.

Denis has taught me to break games into five-minute segments, playing each like a full game and then move on to the next segment. This tactic helps me stay in the moment and play each section like everything is on the line. Today I know my Olympic dream is on the line.

"Great one," Delaney screams as I snag the puck. She's one of my most intense cheerleaders on the ice, and today she has been diving in front of everything. Pucks just bounce my way. We are being badly outshot, and my team is playing on fumes, but I'm there for them. Finally, all my training and work comes to a crescendo. I continue to sprawl to make saves. At the final buzzer, I've faced 51 shots, stopping 50 of them and helping our team claw out a 1–1 tie.

In the dressing room after the game, I'm exhausted, but thrilled.

"Sami, you were so great today," says Jen as we drag ourselves out of the rink at 11:30 p.m.

"Aw, thanks — you guys must be exhausted," I say back. Mel spots us and stops me.

Very stoically, she says, "Sami, it's your start tomorrow — you've earned it," and keeps walking.

•••••••

I awake to my alarm blaring at 6:00 a.m. I'm sore, my hip aches — stopping 50 shots took a lot out of me. I didn't get to sleep until 2:00 a.m., I'm deeply fatigued, and I'm fighting for my existence. I feel like throwing up, like I have the flu, I woke up with my period, and I don't want to move; my eyes are crusted shut. I reach over and press snooze.

The alarm goes off again. Realizing I must be at the rink in an hour, I squirm out of bed.

Today's my game because Mel said *I deserve it*. I'm tired and my body's sore, but I need to prove she made the right decision. Jen's already upstairs ready to go as I emerge from the basement. Her meeting with Mel didn't go as well as mine. Mel told her she was on the bubble. *Is Mel on something?* Jen is one of the best players on this team.

I didn't know how Jen would handle the setback. Initially she was sad, distraught, but she has rebounded to be one of our top players on the ice against the boys. She's proving she not only deserves to be on this team but is one of the most gifted players in the world.

Once at the rink, I prepare in the same way I always do: warm-up, dynamic exercises, stretch. I get a quick massage from our therapist, Mavis Wahl, to loosen up my hips. We're playing against the same team as last night, the Royals, and I feel confident.

I try to do everything the same. I do a mental dance convincing myself to shake off the fatigue. I use adrenaline to mimic fresh legs. I play hard, challenge the shooter, play the puck with smart decisions, yet the puck seems to be nowhere near me. Last night it seemed to bounce my way, screened shots hit my pads, and I corralled rebounds with ease.

Now the puck has eyes of its own, finding its way off shin pads, through screens, and from out of mid-air into the back of the net. Today my team needs me to make huge saves, and my performance is just average.

No matter how hard I try, nothing seems to work. I rebound after each goal, mentally parking it just like our sports psychologist, Dr. Peter Jensen, taught me. I try to stay positive and focus my attention on the next puck. The boys are everywhere. They have open players on the back door. Our players are tired. They have players swarming the front of the net, and no matter what we do, we just can't clear the puck out. Puck after puck finds the mesh.

Thirty-five shots and four goals, and the game is only half done. I see the coach's hand go up, and I know what that means.

I'm being pulled. Humiliated, I find my way to the end of the bench. I try to smile as the girls tap me on the pads, saying sorry. I know they're sorry, I know they wanted to give more, but like me, they're tired. I sit quietly at the end of the bench, willing the game to end.

Hubris is a word I remember learning from Mme. Plamondon in grade 12 English class: "overbearing pride or presumption, esteeming oneself as equal or greater than the gods." I didn't think much about it then; however, I think it very appropriate for this situation. I may have soared too high, been a little too assured of my abilities as a goaltender, and my pride caught up with me.

We lose 6–1, despite Kim's best effort to salvage the game. I wasn't as good as I should have been. There was nothing left to give.

26

The Final Push

The first release came like a bombshell yesterday when they cut Ashley "Riggsy" Riggs. I heard while out for a bite to eat with Dermot and his fiancée, Kim, who had stopped in Calgary on a drive to Banff. Jen and I went to the pub down the road from the rink to commiserate with her and her roommate, Tessa Bonhomme. Riggsy and Tessa are both young and incredibly gifted. Riggsy can dangle around anyone, constantly seeming as though she's been pushed off the puck, only to emerge on the other side in full control. Tessa, a defenceman, captained the recent U-22 team. She can quarter back a powerplay, start a breakout, or join the rush. Both are great additions to the team providing some levity and some fun in an otherwise stressful year. Normally the life of the party, they wore sunglasses, clearly having been through an emotional night. It was tough.

The following day, we board a plane first to Sweden for an exhibition series against the Swedes and then en route to Torino for a pre-Olympic test tournament.

Inside the Palasport Olimpico in Torino, we see the seats are still not in place and the stands look barren, but I try to imagine them full. I try to visualize the Olympic final. Visualization has been a big part of my training this year, thanks to our sports psychologist, Peter Jensen. There are workers everywhere, frantically trying to finish the venue. The workers puff away on cigarettes and their smoke fills the venue. Dust fills the hallways as they scramble to put up drywall.

"Jen, can you take a picture of me?" I ask standing near the glass with the rink in the background.

Jen dutifully grabs my camera and snaps some pictures. She's not really one for taking photos, but I always make sure to make copies of mine for her.

"Now us together," I say, motioning Jen to come down. She hands the camera off to Carla MacLeod.

Jen puts her arm around me and leans in, flashing her smile. I gesture to Delaney Collins, Meghan Agosta, and Cherie Piper. "Come in, guys."

The five of us pose for the camera.

An eclectic crew, our group has become quite close this year. Piper is the friend you want with you in a back alley. She's outgoing, street smart, tough, and quick witted. She tends to snap quickly, but loyalty runs through her veins. She loves the pub and the casino and is always up for doing stuff. She sleeps about four hours a night, on a good night, and if I hosted a party she'd be the first to arrive and help set up and the last one to leave, generally, the next morning after cooking breakfast for everyone in the house.

Jen is more cautious, very structured, and rarely goes out. She grosses out easily, rarely gambles, and seldom drinks. She's the last to arrive at a party and often the first to leave, but she'll have brought the nicest hostess gift and chatted with everyone in the room. She's kind, humble, and sympathetic. In every conversation she makes you feel like you're the only one in the room. She rarely says a bad word about anyone, and she hates offending people.

Delaney, a.k.a. "DC," is reserved and tough to get to know. She has a supreme inner confidence that has served her well through numerous setbacks. She's been left off more teams than any of us and had more injuries to deal with than the rest of us combined. She's a battler and gets her back up quickly; she's feisty, and like Piper, she's loyal to those who are loyal to her. She'll do anything for her friends but is sharp-tongued to anyone who crosses her. She went to Concordia and then most recently has been at the University of Alberta. At both schools she was instrumental in winning National Championships.

Meghan, "Megs" or "Gus," is the most different to the rest of us. She's young, just 18, and recently finished high school but Piper has taken her under her wing, and she's been a pleasant addition to the group. She is extremely considerate and respectful. She's rumoured amongst her younger club teammates to be cocky and brash, but with us, she's anything but. Completely honest, she'll tell you if she was the best player on the ice or not, but not in an arrogant way. The rest of us graduated from some of the top schools in North America, but Megs is still a high schooler. Most conversations go right over her head, but she contributes nonetheless with her own comments in a very endearing way and seems okay when we give her hints of guidance. She's like our project, our mascot, our child we protect and teach to send on to greatness.

After taking photos, the entire team enters our dressing room for the first time at the Torino ice rink, and Robin McDonald, our equipment manager, has it prepared in perfect order. My practice jersey hangs in front of my stall next to Goyette's.

I dress slowly, imagining what this will be like when it's a real Olympic game.

1985: PREPARATION — CHOOSING EQUIPMENT

I am nine years old and I am trying on goalie equipment for the first time, in the main foyer of my local community centre. Every year, Norberry Community Centre goes through the ritual of loaning out goalie equipment to its club's goalies, and this year I've finally convinced my parents to let me play in net.

There's equipment everywhere in all shapes and sizes. *What should I start with?* I see an opening by the upper-body equipment and pull my dad in that direction. I slip a pair of monkey-arms protectors over my head and stretch my upper limbs through the felt cylinders until my fingers poke out the ends. I grab a chest protector — like the kind a catcher in baseball would wear — and buckle it in place. I wiggle my arms. The two pieces seem to fit perfectly together.

My dad checks the length of the arms and makes sure there's enough room to fit on my glove and blocker. He's already been through this with my brother three years ago, and what seemed so foreign to him then is now a habit. I feel invincible, felt and plastic protecting me from the hard rubber pucks that will be my adversaries this coming season. My brother didn't last as a goalie, but I know I will. Watching him play, I knew this was going to be my destiny. He used to get angry when opponents would score on him, but I like the challenge. I have wanted to do this since I saw my first goalie on TV.

Sizing up a pair of pads I see an old, brown pair filled with horsehair. They are ugly and I want something cooler. Every other goalie in the room does too. I jostle for position, trying to see the best gear and position myself to try it on. I'm the only girl in the room, but in full gear, no one notices. I want to look just like the goalies I watch on *Hockey Night in Canada* who have cool pads with modern curves on them.

I'm new to these try-on sessions and I keep missing the best gear. Boys take stuff right out of my arms. With all the good pads taken, I see one last remaining pair. They are straight, brown, and as heavy as the rest of my gear combined.

I look up at my dad with a sad, sullen face.

"Try them on," he says encouragingly. *I don't want them.*

I lay them flat on the floor side by side and lay down flat, stomach on the floor, knees perfectly positioned on top of the pads. My dad begins to tie the buckles. I look around and watch what some of the older goalies do. I scan the room, taking in the aura of goaltending. I can feel the pads slowly becoming part of my body.

As my dad tightens the final buckle, he prompts me to stand up. I push my arm out, raise up my chest. With all my might, I lift my first leg and clumsily stand.

What looked brown and dull are now fortresses on my legs. My pads are perfect.

This is what I've always imagined being a real goalie would feel like.

NOVEMBER 2005: PRE-OLYMPIC TOURNAMENT (CONTINUED)

My first game, and our team's second of this Torino pre-Olympic tournament, is against Finland. Despite this being Kim's tournament, similar to the 4 Nations being mine, I still get one game to feel what it's like to play on the Olympic ice surface. I have one game to formulate my images for future visualizaion sessions.

As I walk down the tunnel into the rink prior to opening faceoff, I can feel the excitement both internally and from the crowd. Kim walks behind me, and Becky Kellar behind her. Kellar has been a constant in my career and her presence is calming. As I step on the ice, the crowd, packed with school children, waves flags and screams.

The Finns come out flying. They're a small quick team. They don't have the stars the Swedes have, but they definitely have more depth. Their goaltending is solid. Maija Hassinen is a short little goalie made up of all pads and seems to be everywhere. They give us a good game, but we execute our plan and come out with the win, 3–1.

Our tournament will finish with two games against the Americans.

We play the first game at what will be the second Olympic rink and site of our round robin games come February. The arena is once again packed to capacity with yelling schoolchildren.

Kim is in net and I back her up. As the game begins, the crowd erupts. I swing around to see the commotion, and our team is already on their feet with joy.

Robin and I look at each other first with bewilderment and then excitement. I think we scored, and I haven't even sat down yet.

"Did you see it?" I shout over the roar.

Wick's the first to the bench for high-fives, so she must have put it in. As the procession passes by, I hold my glove up high to share in the excitement.

The game continues, and the Americans don't look themselves. Their goaltender, Pam Dreyer, is struggling, and despite some of their chances sailing off the crossbar during their power play, they just don't look like a cohesive unit. We celebrate twice more, and the first period ends with us already leading 3–0. The Americans look stunned.

We score a couple more times and eventually win 5–0, as much to our surprise as theirs.

The next day, we have a day off and our team has organized an outing to a Juventus soccer match — Torino's local team. Our three Italian Canadian teammates, Katie Weatherston, Gillian Ferrari, and Meghan Agosta, try to help us understand the cheers and chants from the stands. We scream and join in the fun, even though we have no idea what we're saying.

Because we have the evening to ourselves I walk down to Piper and Megs's room and knock on the door. Megs answers, greeting me with hairdryer in hand and a big smile.

"Sami! C'mon in."

Piper already has her laptop open on a makeshift stand between the two beds.

I get myself comfortable on Megs's bed, as Piper resumes play on the TV series *24*, starring Kiefer Sutherland as Jack Bauer. Piper and I watch captivated as Megs blow-dries her hair in the bathroom.

"Sami, why don't you get to play tomorrow? You should be playing," shouts Megs.

"Megs, it's not my turn."

"That's stupid."

"Yeah, I know," I say without taking my eyes off the screen as a commercial break begins.

"Megs, why are you doing your hair?" Piper asks, looking at me, rolling her eyes.

"I don't know. I hate going to bed with it curly and I want to look good for the game."

Piper returns her gaze to the screen.

·······

I watch the Torino Ice Tournament Final from the stands with the five other scratches for the night. We find seats in the top row of this 7,000-seat arena and nervously talk about the potential outcome. We're coming up on the final stretch of our preparations for the Olympics in February, and each of us wants to make the team too.

We want the American team to give us an exciting game, but as it starts, they look depleted. They really appear to be missing their captain Cammi Granato. No American seems to step up to take her place. We are up 5–0 after the first period. They pull goalie Shari Vogt in favour of Pam Dreyer. Shocked, the six of us alternates chat in disbelief about the lacklustre Americans.

We win 7–0. Kim impressively gets two shutouts in a row against Team USA. The Americans look frustrated and discouraged. They are a much better team than this, and despite what the score indicates, they are still the team that beat us at last year's World Championship, still our fiercest rivals.

DECEMBER 2005: LAST GAME

"Sami, I'm very impressed. Your movement is really coming along. You're looking the part," says goalie coach Dave Jamieson during his week back. I try to gather as much intel as I can from him before his departure.

I hope it's enough. I have one more boys' AAA game to put it all together before Christmas. Last Olympic cycle, the final cuts were made late November so we assume they must be looming. We squish team activities in, but everyone's on eggshells. I'm constantly anxious. Fatigue and pressure are getting to all of us.

I have one more shot to prove I can be the number one, one more game to show the coaches my hard work. Dave emphasizes movement, while Denis, our other goalie coach, emphasizes focusing on the small details. Always be ready and track the puck. Stick to the game plan and try to conserve energy.

I want to leave everything on the ice. Today's game is against the Midget AAA Calgary Flames. We've already lost a 5–3 tilt against them earlier in the season, but I have never played them. I love important games.

The game starts, and I tune the rest of the world out. I am back to my old style of playing calm and conserving energy. I forget about angles, movement, details, cuts, pressure, and anxiety and *just play*.

Our team is struggling, but I'm not. I am making the difference. I stop nearly everything, and despite being outshot 36–16, we come away with a 2–2 tie.

This is exactly how I wanted to play. Everything went right when it mattered most.

This is the last time the remaining 26 of us will be together. The team is being named in two days, and all we can do is nervously wait.

27

Final Team Selection

DECEMBER 2005: COACHES' MEETING

It's incredibly bright as I drive my usual route to the rink through the streets of Calgary. Despite sunglasses, I need to pull the visor down. It's late December and snow lines the streets. My muscles are sore from yesterday's workout.

Lost in thought, I habitually turn my blue Mazda 323 into the parking lot of the Father David Bauer Arena.

Trying to make today's drive feel normal is difficult because it's the day of the final cuts. The day we find out if we are going to the Olympics. Each player has a 10-minute time slot with the three members of the coaching staff. Early, I sit in my car for a couple of minutes. I want to text Jen and ask her how her meeting went, but I'm too nervous. I keep checking my watch.

Finally, it's time.

As I walk up the stairs and through the red door into the arena, assistant coach Margot Page holds the door open. Making small talk about my drive to the rink, she is smiling, nodding, but half in a daze, likely still thinking about her last meeting. She leads me past the dressing room, up the stairs, and into a small meeting room. I'm instantly anxious.

Head coach Mel Davidson and assistant Tim Bothwell sit in chairs facing a vacant chair. Margot takes her seat and I head towards the empty one. No one looks me in the face, their gaze instead down at papers on their laps. Their faces are red, their eyes puffy. I'm sure today has been a long day for them. I'm sure some meetings have been great and some agonizing.

"Sit down." Mel gestures.

My heart races. I can feel my face redden. *Stay calm.*

The silence is ominous. My stomach is turning, and the world slows down. I notice stuff I shouldn't notice. The feeling of the maroon polyester chair on my back, the stain on the wall. Like a soldier's mother about to receive news of her child's death, deep down I know something bad is about to happen.

Mel starts, her voice cracking, "Despite some great performances this year . . ."

My brain buzzes.

Despite . . . ? What, don't say despite, *that's not a good way to start.* I don't want to know where this is going.

I want to storm out of the room, get in my car, drive home back to my bed, and start the day over again.

Mel continues, ". . . we've decided that we're going keep Charlie and Kim as the goaltenders going into the Olympics."

Am I hearing this right? Where is my name? A huge weight lands on my chest.

I am fighting back tears.

Mel's lips are still moving. There's noise in the room, but I can't hear what she is saying. She's still talking. I try to concentrate, but her voice sounds like Charlie Brown's teacher. I can feel all my body's blood in my face, beet-red and hot. My heart thumps so hard it's shaking my entire body.

Mel is still talking; I can see her lips moving, but I have no idea what she's saying. *This can't be happening.*

"So, we'll give you a couple of weeks to make your decision," she ends.

What am I supposed to decide? I have no idea what she just said. How much time went by? What is going on?

I stare.

Mel stares back at me, waiting for an answer.

I stare some more, hurt in my eyes.

Mel's head tilts, confused, she speaks slower. "We'll give you a couple of weeks to decide . . . ?"

Tim Bothwell sees my confusion and adds, "Whether you would consider being the third-string goalie."

Third goalie? Disbelief. I nod slowly, staring straight at Tim, finally having understood the question.

The third-string goalie must train every day knowing that she will not be considered "on the team." The third-string goalie in women's hockey does not receive a medal at the Olympic Games, even though in men's hockey they do.

That's right, in men's hockey they do.

Our official roster is still 20 at the Olympic Games, unlike the men's that is 23. This, despite me being player 21 in Nagano in '98, us having 22 at Worlds in Halifax in '03, and 23 on last year's World Championship squad in Sweden. The International Ice Hockey Federation has changed, but the International Olympic Committee has not.

No one moves. Can I get up and leave? I don't want to break down in front of these people. They don't deserve my grief.

Mel stands, looks towards the door and then back at me. Tim Bothwell scrambles to open the door. "So, I guess we'll give you a couple of weeks, and you can let us know your decision."

I want to scream *no way am I going to help you!* I want to scream *this was rigged right from the beginning!* But I don't. I know as soon as I open my mouth that tears will start to flow.

The news is crippling.

I won't get to play in Torino.

Can I even stand?

Margot walks towards me, her eyes red and welling up. She reaches out her hand.

I stand and reach mine out too, awkwardly shaking her hand. I quickly take it away, avoiding eye contact.

I walk past the coaches and out the door, trying to put one foot in front of the other. *Stand strong, don't let them see you waver. Concentrate.* I don't look back. It takes every single ounce of the good in me to not turn around and say something snide to Mel. Every cell in my brain wants to, but something deep down knows that how I react matters.

As I walk down the stairs, I can feel my contacts starting to swim in eyes. I walk past the championship team photos on the wall to my left. I am in nearly all of them. I glance at the pictures, but it makes me sadder. I will myself not to cry. *Left, right, left, right.*

The door shuts behind me, and I head down the stairs to my car. *What am I supposed do?*

In the driver's seat of the Blue Bomber, I turn the key in the ignition. I need to get out of this parking lot. I see Kelly Bechard pulling in. My lungs are heaving. I can feel blood in the back of my throat. I just need to get somewhere.

I am unravelling. Anger mixed with sadness swirls through my head. The world is falling in on me. *Just breathe, Sami, the world can still see you.* Grief fills every cell of my body. I'm on autopilot; I can barely see. Tears stream down my face. All the tears I held in inside are pushing to get out. I blink, trying to see through the tears. I'm driving, sobbing. *Where am I going?*

My world is that hockey team, my world is Team Canada, and now I'm no longer a part of *that* team. *Now what?* I keep driving.

I turn off my cell phone. Hours go by. I can't talk. I'm still driving. I'm still sobbing.

My dream is over.

Driving along the highway, I see a sign: *Welcome to Saskatchewan.* A whole province has gone by. It's still so bright. I am driving into the horizon with no plan.

My whole life, I've had a plan. I was going to be an Olympic hero. Now I suddenly have no plan. And I'm still driving.

DECEMBER 2005: HOLIDAY TURMOIL

Eventually, somewhere outside Moose Jaw, I turned my car around.

My flight to Toronto to see Allen left yesterday, but I didn't get on it. Lying in bed, I'm avoiding everyone. Jen had left on her flight home to Winnipeg by the time I got back from my drive. I've only called my brother. Through the tears, I told him to tell Mom and Dad. That was yesterday. I'm still in the same clothes.

The light on my cell phone blinks. Fifty-six missed calls. I know people are worried, but I just can't manage a response. I'm profoundly sad.

The dream I've had for so long is over. *How do people find strength in the face of such sadness?* I'm depressed. Back to sleep.

Two days later, on Christmas Eve, I'm finally on a plane back to Toronto. I wear sunglasses on the plane. I still haven't talked to anyone. Time passes in slow motion. Allen picks me up at the airport and asks if I want to grab a bite to eat. I just want to go home. This is the worst I've ever felt.

I stay in Toronto for only a few days, a mess the entire time. Then I get on a plane for Winnipeg where I'm supposed to meet my team for their game against USA on January 1.

I crawl into my childhood bed and turn on the heated blanket that I've had since I was a kid. I pull the covers up to my chin and let the darkness engulf me.

I don't have a reason to wake up anymore. Anguish consumes me. I lose myself in sudoku and sleep. There is no day and no night. One day turns into the next. It's Christmas, and I don't want to be around people.

My brother, Gina, and their new baby girl, Annika, are living in the basement. They've moved back to Winnipeg to take over my dad's optometry practice. Luke brings Annika upstairs to meet me, but she is foreign. I feel nothing. I'm numb. They leave, and I go back to sleep.

I can't process what my parents and my brother say to me, though I see them sitting at the edge of my bed. I can smell the cooking meals, hear my dad cracking jokes, and my brother asking me to go play on the outdoor rinks. Lying in my bed for days, I try to forget life. The only person I talk to is Delaney. Unfortunately, she was released on the same day I was along with other defencemen Tessa Bonhomme and Correne Bredin. Bredin, despite her abilities to play both forward and defence, has devastatingly been the last cut from two straight Olympic teams despite having made two World Championship rosters. Forwards Dana Antal and Kelly Bechard were cut as well. Delaney is the first alternate and will be staying on in Calgary. She understands my pain.

Curled up on our beige-brown speckled couch in the basement, I am 13 years old, trying unsuccessfully to fight back tears. The TV is loud, so no one upstairs can hear my agony. I was cut tonight from my hockey team. I know it's because I am a girl.

I was released from the only team I want to play on: the boys' AAA Bantam Winnipeg Warriors hockey team. They play in the top league in the province. The Warriors are boys from St. Vital, St. Boniface, Transcona, and the outskirts of the city. There are only six teams in the entire city. I was good enough to make our team last year, but the zones have been restructured, and now we have a new coach. I sob some more.

I'm angry, but mostly embarrassed because I wear my white AAA Warriors jacket every day to school — ashamed because I'm known as "that girl that plays hockey." How am I going to make it to the NHL if I can't even make my local AAA team?

Every eyelash I blow away, every candle I blow out, and every coin I toss in a fountain, I always have the same wish. *I'm going to be the first girl to play in the NHL.* This feels like such an injustice. I think I'm good enough to be there. I had a great tryout. I try to get it together, but I can't. I don't want my parents to hear. Thinking of my parents makes me sad. I wanted them to be proud of a daughter who played AAA.

Sitting in the back seat on the way home from the tryout, I knew my dad knew, but I couldn't speak. I hate to have people see me cry. I whimper some more, my eyes stinging.

Ringing in my head are the final words the coach said to me in our meeting after tryouts.

"It just wouldn't work on road trips having a girl on the team."

It just wouldn't work? What does that even mean? I wasn't allowed to play in the boys' baseball provincial championships with my team when I was 10, but I've never had this happen in hockey. If I'm good enough, I'm good enough. I stood up from the meeting with the coach, shook his hand, and wished the team well. I didn't let him see my sadness.

It just wouldn't work plays in my head. I continue to sob. *Why do I have to be the only girl?* My life is hockey. I feel like a failure, like a fraud. Everything I am is falling apart.

It's New Year's Day. I sit on a solitary lawn chair in the middle of my living room in Calgary. I rarely drink, but I have a Diet Coke and vodka to my right and my cell phone to my left. The only light comes from the television set. I'm wearing the same sweatpants I flew in yesterday.

In front of me, the TV plays a commercial before the opening faceoff of Team Canada versus Team USA in Winnipeg. It was supposed to be my game, my team. I flew back from Winnipeg yesterday even though the game is today. I just couldn't be there. I hated all the questions, all the excitement surrounding this big game. Team Canada's last against the Americans before the Olympics.

With anger in my heart, I watch the game. More than 14,000 people are jammed into the MTS Centre. It hurts so much to see my teammates on TV, I'm not sure I can see them every day in person. I'm not sure I can give the team what they need.

My phone rings again. I reach down to see who it is. I don't want to talk. I flip over the grey phone. It's my friend Dermot. I know he's at the game. I take a sip of my drink and answer.

"This arena is awesome; the place is jammed!" he yells above the noise of the crowd, trying to include me in the excitement.

"Oh, great," I say with a sarcastic tone. Dermot instantly changes his tactics.

"I'll cheer for Team USA! Screw them." I laugh that one of my best friends, dressed head to toe in red and white, would even contemplate cheering for the opposition.

I want my team not to be able to go on without me. I hate that I'm not needed, that I'm not deemed good enough to be there. Then I think of Jen playing at home and I want the game to go well for her.

"Let's just hope we win, but that Team USA scores lots of goals?" suggests Dermot, barely audible as the teams line up for the opening faceoff.

"Perfect." I hang up the phone with a mixture of guilt, sadness, and jealousy. I want to be where my teammates are. I take another drink and stare blankly at the TV screen.

Ruggiero goes top shelf on Charlie. 1–0 Team USA. I take a drink.

Wendell redirects a puck past Charlie. 2–0 Team USA. I take another drink.

Team Canada looks exhausted. Charlie's struggling. I feel a tinge of guilt feeling like I am contributing to their demise.

I *will* my teammates to make a comeback. Slowly, they do, but it's not enough. Team Canada loses 5–4.

Their faces show their pain.

Team Canada returns from Winnipeg the following day, including Jen. I know this is going to be hard. We had this dream together. She's been worried, she's reached out numerous times, but I've felt too embarrassed to reach back.

Jen walks in the house, tears in her eyes, and rushes towards me. She knows I hate hugs, but I concede and start crying at her tears. Her embrace seems to last forever. Eventually I pull away, not knowing what to say.

"Sorry I didn't answer the phone."

"Sami, don't be sorry. I was just worried. Everyone was worried. Everyone just wants to make sure you're okay. Are you coming to practice tomorrow?"

"I just . . . just don't know."

．．．．．．．

The next morning, I'm still sleeping when Jen knocks at my closed bedroom door.

"I'm leaving now for practice. I think you should come."

I reluctantly join her and my eyes well up as I slowly climb the stairs of the arena to the red dressing room door. Fifty-one more days. *I can do this.* I pretend to be normal, but I am not. I walk into the dressing room and see Delaney. Piper sits beside her. She catches my gaze, and they make their way to me. Piper and Megs give me a big hug. I hate this. I don't want hugs. Jen is still by my side.

Every moment, Jen, Piper, or Megs is beside me. They are taking turns with Delaney and me, shielding us from the pain, diverting our attention by telling stories or making us laugh. Somehow they know just how difficult the small tasks are.

I want to be anywhere but this dressing room.

Time moves in slow motion. I can tell the rest of my teammates feel awkward not knowing how to express their joy while seeing my pain. I get more hugs, more sympathetic head tilts, and courageous well wishes, but I just want to blend in.

JANUARY 2006: FINAL MONTHS BEFORE TORINO

The following day, I head to the rink again. I don't really know what else to do. I never formally stated that I'd be rejoining the team, but I assume the coaches know.

I figure that being here in Calgary with the team is better than moping on my couch back home in Toronto while Allen is at work. I don't know how to express myself. There is too much grief behind my words. I have a brand-new painted team Canada mask. One painted just for me, with my designs, my first one ever. Up until now they have all been stock helmets that I've used, often also used by other Team Canadas, whether U-22 women or World Junior men. Yet despite my sparkly new Olympic mask, I feel like an imposter. I don't know what to say to people's sympathies; the only place I feel normal is on the ice.

Every morning, I struggle to put my own feelings aside and be there for others. Our team is going through its final preparations for the Olympic Games, so every practice matters.

The hour-and-a-half practices we have every day are my sanctuary. No one asks questions, no one takes pity on me. I forget briefly about the truth.

I step off the ice surface after practice and reality hits. *I'm not going to get to play.* I suck back the emotion. How did Bredo and Benny do this last time? Even with my close friends, I try to put my emotions aside and listen to their struggles, however it is very taxing to stay positive and often difficult to stay in the moment.

Time helps me to feel somewhat normal again, but I still hurt. Slowly I start to find joy in others' successes. We have played six games against boys' Midget AAA teams since Christmas. It's never easy to watch, but I'm becoming more observant. I'm learning to analyze all the positions and try to give feedback to my teammates between periods. Delaney plays in most games, often filling in for an injured player.

My body is depleted; my emotional stores are empty. I call my parents and devastatingly tell them not to come to Torino. They are extremely hurt, but understand this is my choice and I must use my emotions for my team.

Some days I drive with Jen, and some days I need my space. Delaney and I have been spending a lot of time together, watching games and venting. Today, just two weeks before leaving for Torino, she found out she won't be travelling with the team. There's no space for her in the Village. She's heading home tomorrow and is understandably upset.

To manage this on my own, I'll need to find a way to embrace my role.

28

Accepting My Role

JANUARY 2006: PRE-OLYMPIC TRAINING CAMP

Team Canada lands in Frankfurt, Germany. We then board a flight to Torino, Italy, the site of the 2006 Olympic Games. However, this is not our destination, at least not yet; we still have a weeklong training camp to get us used to the time change and to make our final preparations prior to entering the Village. From Torino we get on a bus bound for Torre Pellice, a small town an hour north and our training ground for the next week.

My roommate for the camp is Cherie Piper. This is the first time this year we get to room together. Selfishly, this is great for me because around Piper I don't have to put on a mask, and it probably gives Jen a bit of a break to get herself ready.

We have a few sleepless nights trying to adjust to the time change, but we quickly settle into the routine of morning training, afternoon ice time, and Jack Bauer and the TV series *24* at night.

Torre Pellice, in the valley of Val Pellice, is perhaps the only town in Italy more interested in hockey than soccer. The town is at the base of the Alps, so the views are incredible. Storefronts are decorated with hockey memorabilia, and signs everywhere welcome Team Canada.

Our third day in Italy begins with an on-ice practice. After practice, I walk in the sunshine with Denis Sproxton, one of our goalie coaches, back to the hotel.

"Sami, you moved really well laterally at practice this morning," he says. I try to take the compliment, but reality always comes back to haunt me.

"Doesn't really mean much at this point, though, does it?"

"It should mean something."

"To whom?"

"To you."

"It only makes me more frustrated when I get off the ice."

"But you're making your teammates better. Looks bad on the other goalies if you're the best one on the ice. Makes them have to work harder."

"Yeah, I guess, but I'm tired of making others better."

"That's life. As much as this sucks, it's important. Your attitude is important. If ever you think no one else cares, know that I do, I'm watching, and I get it."

We continue the walk, talking about life after the Olympics, about life back home. I vent a lot, but he remains positive. I'm grateful he's here.

We have the rest of the day to ourselves, so Jen, Megs, Piper, and I decide to walk downtown for dinner. We spy a pizzeria, venture in, and are surprised to find several other teammates have found the same spot. We have a great meal, laughing and reminiscing about the year. For the first time in a long time, most of the team is just hanging out as friends.

I try calling Allen, but he's not answering. We haven't talked in days. He's no longer the person I turn to. He's busy, the time change is hard, and I'm different.

The day concludes as we tuck ourselves in with Piper's computer propped between the two beds. She presses play on *24*, and I realize that today was unexpectedly fun. My first day in a long time when I didn't feel I had to be a different person. Maybe I'm starting to face the reality of my role, maybe I've accepted the loss, but more than that, I feel like others around me are back to treating me normally. I'm feeling a part of the process and want to see my teammates succeed.

FEBRUARY 5, 2006: OLYMPIC VILLAGE

Canada has four buildings in the Olympic Village, all next to each other, all covered with Canadian flags. We walk towards the building with one enormous flag hanging down one side. I've never seen such an enormous flag — it must be six storeys high. At reception, I wait with my teammates as the keys are distributed.

Jen and I are roommates, but she's at her Olympic clothes fitting. I make my way to the room to unpack all my clothing and put it neatly in my closet. We have two very plain rooms. One has two single beds and one is the living area with some lounge chairs, but there is no TV.

I hurry to join my teammates at the fitting. Cassie smiles, surrounded by a mound of clothes as she pulls each item out of her bag to try it on. Cassie has always been known for her fashion sense. A model in high school, she was best known early in her career for her sweater jacket, or "swacket." She could make anything look trendy.

This year's HBC outfits look amazing. There are clothes for working out, for warming-up outdoors and indoors, and formal wear all emblazoned with Canada in large letters. I love the reds. There's a tailor on site to do any alterations. I stand in line and wait my turn. This is one of the things I've been most looking forward to in Torino.

"Sami Jo Small," I say as the seated receptionist runs her finger down the list of names on a paper. She flips the page.

"I'm sorry, we have no Sami Jo Small. Could it be under another name?"

"Samantha Small?" I say hesitantly, now painfully aware of a potential mix-up. The woman turns and rushes to a back room. I can hear her voice in the distance. Seconds later she's back.

"I'm so sorry . . . your clothes won't be ready until tomorrow."

I try to keep smiling.

"Yeah. Of course. No worries." But I feel like I'm back in the meeting with the coaches. I wave goodbye to Cassie and the rest of the girls, head towards my room, and crawl into bed. Minor setback.

FEBRUARY 10, 2006: OPENING CEREMONY — TORINO

Today is the Opening Ceremony, but it's also my mom's birthday. I feel horrible that I've broken my parents hearts by telling them not to come; but I know I must focus on myself to be there for my teammates. Sometimes, sport can make me extremely selfish.

I convinced them not to come — they are Sami fans first, and Team Canada fans second. I know it's difficult for them not to see me play, and I want them to save their money and use it for a trip where we can really spend time together. Also, selfishly, I don't want the distraction of sympathy at such a difficult time. This is an easier way for me to focus on my teammates.

We didn't practice today, but we did do a workout on the bikes in the Canadian athletes' lounge. I just showered, and now I'm staring into my closet. I hung the Opening Ceremony clothes in my closet, on the right, so I wouldn't wear them until now. I throw my towel on the bed and pull on my white Ceremony snow pants, followed by the rest of the garments.

Jen's sitting on one of the orange chairs in our living area, checking emails on her computer.

We stuff our cameras and ID in our pockets and make our way to the stadium. I stay close to Jen, hoping we can march side by side again.

My teammate Danielle Goyette has the incredible honour of carrying the flag. We walk through the bowels of the stadium, and the rest of Team Canada follows.

Danielle seems nervous as she fidgets with her hold on the flag post. I am fiercely proud of her. "Go-yet-tee," as we call her, is a dominant force on the ice but is too often forgotten off the ice. She is quiet and prefers one-on-one interactions. She always makes an effort to make me feel included and valued.

Danielle didn't play organized hockey until she was 18, despite growing up playing shinny with her brothers. She first played at the World Championship in 1992 yet has rarely been given a captain's letter. She wore an A in Nagano, but nothing since. It never seemed right. Her work ethic and her drive to excel are unparalleled. She is a leader, and it's good that she's finally being recognized as one.

The excitement and the thrill of walking out wearing the maple leaf are still incredible.

Our entire team is near the front, behind Danielle. Jen and I wave to the crowd, giggling, looking for Canadian flags among spectators. We tour the stadium, pointing at the randomly scattered Canadian fans dotting the crowd.

At the end of the lap, we make our way to the designated seating section in the middle of the infield. Carla MacLeod is to my right, and Jen is to my left. Carla, a defenceman, also known as "Crib," is an incredibly gifted skater with a strong sense of positioning. Her quirky sense of humour and even-keeled demeanor is refreshing to be around. Piper and Megs are beside Jen. I unzip my parka to let some heat escape into the crisp air. The main stage is directly in the centre of the stadium, immediately in front of us, about 12 feet up.

We can hear the festivities but can't see much, the stage is too close and too high. Unless the performers come right to the edge of the stage, we are forced to watch the incredible show on one of the four Jumbotrons around the stadium.

It's fun to watch Megs as she experiences the Opening Ceremony for the first time. She catches me staring at her and gives me a gigantic smile.

"Delaney should be here with us," she says sadly, her bottom lip extending.

I nod my head slowly.

FEBRUARY 14, 2006: ROUND ROBIN

Four days later, I'm settling into my role as cheerleader. Today is our third round robin game of the Olympic tournament, and it's against Sweden. I am sitting in a meeting room near the cafeteria in the Olympic Village as Mel goes over last-minute notes about our opponents.

"They will clog up the middle. We need good shots on net — and crash the net for rebounds." Mel gestures with her blue dry-erase pen at the makeshift hockey board in front of her.

Before every game at these Olympics, the coaches have a pre-game meeting prior to departing the Village for the short walk over to the rink. Last-minute lineup changes are announced; tactical reminders are stressed.

The team nods their heads. They look to be listening, but I know some already have their brains at the rink, visualizing the game. Mel wraps up her pre-game speech and looks at her assistant coaches. "Anything to add?"

The other coaches shake their heads and Mel motions to our video coach to play the DVD of highlights from our past two games.

Our first Olympic game was against Italy. It ended 16–0, plenty of highlights of us scoring. The Italians remained loyal to the home team to the end, cheering fanatically whenever the Italian women cleared the puck from their own zone.

Our second game was against Russia. I had hoped the Russian game was going to be a bit closer; the lopsided 12–0 didn't leave fans with a great game to watch.

I am proud of my teammates who, despite the predictable games, have continued to play as a team. In games like these, players often fight about points or shifts, especially when it's the Olympic Games and everyone is watching. Everyone seems to be in on goals. Even our "fire-bug line," which has four players — Katie Weatherston, Gina Kingsbury, Sarah Vaillancourt, and Meghan Agosta — who interchange, has been exceptional. However, my biggest cheer thus far was for Megs when she scored a hat trick against Russia on her 19th birthday.

As the video wraps up, players become fidgety in their seats as tension mounts. It's almost game time.

The Palasport Olimpico, the arena where we play, is only a 15-minute walk from the Village so I can walk over when I'm ready, rather than getting on the bus with the team three hours before game time. I have a quick chat with GM Julie Healy. She checks in to see if I need anything and if not she'll see me at the rink. Julie's been with us since '99 and is always looking out for the players. She coached the Montreal Axion (formerly Wingstar) in the NWHL and therefore truly understands the demands on high performance athletes. After the meeting, I wish them good luck and make my way back to my room.

I think about calling Allen, for Valentine's Day, but I'm still disappointed with him. We've talked a total of 10 minutes in the last week. I wish I could just pick up the phone and call him, but he's always busy with work. I'm not communicating very well how much I need him right now, even though I'm sure I'm probably not much fun to talk to. I feel like he stopped caring, likely tired of my emotional mood swings.

Eventually I make my way to the arena. I arrive during the team's off-ice warm-ups. I chat with some players, make some jokes, and try to encourage or distract as needed.

I watch the on-ice warm-up from our bench, mostly watching Kim and

Charlie. They look ready. Kim is starting today. She takes some shots feeling the puck. When she's done, Charlie replaces her to finish off the drill.

After Mel's final pre-game speech in the dressing room, I make my way up to the rafters to the accredited athlete's section. Alone, I unscrew the lid on the Coke Light, and the Sweden game begins.

FEBRUARY 17, 2006: SEMIFINALS

It's the afternoon of our semifinal game against Finland, and our pre-game meeting has just finished. I wished the girls well and then turned and headed in the opposite direction.

I got Wick's room key in order to watch the other women's hockey semifinal (Sweden vs. the United States) since her room has a TV.

The Swedes are the underdogs in this game. Only 10 minutes in, it's 1–0 for the American side with a goal by Katie King. I open my bag of pretzels and prepare for an onslaught. We beat the Swedes 8-1 in our prelim game. Kim got the start for us and Gillian Apps scored a hat trick, though they opted not to start their top goalie, Kim Martin, likely saving her for this game.

The second period begins with another goal by Team USA, this time by Kelly Stephens. I wait for the Americans to put down the hammer and score some more goals, but they don't have the jump I expected.

The Swedes do everything to prevent the Americans from scoring a third. They dive in front of shots, muck it up in the corners, and out-hustle their more talented rivals. Then, suddenly, the Swedes find an opening, and Maria Rooth scores, making the game 2–1.

The Swedes gain more confidence with each shift as their passes become more crisp, their forecheck more intolerable and Kim Martin more unbeatable. Five minutes later Sweden's captain, Erika Holst, strips American Lyndsay Wall of the puck in the corner and dishes to a wide-open Maria Rooth who shelves it over American goalie Chanda Gunn, scoring again. Chanda was the top goalie at last year's World Championships in Sweden, shutting us out in the finals.

Incredibly, the game is tied 2–2 after two periods.

I usually head over to the rink around now. I rush to my room to pack up my camera and a good luck Coke Light for Meghan Agosta. It's our thing. I've written in a Sharpie marker on the label, *Good Luck, Megs! I'm excited to see you play!* I grab a pair of Canada mitts and my accreditation, and I also throw in an extra Olympic-issued Canada t-shirt for Delaney who's flying in today. This will be the first time I see her since the Games started, and I want her to share a little piece of the Canada kit so she feels more a part of the team.

I rush back to the TV room in time for the start of the third period. I'm going to leave as soon as the Americans score another goal.

Swedish goalie Kim Martin's play is unreal with amazing acrobatic saves. Martin's only 19 and made her Olympic debut in 2002 at only 15. After being out-shot in the first two periods, the Swedes are now, unbelievably, out-shooting their rivals. Only an hour until our game time. I really should be at the rink, but I can't leave now.

The Americans look disjointed, unsure. They miss Cammi Granato and though they have many familiar faces, there has been a lot of turnover from 2002. The Swedes look tired but energized.

The third period ends without a goal. My heart is racing and I can't sit still. I stand and pace.

After a 10-minute overtime ends without a goal, a five-person shootout will decide who will play for the gold medal.

I'm stunned that the Americans might not be playing for gold; this could be the first Olympic gold medal game in the history of the sport that won't be a North American match-up. But still, it's a great feat for women's hockey. Our sport has been torn up in the newspapers with complaints of lopsided scores and the inequality of teams outside North America. Now suddenly, this is more than a two-team tournament.

The first shooter for the Americans is Natalie Darwitz. She has speed and hands. She makes her move, Martin goes down, and the net is open. Darwitz fires it over the glove hand.

Bing! No goal. The puck ricochets off the post and lands safely in the corner.

The first Swedish shooter, sniper Erika Holst, also misses.

Angela Ruggiero gets not one, but two chances to beat Martin, because the Swedish goalie left her line early, but still can't beat her. Gunn stops Swede Nanna Jansson to continue the tie.

After Jenny Potter misses on the American's third attempt, finally,

16-year-old Pernilla Winberg puts the Swedes on the board in the third round.

The American's fourth shooter, Krissy Wendell holds the puck too long and the Americans are still shut out. Sixty minutes of regular play, plus a 10 minute overtime period, and the whole game comes down to the Swede's fourth shooter, Maria Rooth.

If she scores, Sweden will win the game.

The referee blows her whistle to signal for Rooth to start at centre ice. As she pushes the puck off the faceoff dot past the blue line, I can already see that goalie Chanda Gunn is too far back. *There's too much open net. Can Rooth see that?* In an instant, Rooth, with two goals already in the game, shoots far side at the opening. Gunn goes down in a butterfly and stretches her blocker as far as it will go, but it's not far enough.

The crowd erupts, and Rooth can't believe her fate.

Sweden wins.

They will be playing in their first ever gold medal game. I turn off the TV in amazement, and run as fast as I can to the rink.

I know our coaches will be scrambling, changing their pre-game talk. Four years of training doesn't guarantee anything.

As I arrive at the rink, my teammates are putting on their equipment while talk surrounds the Swedish win. Some are motivated by Sweden's play, others are angry they won't get to play our long-time rivals in the finals, but everyone realizes our semi against Finland is not to be taken lightly.

Charlie gets the start, and we dominate from start to finish. Scoring is spread around, and five goals come on the power play. Piper's grit and tenacity help her score two goals in the third period, giving us a 6–0 victory, and together dressed in red and white, waving maple leaf flags and scarves that I've brought with me, Delaney and I wave our arms above our heads in celebration.

FEBRUARY 18, 2006: WE ALL MAKE A DIFFERENCE

We have two days off before the final. Today I am hanging out with my long-time friend Gillian Russell. She paid the equivalent of $50 to fly roundtrip from London, England — where she is living — with her boyfriend, Fred, and his aunt. I bring Gillian to our friends and family dinner at a local restaurant. She lets me vent for a bit but keeps me on track. She knows most of the girls on the team and cheers loudly for Canada but, like a good friend, wore a *SMALL* jersey in the stands to show her allegiance.

Having put my hurt to one side, I spend the remaining part of the two days trying to build others up, breaking down details of the games and encouraging each person. The pressure seems less than a Canada-USA final, but it's still an Olympic final, and each player still wants their share of the ice time. I practise hard but give Kim and Charlie most of the net time to ensure they are feeling prepared. I spend my alone time building my strength to be there for others. I read, watch videos, do crosswords — anything to take my mind off hockey so that I can be re-energized, happy, and rah-rah with my teammates. This is my role.

Finally, it's the night before the final game. I'm in our makeshift computer room, which is just Piper's foyer, writing on note cards that I purchased yesterday at the Olympic fan store. Wick wrote note cards to each of us before the Salt Lake City Games, telling us how much we meant to the team, and I want to duplicate the sentiment. I write feverishly and know I won't get to everyone, so I pick those whom it might impact the most.

I start with Cassie Campbell, our captain, who has led us through some tumultuous times. She has been the face of this team, taking on the public scrutiny head on. As a player she started off as a defenceman and then post-Nagano was made a forward. She has played nearly every role on this team and has come to understand each position. The coaches have made her be hard on players, motivate players, push players, and it can't have been easy. We often come at problems from very different perspectives, but the mark of a great leader is that she always listens with an open mind and isn't afraid to change her viewpoint. She's notorious for easing stressful situations with a prank or a joke, often at her own expense. She's reached out to acknowledge my role, noticing things others often miss. She's matured into an incredible leader whose value extends far beyond the rink. I want her to know that.

I then write one to Wick, repaying the favour of four years ago. With Wick, it's hard to know what she's thinking or if I'm in her way. She surprised me by writing note cards, revealing a side not often seen. She's always led by her work ethic, pushing each of us to be better. She's tough to play with because she's incredibly hard on herself and takes it out on her teammates, and is the prime reason Team Canada has continued to elevate it's game and remain dominant for the last decade. She expects the best of herself and, in turn, of those around her. She's very guarded and private, but I hope she's happy, genuinely happy, with what hockey has given her. She never seems satisfied. I urge her to find the joy in the game, to understand her impact on this team and that her incredible skills can carry us through the game tomorrow.

I write a note to Danielle Goyette saying how proud I was to walk behind her when she carried the flag for Canada and thanking her for always taking the time to see how I was doing.

I compose cards for Vicky and Jayna, both teammates with me from the beginning with the Thunder, and two who have had a tremendous impact on my career.

Writing to Jen, Piper, and Megs, I smile with each pen stroke, my eyes welling up as I tell them each how much they've helped me and how privileged I feel to be a part of their journey.

I then pen one to Charlie, who's been chosen to play in the finals tomorrow. I tell her how proud I am of her, how much I admire her work ethic, and how much she deserves this.

Last, I write a note to Kim St-Pierre. This one is the hardest. She was just told she won't be playing in tomorrow's final and I know the anguish I felt the night I was told I wasn't playing.

Kim had shut out the American side twice this year, letting in only four goals in five games, every single game a win. She played in last year's World Championship Finals and, despite losing the final game in a shootout, she didn't allow a goal during the entire tournament. Perhaps, if we were playing the Americans she may have gotten the start. Kim was the go-to goalie that won us the gold medal in Salt Lake City, but tomorrow she'll be the backup.

In Kim's note, I tell her I know her pain. Yet, despite the pain, I write that we need her more than ever. That Charlie, who has looked up to her for the past decade, will need her support. It won't be easy, but I know she has the strength. We all have more strength than we ever thought.

29

Gold Medal Day

It's gold medal day and I'm at breakfast in the Olympic cafeteria with my teammates. Our team has taken over a small section upstairs.

The table to my right includes most of our defencemen. Our defence have a special bond, having many insider jokes. There are only five of them since the coaching staff opted to take an extra forward instead of the usual six defencemen. Even a harder pill for Delaney to swallow. Mel has slotted Caroline Ouellette back there, but she's not really a D. She'll mostly be called back during odd-man advantages. On our power play, our defence don't play — the coaches prefer offence — nevertheless, this predicament has only served to bring them closer.

At the table to my left, Heff sits across from Vicky. Joining them are Gilly, Appsy, and Katie Weatherston. All but Katie have lived together all year in what we call the "Ontario House."

The rest of the team fills out the adjacent three tables. Laughter dominates despite the pressure of the game ahead. Sos is upset that we don't get to play the Americans in the finals. The team has been making up nicknames for them all year and she wants to be able to trash talk them on the ice. "Tammy Toe-Drag" and "Susie Make-Up" make us laugh, but she resorts to making up names for the Swedes. "Sticky-Bird," for one of their tall players who often has her stick in inappropriate places, makes us laugh the hardest.

Even Wick is laughing, and she rarely laughs on game day.

Pounder's phone rings. She steps away from the table, phone to her ear.

"It's a boy!" says Pounder, turning, tears streaming down her face.

Pounder's sister, Karen, couldn't make the trip to Torino because she was already nine months pregnant. The baby picked a good day to come.

Pounder rejoins us at our table ending her phone conversation with saying, "Yeah, yeah, I'll make sure Mom and Dad know. So proud of you."

Her pink Hockey Canada hat pushed back on her head, covering her uncombed curly locks, Pounder is suddenly gushing. "Five pounds — emergency C-section! They named him Blake. I can't believe it was today. This is a sign."

We all smile at Pounder. There have been many so-called signs, but this is the most significant yet. She turns to me.

"Sami, can you get this message to my parents? Take my phone — tell them it's a boy," she says through the tears. Her parents don't have a cell phone with them, so they don't yet know their first grandchild has just been born.

"For sure, Poundy, I'd love to." Suddenly, I have a purpose.

I sit through our pre-game meeting in the Village, Pounder's flip-phone sweaty in my palm. The coaches' message is always the same: "out-work their goalie," "sixty minutes of hockey," "four-point attack," "keep your feet moving."

After the pre-game video of Sweden's power play and forecheck, we watch a montage that Jen Spencer, our video coach, put together of our incredible journey through the year: our long gruelling bike rides back in May on Prince Edward Island, our makeshift family in Calgary, our hard training regimen on and off the ice, and highlighting jokes and horseplay, including a picture of even-keeled Gina Kingsbury moments after chasing down a purse snatcher yesterday in downtown Torino.

Most of us are laughing while trying to hold back tears. Our journey is almost over. The video ends, the lights come back on, and we all stand to cheer not only for the video, but also for having made it through this incredible journey together.

As I walk out of the meeting room, I reach into my pocket and feel the gold coin that each member of the team received, and I feel like my job is nearly done.

The coin reads, *Take Care of Yourself. Take Care of One Another.*

I walk towards my room for the last time. I have plenty of time before I must find Pounder's parents in the crowd. I've done everything I can for this team and now the hardest part is about to begin. I'll have to watch my teammates receive their medals at the end of this game and everything will change.

It's still two days before the Closing Ceremony, but I pack my bags. There are bound to be festivities after this game, and the last thing I'll want to do is pack. In Nagano, I didn't pack prior to the Closing Ceremony and was forced to throw everything in bags five minutes before departure. Rookie mistake. Not this time.

Time moves in slow motion.

With two hours until game time, I'm bored, so I make my way to the rink to watch our team warm up. I chat with some of our staff and congratulate Peter Elander, Team Sweden's head coach, on an amazing win in the semis. I wander the halls of the arena and eventually end up in a volunteers' snack room. I walk in and grab a Coke Light and pull up a seat next to Darren Boyko, from the Hockey Hall of Fame. He's been really good to me and my teammates; he's the one who hooked me up to play pro in Switzerland. We chat while watching live feeds from other venues on TV.

Eventually I make my way to the rink surface, sitting on the players bench to watch the warm-up and scout the stands for Pounder's parents. I still can't see them. It's not a big venue, and the Canadian fans are noticeable in their red and white gear. They stand out against the majority of local Italians. Pounder's husband, Mike, will be with them too, but I also can't see him yet. I continue to watch warm-up, occasionally glancing throughout the stands.

No one is truly warming up — everyone is in high tempo right from their blades touching the ice as they attempt to demonstrate that their line should start. Usually, players fire pucks from further out on the starting goalie allowing her to "feel" the puck. However, our team started to deviate from this months ago. Now the goaltenders aren't lucky enough to have practice shots to get into the moment, pucks are buzzing right by their ears as players' egos take over and they shoot to score. It's become the Team Canada way. One hundred percent all the time, or the coaches think you're not ready. There are very few smiles on the ice, just fierce determination.

Warm-up ends, and I make my way back to the dressing room, squishing in between Piper and Vicky. Piper is always relaxed, so I know that talking to her won't interrupt her focus.

"You guys looked good out there," I say over the music blaring in the background.

"Yeah, did you see Charlie get nailed in the head, not once but twice?" she says almost horrified at her teammates.

"Did you find them?" Pounder shouts across the room.

"No, I don't think they're here yet."

Mel walks in the room and the music stops. Margot and Tim follow. Tim has a white board and a dry-erase marker in his hand.

Listening, I nod at appropriate times, but the message is not for me. Tim goes over the Swedes' power play one last time on the white board as I scan everyone's face. I stop on Kim. She's looking down. I can empathize.

Everyone has their pre-game routines, and as I sit and watch my teammates go through their final prep, I know this team is ready; maybe it's a feeling, but having spent eight months in close quarters together, people become easier to read. Sure, there are some nerves, especially amongst the younger players, but most have visualized this exact moment. Inwardly jealous, I say my good-lucks, give some taps on the shoulders, and then make my way out to find the Pounders.

I search frantically among the crazy Canadian fans in order to deliver the great news and get back to my seat before puck drop. Unfortunately, I keep getting stopped by well-wishers and drunken fans who simply want autographs. Eventually, just before the puck drop, I find Mr. and Mrs. Pounder.

Tears stream down Pounder's mom's face as I hand her the phone, give her the number at the hospital, and say I'll be back after the period to collect the phone. They hug me as if I had a part in the amazing moment, and I turn and push my way through the rabid fans to get upstairs and meet Delaney.

I miss the opening faceoff trying to get to the rafters, but eventually find Delaney in the athletes' section with Team Finland stickers stuck to her black jacket. I sit down beside her with a quizzical look.

"I was watching the bronze medal game, and the guys beside me were staff members of Team Finland." With a sheepish grin, she says, "They made me wear them." I laugh, glad that she's enjoying herself.

It's not easy to watch our team play — they are living my dream as I observe from way up in the stands — but despite my envy I'm still exceedingly proud of my teammates.

I've seen first-hand how hard they've worked nearly every day pushing to exhaustion, gaining strength in each other's commitment, and each one of our 20 players deserves the recognition they are about to receive. This may be the greatest team of which I have had the privilege to be a part of.

Our players could have been a different 20, depending on who was coaching. There are a few back home who have toiled just as hard, put just as much of their lives on the line, only to have others take the spotlight. My thoughts wander to all those that came up just short of being on this team and those that helped make this team better.

I think about the players who began our centralization with us, rookies Ashley Riggs and Tessa Bonhomme, who will surely make future national teams. And the veterans released, Dana Antal, Kelly Bechard, and Correne Bredin whose dreams were cut short, each more than capable of playing on this team.

I think of Delaney and of her courage to fly to Italy of her own volition — thanks to a generous donation from Team Canada supporters at the Good As Gold golf tournament — to watch the semis and the finals through tears, wanting to be a part of this, even if only from a distance.

Lastly, I think of Kim, sitting at one end of the players box, who I believe is the most accomplished goalie of all time but wasn't chosen to start tonight's game and must watch one of her best friends, Charlie, take her spot.

I smile, greet familiar faces, recount dressing room stories, and tell anyone who will listen that the team is ready. I cheer. I scream.

Yes, my team has scored. My friends are winning. I see the familiar fist pumps — they do that all the time in practice when they score against me. Replay after replay plays on the Jumbotron, and I'm trying to cherish the moments. *I taught them that move, told them to shoot there, I knew it would work.* Despite heroic goaltending by the Swedish goaltender, Kim Martin, Gillian Apps, and Caroline Ouellette both find the back of the net in the opening stanza causing the fans in red and white to erupt in the stands.

I make the familiar trek from my perch down to the dressing room between periods. Instead of yelling with excitement, I fill water bottles, run errands, find tape, and then sit among all my unused equipment in my stall. My jersey catches the slight wind from the dryers now working to dry the equipment of sweaty hockey players.

I'm nervous that I'll say the wrong thing, nervous that my emotions are going to boil over and reveal what's behind the smiling, supportive face. I scan the room — the feeling is light. We're already up by two goals, and we've never lost to Sweden. Charlie's not seeing much action but I give her the habitual encouraging words: "Keep it up." She gives me a knowing smile.

As I walk back up to the rafters for the second period, I join Delaney and our friend Tyler Stewart, from the Barenaked Ladies who is a huge supporter of women's hockey. I first met Tyler at the Tragically Hip concert in the Village after our gold medal win in Salt Lake, and then got to know him at the very first Good as Gold golf tournament up at Windermere House in Muskoka. He plays on occasion in my Friday Moss Park Arena games.

Focusing on the game helps me put my emotions aside. Piper scores off a pass from Wick, triggering Delaney, Tyler, and I to leap out of our seats high-fiving each other. Minutes later, Jen finds Hefford at the side of the net for our fourth goal: it's 4–0 at the end of the second period.

After a brief visit down to the dressing room, I rejoin Delaney for the final period, the game already pretty much in the bag. I don't know what to feel. I love watching women's hockey at this level, but I am tired of living vicariously through others. I want this to be over, but I don't want to experience the emotions at the end of the game.

This is my final period with Delaney. After the game, she'll get on a flight tonight back to Calgary, and I'll make my way down to ice level to be a part of the team photo. Nothing about this seems fair.

We watch the third period unfold without anything too exciting except for a point shot from Sweden that found the back of the net. The whole team looked like they were already preparing for the celebration. This has been a long and trying year, and these last moments before the final buzzer are being savoured.

With just under five minutes left in the game, I sadly say goodbye to Delaney. I can barely look at her face.

"I'll miss you," I say in an awkwardly long embrace knowing I won't see her for a very long time.

I make my way slowly through the crowd down towards the rink; the Canadians are on their feet, joined by all the locals, and the noise is deafening as the buzzer sounds.

We are Olympic champions.

The bench erupts and our players storm the ice. Charlie throws her stick high in the air, and the team jumps on top of her. My teammates' joy fills the entire stadium. All the players are in the melee as I make my way with our other staff members to join in the celebration.

As the players line up on the blue line to receive their gold medals, I join the staff in the player's box. My dream unfolds in front of me, but I'm on the other side of the action and may as well be on the other side of the world. I'm not sure what I feel. I force myself to cheer. You're supposed to smile and laugh and support the home side. You're supposed to deck yourself out in red and white and wear the maple leaf with pride. I know all that, so that's what I've done, but as our flag rises high into the rafters, I feel everything I'm not supposed to feel and fight back the tears.

FEBRUARY 22, 2006: CLOSING CEREMONY

Piper's hand jiggles my arm. "Sami, you have to get up."

The room is dark. I have no idea what time it is. I can smell last night's alcohol on my friends.

"Yeah, yeah, I will." I try to sound awake. Jen's been in and out of the room all day, urging me to get up, but I manage to brush her off every time.

"No, now!" Megs says as she tears off my covers. They all giggle. The cold air hits me, and I'm angry, but I don't move.

Piper flips the light switch as Jen enters the room. "Sami, we want you to come with us," Jen says. "C'mon, we have tickets to speed skating tonight."

"Let's go get some Egg McMuffins," says Piper. Megs sits on the edge of the bed flipping through the athletes' Media Guide. I know they won't leave without me. Megs has already laid out my clothes.

Food cheers me up, especially unhealthy food. Sitting with Megs, Piper, and Jen at the cafeteria, I start to feel normal again. They are beaming coming off their gold medal win. Most of our group is reunited, but I think of Delaney on a flight home.

I reluctantly follow my friends to cheer on Canada's long track speed skaters. Once seated at the arena, Piper brings us beer and hot dogs, and gradually I get caught up in the event. I don't really like beer, but I drink it anyway. We witness on fellow Manitobans Cindy Klassen and Clara Hughes skate to gold medal victories, and I become a super fan cheering them on.

My friends don't let me out of their sights. I know I'm being watched, and I'm trying my best to be jovial. I'm a sports nut, so having the opportunity to watch other Olympic events is truly enticing. The next couple of days we cram in several events before the Closing Ceremony. We cheer the chaos of short track speed skating and take a train out to the curling venue to watch our Canadian men win gold. We drink lots of beer and eat lots of Egg McMuffins.

I know my role has come to an end here in Torino, but I have no idea what the future holds. This has been my dream for so long, a tortuous, often jilting dream that has landed me walking the stadium at the Closing Ceremony among the best athletes in the world. *There is nowhere else I'd rather be, but what about the future? Is it time to move on?*

PART 4

30

Finding the Love

My boyfriend, Allen, expected *his* Sami to come back to her daily routine, but that Sami never returned. If there was a lesson to be learned in all the hardship, I haven't learned it. I just hurt. Some days I can't fathom getting out of bed. Weeks go by. I'm depressed. I have no love to give, either to Allen or to myself. I have a tough time reasoning why I'd want to put myself through gruelling runs or long sessions in the gym. So, I don't.

Similar to after Salt Lake City, the demands on our team are endless. For the next few months, we travel around the country, heroes basking in the glow of an Olympic gold medal. I go from event to event but I always feel like an outsider. Every week it seems like there's something new. From parade marshals at the Calgary Stampede, to the Briar in Regina, from Hockey Canada's ring ceremony at the Hockey Hall of Fame, to the Junos in Halifax and Hockey Day in Rankin Inlet, Nunuvut, and many other stops in between. Life is spinning out of control as accolades pour onto us from all parts of the country, but I often feel like a fraud.

At countless functions, Jen shares her medal with me, pretending it is ours. I display it proudly as if it is my own, but deep down I know it isn't. Grief is complicated. I resent that medal. I want that medal. I'm jealous of that medal.

I'm tired of answering the question, "Where's your medal?"

I've told the story such an innumerable amount of times that I've stopped caring. I start to lie, or I glaze over the truth. If I'm with one of my teammates, I pretend we didn't want to bring more than one medal. Often, my teammates even forget that I don't have one, but everywhere I go, there's that damn gold medal staring back at me.

On the road and at events, I smile through the pain, but I can't mask it at home. I don't have the emotional fortitude to be there for Allen and I right now. As the summer progresses, I travel more and more. I choose to be away because it's just easier. Using up all my happiness at events, at home I become melancholy and selfish.

I celebrate my 30th birthday with friends and family back in Winnipeg.

"So, are you getting a 'real' job now?" they ask.

Smiling, I acknowledge their question, but it angers me. The question hurts.

As spring turns into summer, I try to put my life back together, try to find some semblance of normalcy. I start going to the gym, and despite not doing much, the activity makes me feel better. July comes, and I run my girls' hockey school in Winnipeg. For eight straight hours a day, I'm on the ice — the rink is still my sanctuary.

On the ice, in the eyes of the young players, I find my joy.

Despite the pain, I still enjoy the game. I love the small moments like lacing your skates in the middle of a noisy dressing room or wobbling on both edges to stretch out my ankles. I like how my body feels while participating in sports and I love that it still makes me smile. However, I mostly love that when I play, there's always a storyline that's being constructed, and it's there for me alone to enjoy.

SUMMER 2006: FULL CIRCLE

I'm trying to stay asleep for a little longer, but the Ontario sun irritatingly fills my car. Lying in the back, I cover my face with my sleeping bag until finally my eyes are forced open. It's got to be after 9:00 a.m. because the Valu-mart parking lot is full. In the front seat is a small duffle bag of belongings, and my hockey bag stuffed into the passenger seat. The rest of my belongings are in storage until after Team Canada camp next month.

Allen and I are officially over. I wasn't myself and I wasn't being fair to him. We parted ways when our lease was up yesterday. This is likely for the best, but it hurts.

My out of province plates are still on the Bomber, which once again is command central.

My stomach's starting to rumble.

I finish writing in my journal my list for the day:

1. Head to the gym
2. Eat breakfast
3. Workout
4. Shower
5. Follow up with Chris Dalcin about his spare room

That's enough of a list for today.

Still in my matching Team Canada red sweatsuit, I rifle through bags in the front of the car for some workout clothes. I grab a small grocery bag and pile everything in it. Next stop is the Fitness Institute for a training session.

I have nowhere to be, and no one is expecting me.

Most mornings I wake up with the sun. Slowly I move back to the reality of training. Without Allen in my life, I have the ability or, perhaps, the necessity to find myself again. I embrace being a full-time athlete and what that represents. It gives me daily goals to focus on as I slowly regain hope.

SEPTEMBER 2006: FIRST CAMP BACK

Eventually our Toronto Aeros practices start up and I move into Chris's spare room to start a new hockey season. Mentally, I'm starting to feel direction again. Training is going well. It's what I know. Perhaps it's my ego, but I still think I'm good enough to play for Team Canada. The World Championship are in Winnipeg this year, and I don't want to miss the opportunity to play at home. In all the years on the team, I've never played in Winnipeg in front of friends and family, missing both the games leading up to Nagano and Torino.

The road to Worlds starts at the Team Canada selection camp in Kenora, Ontario. Because it's the start of an Olympic cycle, this is the largest camp of the next four years. Our first inter-squad game is tomorrow. I often close my eyes and think of making important saves and dressing room laughter. *This is the right decision. This is something I still love to do.*

I reflect on the impact of my friend Adam, who passed away in 2002. I habitually think about him when faced with difficult life choices. To him, sport and life were never about the medal, but rather about constantly striving to be better. He always believed that if you put in the work and gave it your all right until the finish line, that you should be proud. And ultimately, regardless of the outcome in Torino, I was proud. I was proud of the role I played and proud of having been a member of such an incredible team. Proud to be a part of the dynasty.

Walking near the lake with Jen during one of our few shared breaks, this is our first chance to catch up, as we are on different teams.

"I've been looking at spots down near the lake in Mississauga . . ." She says.

"I just don't know. I don't know if I'm ready for a roommate."

"We could get separate apartments, but in the same complex?" Jen's voice is hopeful; she knows the difficult time I've had moving on from Allen.

"Mississauga is so far," I say, finding more excuses.

"Yeah, but our team is going to be playing in Mississauga, and there's another gym we can train at down there. We could work out with Pounder and Kellar." Our Aeros franchise was sold by founder Colin MacKenzie to a new owner, making us the Mississauga Aeros. Living out that way would be more convenient, and it's likely the right thing to do, however, it would mean I will finally have to accept my relationship with Allen is truly over.

The final night of the tournament becomes a shooting gallery, but I make key saves. I see my parents beaming with pride in their seats, but it still hurts to know that I was the reason they weren't in Torino. We went to Newfoundland together as a family since I had to attend Hockey Canada's AGM, but I know it wasn't the same for them.

Being back in action with the team feels good. I contributed to our tournament win, playing half of every game, but my goalie partner and roommate, rookie Shannon Szabados, really impressed. I'm not sure what the coaches will make of my performance, but I'm satisfied. I left everything on the ice, and I was glad to come out with a win.

As we congregate on the ice for our celebratory photo after securing the camp championship, I have a new appreciation for the game. The familiar is heightened. The smell of the rink. The feel of my pads. The look of the score clock. I notice everything, wondering if in the familiar, I will be able harness significant games of the past. I'm going to have to be spectacular this season to usurp Kim or Charlie.

APRIL 2007: WORLD CHAMPIONSHIP — WINNIPEG

I move my stuff out of storage and find a place with Jen along Lake Ontario in southern Mississauga. I've come to terms with my life in the eastern part of the GTA being over. She has found an amazing place mere metres from the lakeshore and moving in with her is easy. I need her positive energy in my life.

We start training together at the Fitness Institute in Mississauga and commuting together to practices. I must do more, be better to get into a playing role this year. I work out with more efficiency and a renewed desire.

There are not many returning faces to Aeros this season as most retired or left to play on other teams when the team moved to Mississauga. Sommer West is our new captain. Heather Logan is back after leaving the Aeros to pursue her Olympic hockey dreams at the Calgary Oval. While there, she was recruited by a professional cycling club to tour in Europe. She is still travelling the world with her cycling club but moonlights with us.

Last year, while we were at centralization, the Aeros had their first losing season on record, but we're rebuilding. We've picked up Olympian Kelly Bechard who was a late cut from the Torino team, and Team USA member Tiffany Hagge as well as 18-year-olds Haley Irwin, Mallory Deluce, and Tara Gray.

Also, to help with the transition, we have rookie Ashley Stephenson, a member of Canada's national baseball team, fresh off a Canadian university hockey championship with Laurier where she was the MVP of the league and Jen Raimondi, a recent Harvard grad. Kendra left prior to Torino to play for Durham, now the Vaughan Flames, so I have a new goalie partner, Sarah Love, who has a quiet work ethic and endearing sense of humour.

In November, Kim St-Pierre and Shannon Szabados are chosen to go to the 4 Nations Cup in Kitchener. Shannon shuts out the Americans 2–0 in the round robin (her first shutout at the senior level). Kim plays against the Americans in the finals and Canada wins 5–2.

The Mississauga Aeros are on a roll as Charlie Labonté and I head to Calgary for the January camp. We play against local boys' teams, concluding with a four on four inter-squad scrimmage. I save my best game for last, helping our team win by turning away 48 shots.

Despite this, head coach Melody Davidson calls mid-February to inform me, "I'm sorry, Sami, but you'll be in the third spot again this year for the World Championship in Winnipeg."

·······

Despite the pain felt not playing, I'm relieved that Mel and her assistants, Peter Smith, Barry Medori, and Steph White from my Mississauga team, let me start a pre-tournament exhibition game in Selkirk, Manitoba, allowing my friends and family the opportunity to watch me play at home. Nearly 40 of my friends and family make the hour drive, including my parents; my brother, Luke, and his family; Dermot and his fiancée, Kim; and Anders, Kathryn, and Stacey. This will be my only game in uniform, and I embrace the opportunity to shine. I shut out the Finns and help Canada with their final preparations prior to the tournament with a victory.

At the games in Winnipeg, joining me in the press box at the MTS Centre are rookies Annie Guay, Cathy Chartrand, and Rebecca Johnston who, like me, are alternates.

"What a crowd," Rebecca says.

"This is Winnipeg! We love our hockey," I say as I watch the player introductions for the final game against the Americans. While I wish I was experiencing the excitement from ice level, I am incredibly proud of my city and the support they've shown women's hockey.

Cassie Campbell has retired and Hayley Wickenheiser has been promoted to our new captain. Cherie Piper unfortunately tore her ACL and is replaced on the roster by veteran Kelly Bechard. Becky Kellar is pregnant with her second child and after a year of incredibly hard work, Delaney Collins replaces her and is back on the Team Canada roster.

There are several "SMALL" jerseys in the crowd, but also many "BOTTERILL" and "COLLINS" for the other local Manitobans. Piper, who has been staying with my parents, is sitting next to my two-year-old niece Annika and the rest of my family. It's been a nice change of focus for my parents to have Piper around.

"Is that your friend Susie?" Cathy says pointing to a section near the ice. We're so high I squint.

Before our round robin game against Team USA, Hockey Canada honoured the first Canadian World Championship team from 1990 on the ice, including my friend Susie Yuen.

We celebrated Canada's first ever World Champions. Many of us feathered our hair like Vicky Sunohara did in 1990 for the pre-game meeting — she's the last remaining member of the '90 team on the National Team. In 1990 Hockey Canada made the team wear pink jerseys thinking it would generate more hype and be more feminine, but the players were upset and they wanted to represent Canada wearing the traditional red. We wore replica pink jerseys from that team, this time, with pride, knowing our heroes wore these jerseys, eventually with pride cementing their rightful place in women's hockey history. The euphoric crowd cheered Charlie Labonté and our team to a 5–4 shootout victory over the Americans thanks to a game winning shootout goal by Hayley Wickenheiser.

As the play develops, I spot Susie Yuen in the crowd wearing her volunteer jacket. Seeing her on the ice with her 1990 teammates at the throwback game was a thrill, but my eyes well up seeing her today. She is the true matriarch of women's hockey in this city and every young girl in the crowd today has been influenced either directly or indirectly by Susie. Most will never have the privilege of knowing her like I do, but she sparked a dream for many in Manitoba that has manifested with three girls on the National Team from this tiny province. Who knows who is sitting in this crowd today who, because of seeing their heroes on the ice, will someday represent Canada as well.

"Et le but," Annie shouts as Jen puts in the first goal of the game for Canada. The crowd loves the hometown girl. I instinctively look to Kim St-Pierre in net. She looks calm and in control. Thanks to help from the crowd, we skate to a relatively easy 5–1 victory, reclaiming the World Championship crown.

Wick led the tournament in scoring and is named the MVP. My biggest cheer is for Delaney who is named to the Media All-Star team. I think about the 14-kilometre river valley runs that she did nearly everyday after being released from the Olympic team and her obsessive work ethic this season. Not only did she make the team after the devastation in Torino, she is also named best defenceman in the world.

·······

After the final game, we celebrate as a team at a local pub.

"This is Billy," Piper says, introducing her friend to me, Jen, Megs, and Delaney. "He plays for Canada's men's sledge hockey team."

"Did you see our demo?" Billy says to Piper, referring to the sledge hockey demonstration he and his teammates did between periods of the final game.

"No, we must have been in the room. How'd it go?"

His smile is contagious. The girls and I have a little fun trying to set him up with a Finnish player, but as the evening draws to a close, there feels like something between us. But unsure, I say nothing, and our cabs head in different directions.

The following weekend, we beat out Brampton for a spot in the upcoming Esso Women's Nationals in Salmon Arm, BC. Unfortunately at Nationals, our Mississauga Aeros team loses 1–0 in the semifinals to an unheralded upstart Etobicoke Dolphins squad that includes American captain Krissy Wendell, who moved to Toronto from Minnesota to be close to her boyfriend who played for the Maple Leafs.

It's a tough loss to handle, because I always want to win important games, but the pill is made easier to swallow by the fact that nearly a year after the demise of my relationship with Allen, I finally feel my heart flutter at the prospect of someone new.

Being with Billy is unlike any other relationship. He is also an elite athlete, having competed at two Paralympic Games, and he makes me want to do more, to be better. It took me a full year to find balance again, to feel like myself again, and to be ready to let someone else in. When he spent the entire night in a hospital with me when I had gallbladder surgery, I knew Billy felt the same way.

This year has been a struggle. First, breaking up with Allen was hard, but I needed space to find my confidence again, to find out what really motivated me, and to find the joy in playing again.

Second, transitioning from Calgary with the National Team where every single moment is mapped out for you, back to Toronto where we insert ourselves into club teams amongst players who have their own lives was difficult. I questioned everything, not trusting my instincts, thinking I was contributing to my own demise.

But meeting Billy has made the struggle mean something. With Billy, I have the space to be me. With him, I have rediscovered my love of sports, my love of playing, and my love of me.

My Legacy

SPRING 2007: THE START OF A NEW LEAGUE

"They can't really fold an entire league, can they?" Vicky Sunohara says. She's on the stationary bike beside me. Jayna Hefford, Gillian Ferrari, and Jen ride beside us.

Last season was a tough one for the owners of the respective clubs, but my focus was on the ice. There have been rumours swirling around the gym about changes. Our Aeros team was under new management and in a new location, but I hadn't thought our issues were *league* issues. Despite playing on different teams, we see the Brampton girls at training, but unfortunately, no one has insights on the future of the league. *Why are we, as players, not a part of these conversations?*

"Hockey Canada would never let that happen. Where would we play?" I say as we are about to start another sprint.

"Cass says the owners are upset with league governance: they put so much money in, they want a say," Hefford says, referring to Cassie Campbell, now retired, who has attempted to get all the league owners to the same table.

"I'm sure it'll work out; they just won't let that happen," I say.

"Who won't? Who are *they*?" asks Jen.

"Humph, I actually have no idea," I reply as Gilly yells "Go!" to start the two-minute sprint.

Two minutes are up, and Jen, breathing hard says, "We were emailed that our owner wants to see changes . . . what *are* those changes?"

Vicky responds, "I heard they want fewer teams and some guarantee players will stay with their teams. Also, something about face shields, and maybe some of the rule stuff, but it sounds like the owners don't get along."

On the drive home from the gym, I say to Jen, "I'm sure no one wants to see the league die. Surely someone will step in and make it work."

"I hope so," she says in reply.

• • • • • • •

Sent: Friday, May 18, 2007
Subject: NWHL

Hello to all,

The N.W.H.L. has decided to suspend operations for the upcoming 2007–08 season. The league will be using the year to restructure. An announcement will be forthcoming regarding the status of the Mississauga Aeros and its position within the N.W.H.L.

Regards,
Mississauga Aeros Management

1991: MAKE A DIFFERENCE — '91 CANADA GAMES

It's the first ever Canada Games to include women's hockey and I am a 14-year-old defenceman. I am sitting in the back section of an energetic auditorium in Charlottetown with my Team Manitoba teammates.

I started tryouts for the Manitoba team in net, but as a boys' AA goalie, the level of play wasn't challenging enough. There weren't many actual hockey players on the ice, mostly converted ringette players. Not knowing how huge the Canada Games would be, and with a slight chauvinistic attitude, thinking very few girls played hockey, I showed up at the second tryout and made the team on defence.

After our morning skate and lunch, we proceeded to the auditorium for the women's hockey pep rally. The host of the afternoon speaks at the podium on stage below, although my mind has wandered to the games that start tomorrow. We begin the tournament against Alberta. Our coach Darren Juby went over their systems this morning at practice and warned us about their best player, a 13-year-old named Hayley Wickenheiser.

Our fluorescent yellow jackets stand out as we perch in the top section. All the women's hockey teams are jammed into the seats, and the crowd is abuzz. We were the second-last team to belt out our cheer, and my throat is still burning from the screaming. I led our girls in a "Go, 'Toba, go!" chant based on one of my brother's swimming cheers. I am sure we were the loudest — we certainly gave the most effort — but Manitoba has always been known for our team spirit.

The lights dim, and a video starts to play on the screen.

The video is a highlight compilation of the 1990 World Women's Hockey Championships that took place last year in Ottawa. It was the first ever Worlds for women. My heart rate quickens. I can see myself there. Not just in the stands as a fan, but as a player. I picture myself playing with those women on the screen, not as a D, but as a goalie.

Great saves by Cathy Phillips and great goals propel Canada over Team USA 5–3. I see the lone Manitoban, Susie Yuen, the smallest player on the team at 4 foot 11, being hoisted high in the air with the Championship Plate. Susie spoke to our Manitoba team shortly before we left and inspired us to believe we could win, despite being huge underdogs.

I look around at the other athletes. The crowd is silent.

Our new heroes are on the screen.

Two hundred of the best female hockey players under 18 are here in this room. I look around. *Who will be the next ones on the national team? Who will shine here over the next week? Who will propel their team to victory?* I want the answer to all those questions to be me.

I hope the scouts know I'm a goalie on a boys' AA team back home. I'm sure they do. No matter. No excuses.

Sue Scherer, captain of Team Canada, comes to the podium. She has on a white tracksuit top that is clearly a Team Canada issue even though it has pink trim. The lights slowly turn on as Sue takes the microphone in front of a mesmerized audience. We all want to be her. Just under a year ago, I watched from my living room in Winnipeg as she led her team to victory. I didn't care for the pink jerseys, but I wanted to be on that team.

"To be a part of the future, dream big. This is only the beginning. Each of you has an opportunity to leave a legacy, to impact our game."

This is only the beginning. I repeat the words in my head. I let the words sink in.

Leave a legacy.

SUMMER 2007: WHAT NEEDS TO BE DONE

Quickly I grab the last of the documents I just printed out for tonight's meeting.

"Jen, do you want to drive, or should I?" I ask loudly to Jen in the kitchen.

She pops her head into our shared office. "So sorry, but I have to head to physio first. I think I'm just going to call in."

I try not to seem too disappointed; I know physio is important, but I'm dreading having to make the hour commute downtown in rush hour traffic alone. "Okay, no problem."

I pass by Jen in the living room. "Don't forget to mention that amendment to the budget you were talking about. I think it's a great idea," she says.

Our apartment has become the unofficial headquarters as we attempt to build a league. Documents are spread all over the place, sponsorship and marketing proposals, bylaws, meeting minutes, business plans, and logo designs amongst others. Every waking moment has been focused on ensuring the league's existence.

I jump in my car and quickly call Billy. "Hieeeee," I say sweetly, knowing I'm about to disappoint him. "So, I totally forgot we have a face-to-face meeting at Birch Hill again tonight." Birch Hill Equity is the firm where Michael Salamon works. He has provided his office for weekly meetings. One of the players, Mandy Cronin, met him while at a charity ball hockey tournament. She explained the situation of our league to him. Not only did he listen, but with an infant daughter at home, she struck a chord and he asked how he could help. He has been incredibly generous with his time and worked hard for the past few months on the league, and he has involved many of his high-powered friends to help us and most importantly, guide us as we navigate the road towards a fully functioning league.

"Didn't you just meet?" he says. We had dinner plans for tonight.

"Yeah, that was last Wednesday, but lots has happened. We only have a month until the potential start of the season." I start to rattle off all the bullet points on the docket for tonight's meeting. Billy listens patiently, giving feedback from his years of playing sport at the highest level. I look down at my console and realize the time. "I'm so sorry, maybe we can meet up after?"

The last few months have been an incredible learning curve for me. From having no idea how each team ran to being fully entrenched in the day-to-day operations of an entire league, I feel as if I've earned a mini-MBA along the way. I have put in more than 50 hours a week for three months in the hopes that we will have something solid come September.

It's been a lot of work, but for some reason, I felt compelled to do it. Selfishly I want a league where I can play, but also I have the knowledge, the time, and the will. Maybe also because I'm the player rep for the National Team, or perhaps because both my mom and dad volunteered for nearly every organization my brother and I were a part of growing up, or maybe just to feel needed. Regardless, the work consumes me.

"Sami, you know what you need to do. No one knows the work you've put in, but I do. Maybe they won't appreciate it, but you'll know what you've built. Good luck tonight. Love you."

He ends the call, and I begin the trip downtown. I make a few more quick calls on my headset to prospective league sponsors always with the same message: "We have an amazing product, we just need funding quickly." I don't say exactly that, but I try to sell our game with as much passion and excitement as I feel when I play.

OCTOBER 2007: GAME TIME

Sitting, drenched in sweat, in the dressing room post-game, I listen to our coach, Stephanie White, excitedly talk about our enormous win tonight against Montreal. My goalie partner, Sarah Love, taps me on the pads as Coach White summarizes key moments from the game.

"Good job capitalizing on our chances," She says smiling, scanning the room. I turn to Jen on my left and flash her a smile. Her two goals solidified our win in our first league game at home.

Together, we managed to get the new Canadian Women's Hockey League up and running by September. The board of directors went back and forth on league names. Initially, we thought we should be the Eastern Women's Hockey League as there's still a Western Women's Hockey League in existence, or perhaps a name more aligned to our future aspirations, the North American Women's Hockey League; but ultimately the board settled on the CWHL because it best positioned us with local sponsors.

I'm the vice-chairman of the league — Michael Salamon is the chairman. Ultimately, we hope to have the board populated with non-playing individuals. Under my portfolio falls fundraising and sponsorship as well as the management of my team.

"Great job by all the penalty-killers — you kept them from getting shots through. Those penalties were bad calls, but no one lost their focus. Great job tonight," says Steph as she paces around the room. I look down at my jersey and feel the giant cursive *Mississauga* patch that has been ironed on the front. Thanks to a partnership with the Mississauga Girls Hockey League, that has not only provided us with ice time, and a dressing room, we have their hand-me-down blue and gold Mississauga Chiefs jerseys. With the CWHL board decision against team names this year, we are simply the Mississauga Hockey Club. I am relieved. It doesn't feel right. I was hesitant to be called the Chiefs because of my admiration and respect for Indigenous Peoples.

Even though we are no longer the Aeros, the team has the same core as last year. In addition, we have Olympian Cherie Piper back who has graduated from Dartmouth College. Our team is strong, and it looks like once again, we will join Brampton and Montreal as the front-runners, which makes today's win an important one.

As Stephanie leaves the room, I quickly take off my jersey and chest protector. Walking out the door still in skates and goalie pads, I shuffle along the rubber matting through to the main doors. I wave and smile at our fans, many looking for autographs, but I say that I must do something first.

I find our volunteers, Leigh and Gabby.

"How'd the game go?" I ask Leigh as she counts out the ticket sales.

"What a game — you guys know how to give me a heart attack!" says Gabby with a huge smile on her face. These two never missed a Toronto Aeros game, and now volunteer with us.

Leigh hands me the money she's collected selling tickets.

"Thanks, guys!" I say as I walk away, pushing my way through the doors back into the frigid temperatures of the rink. I march all the way around the rink and knock on the referees' room door.

"Hello?" I say, gently pushing open the door.

"Yeah, c'mon in." I turn sideways with my pads to fit through the door.

"It's ninety for the ref and sixty each for lines, right?"

"No, no, no. Now that we're the CWHL we get five hundred dollars." The refs all laugh in unison as I tilt my head with a sly smile while counting out payments, omitting our coach's negative comments from the dressing room.

"Thanks guys, we really appreciate it."

As I make my way back to our dressing room, I am filled with such a sense of gratification. Montreal made it to Toronto safely. The refs showed up and got paid, the game went off without a hitch, the seats were filled with over a couple hundred excited fans, and we won. What a night. As I shuffle back to our room, I see Lisa-Marie Breton, captain of the Montreal team, with her bag slung over her shoulder.

"Bien faites, Sami Jo."

"Toi aussi," I say, smiling back. "Thanks so much for all your hard work. There'd be no Montreal team without you. I hope your team appreciates that."

"Ah, merci. But Sami, there'd be no league without you."

APRIL 2008: CHAMPIONSHIP SEASON

A few months later, I travel with Team Canada to the 4 Nations Cup in Leksand, Sweden, along with goalie partner Shannon Szabados. I beat the Americans in the round robin, but Shannon gets the final, shutting out the Americans in her first game ever against our main rivals.

In February, Melody Davidson calls. She's no longer the head coach but is still in the position of general manager.

"We are going with Shannon this year as the third goalie."

"What does that mean for me?"

"Well, you're not completely out of the program — we'll re-evaluate where you are come September."

"So, I just train until September?"

"You can train, you can not train, it's up to you, but I'll let you know in September."

········

As the inaugural season of the CWHL ends, we embark on our quest to win both the Esso National Championships and the first ever CWHL Cup. We beat the Vaughn Hockey Club (formerly the Etobicoke Dolphins) in the first round of playoffs and must travel to Montreal to play a best of three against Kim St-Pierre's team.

Montreal finished in top spot in the league with 47 points, Brampton had 45, and we had 43. It was a tight season, but since being cut, my head's all over the place and I am finding it difficult to think about our upcoming playoffs.

Billy's been in Spain, playing professional wheelchair basketball, but he had to fly back yesterday for a Team Canada sledge hockey camp. In his arms, I broke down; I told him this year was all for nothing.

"Sami, you've built something larger than yourself. We'll train hard this summer, and you can show them you deserve to be there. Go to Montreal and just play. Who cares what anyone else thinks? You're still the best in my eyes."

In Montreal, we narrowly win the first game. During the second game with less than three minutes left, we are tied 4–4. Montreal's forward and National Team member Katie Weatherston drives the net and in tight, shovels the puck trying to find an opening five-hole. From the hashmarks down, Weatherston is dominant. Her ability to score when there looks to be no opening is unparalleled. I know I need to play her strong, be big, stay solid.

I make the save, but I am vulnerable, too focused on the puck to notice where Katie's momentum is taking her. She lands right on top of me while I'm in the butterfly position, forcing me back. I feel my left knee snap.

Claire Moscone, our athletic therapist, rushes from the bench to my side.

"I'm fine, I'm fine," I mouth to Claire, her face directly over mine as I lay on my back. She reaches her hand down into my pad and presses on the inside of my knee.

I let out a small whimper, grimacing, trying to fight the pain. I'm more frustrated than anything.

"You are not fine. Can you get up?"

I struggle but manage to get to my feet. My knee is not good, but I look down the ice and see Kim standing in the other net. She, perhaps undeservedly, represents every demon in my head and I become more resolute to not let her win this way.

I try to do a butterfly but am slow to get up. I see Sarah Love, our other goalie, putting on her gloves and helmet. *It can't end this way.*

"I'm fine," I lie to Claire as I stubbornly take my spot back in the net.

I merely need to get to overtime. Every shot hurts, but adrenaline makes winning my sole focus. *If this is the last game I ever play, we better damn well win.*

We play five minutes of overtime, and it proves nothing. We are headed to a shootout.

I don't even skate to my bench, opting to simply stand and wait. Montreal has some of the best players in the world, including 16-year-old phenom Marie-Philip Poulin, but I have no nerves, only pain.

I stoically make save after save until finally, one of our forwards, Jen Raimondi, a rookie from Vancouver and recent graduate of Harvard, scores the shootout winner.

We win.

I struggle to make it to the ensuing scrum. Sarah meets me halfway and, smiling, helps me make it to my teammates for the celebration.

Sommer West, excited to be heading to the CWHL Cup championships, carries my bag out to the bus for the trip home as I hobble on one leg, unsure if this is truly the end of my career. Despite the injury, this game was one of the most satisfactory of my career. One last time,

I showed the National Team scouts I save my greatest performances for when it matters most.

....

Watching the 2008 World Championship in Beijing at home from my sofa is shattering, but I still want my friends to do well. It's a roster that includes Jen, Piper (back from ACL surgery), Delaney, and Megs. Newbies on the team include Rebecca Johnston, who was an alternate with me last year, Meghan Mikkelson, and Valerie Chouinard.

Left off this year's squad was Cheryl Pounder, who recently had her baby, and Danielle Goyette, who after an illustrious career has decided to move on to coaching at the University of Calgary.

Perhaps the most shocking cut was Vicky Sunohara. Vicky is still an amazing hockey player. At 37 she dominated the CWHL, finishing fifth overall in the league in scoring. Night after night, she is one of the best players on the ice, centring one of the best lines in women's hockey history that includes Jayna Hefford and Lori Dupuis. Her speed at 37 may not be the same as when she was 21 but she sees the game better than anyone. I have had the privilege of playing with some amazing players, but none match Vicky for charisma and brilliant leadership skills. She will be sorely missed.

In Beijing, Canada struggles, as do both Kim and Charlie. I've never seen that happen on a world stage before. Kim plays in the 4–2 round robin loss to the Americans, and Charlie starts the final but gets pulled after the second period, replaced by Kim. Canada clawed back from a 4–1 deficit to make it a 4–3 score but ultimately were unable to defend the world title from a year ago. It's emotionally complicated as I see on the screen the devastation in my friend's eyes, but I take a guilty satisfaction in the loss, selfishly believing it increases my chances to regain a spot for next season.

....

At the club level, we still have two championships in women's hockey, but we are working to rectify that. This will be the final year that we fight for both an Esso Women's Nationals and a league championship.

Hockey Canada has decided to stop funding senior women's hockey, so this will be the last Esso Women's Nationals.

We qualify to represent the CWHL at the National Championships in Prince Edward Island along with Brampton. Prior to departure, I am a mess, still unable to put any pressure on my leg. Our team doctor, Dr. Laura Cruz, says it will heal in six to eight weeks, but it's only been two since the injury. The morning of the flights, too depressed to get out of bed, I miss my flight to Charlottetown. But later, I think about my friends that are on that team. They are the ones who have believed in my vision, and have stuck with the league this season, despite the hiccups. I decide I want to be there for them.

Cheryl Pounder is back playing for us after the birth of her daughter, Jaime, less than three months ago. She wants to show the National Team coaches she's ready to fight for a spot at the 2010 Vancouver Olympics.

I watch as one of the Western Women's Hockey League representatives and last year's champs, the Calgary Oval X-Treme, start the tournament by clobbering us 6–1 in front of a sold-out crowd of 1,200 at the CARI Complex in Charlottetown. We don't look like ourselves; we're disjointed and tentative. Brampton also loses their opener 6–4 to the other WWHL representative, the Minnesota Whitecaps.

This sets up a semifinal that pits us against a strong Minnesota team that includes Canadian Olympian Caroline Ouellette and Americans Julie Chu, Angela Ruggiero, Jenny Potter, and Natalie Darwitz. We finally find our groove. Cherie Piper is the star, scoring twice, and Jen scores the game winner to beat the Whitecaps 5–3. Miraculously, Brampton also beats Calgary in a major upset 3–2, to give Calgary its first loss of the entire season. This sets up an all CWHL final.

I cheer, once again from the sidelines. It's a nail biter, as we play our rivals Brampton. Down 1–0 most of the game, Brampton takes a two-goal lead in the middle of the third period. Our two call-ups, 17-year-olds Natalie Spooner and Brianne Jenner, are looking strong and add offence to the team. Unfortunately, Natalie has to leave after the second period to get back to Toronto in time for her Junior game back home.

As the third period progresses, we start slowly to grind away at the deficit, thanks in large part to Piper and Sarah Love. Piper's had a rough year after graduating from university. The transition year back to the real world is never easy on hockey players, but hers was made more difficult with the loss of her dad. She's been very sad, often without focus or direction, but this week she looks incredible on the ice.

Sarah is shining, keeping us in the game. She sprawls to make saves she has no business making, turning away nearly 40 shots, and helping us to believe we can win. Playing behind me for the last two years can't have been easy — especially since she was the star at Yale — but she's been a great support and friend, and I'm so proud of her play today.

First, Jen Raimondi scores for us, followed 11 seconds later by a goal from Piper, with the assist to Cheryl Pounder who badly needs to breast-feed her baby waiting in the arms of GM Maria Quinto near the players entrance. Piper's goal sends us into overtime.

I squirm and fidget like a nervous parent behind the glass. The Esso Nationals have been *the* event for women's hockey since its inception in 1982 and this is the last one. I want us to win it.

Almost 10 minutes into overtime, Piper takes a feed in front of the net from Jen and beats Brampton's goalie, Cindy Eadie, low on the blocker side. I thrust my arms in the air, hear the crowd erupt, and proudly watch Sarah make her way to the pileup celebration on top of Piper.

●●●●●●●●

With a two Championship season, the Nationals win is not the denoue-ment to our story. The following weekend, we play Brampton again for the inaugural CWHL Championship. Thanks to the mayor of Brampton, Susan Fennell, we play at Brampton's Powerade Centre, the same site of the previous NWHL's Championships. As the founder, commissioner, and an owner in the NWHL, she could have turned her back on us, but she didn't. She's proof that working together will help make our fledgling league succeed.

I watch from the stands adjacent to our bench. The arena is packed with over 5,000 fans, most of whom are cheering for the home team. The game is a rematch of last week's Nationals final, and there is clear tension between the two teams. The game is back and forth, with exciting plays at each end.

With 10 minutes left in the third period, we are tied. Again.

Brampton clears the puck out of their zone and Jayna Hefford comes storming down the right wing trying to catch up to the puck. Like Piper, she also plays with a heavy heart having lost her dad this year. She looks to have a breakaway if only she can catch up with the puck.

I see Sarah hesitate and then pounce. It looks like she can outrace Hefford to the puck. Sarah takes a few strides and dives headfirst to poke the puck. Hefford sees this and also dives to thwart Sarah's attempt, but a prone Sarah is first and swats the puck out of harm's way. Hefford collides with her outstretched goalie pads and then hops up to pursue the play.

Sarah does not hop up. She lies motionless on the ice as the play continues in the corner.

I yell at the ref through the glass, "Goalie's down, blow the whistle!" Our net is gaping, and Brampton is salivating, but finally a whistle echoes throughout the arena to halt play. Brampton is upset at the stoppage. They are petitioning the referee as our therapist, Claire Moscone, runs towards Sarah. She still hasn't moved.

Claire's head is next to Sarah's on the ice. Then Claire glances up and motions for a stretcher. This can't be. I head towards our players entrance. She gets Sarah to sit up, and eventually two of our Mississauga players put their arms under Sarah's shoulders and hoist her to her feet. She can only put pressure on one foot. The stretcher doesn't arrive in time, so the two players, with Claire by their side, skate her right towards me at the players entrance. Suddenly her contorted face is next to mine, tears stream down her cheeks and she puts her arm around me.

Claire takes position under Sarah's other arm, and we carry her back to the dressing room. The game resumes with our call-up goaltender, Megan Takeda, taking her spot for the final seven minutes of the game.

I help Sarah remove her gear while Claire checks her knee. Every touch she lets out a shriek. It's not good; even worse, we head into overtime in the CWHL Championships with a goaltender who hasn't played or practised all season at this level. Brampton eventually pots the winner, but our goalie played valiantly, calmly turning away some of the top shooters in the game.

I miss it all, holding my friend's hand in the dressing room: I miss the goal, I miss Michael Salamon presenting the trophy, and I miss Brampton's celebration. But I can hear the roar of the crowd and know that what we have created is bigger than us — it's the future of women's hockey.

32

Finally, a Medal

SEPTEMBER 2008: FINAL PUSH

When Billy finishes his pro wheelchair basketball season in Spain we decide to move in together. It feels like the natural evolution of our relationship. Jen bought a house and will move out of our apartment in a couple months, and our teammate Tara French, a stay at home defenceman from Canada's U-22 team from Truro, Nova Scotia, will move into Jen's old room.

I put everything I have into training for the next five months. I train with Chris every day, sometimes twice a day, breaking all my own testing records and exceeding all my previous fitness benchmarks. My knee heels and by the end of a gruelling summer of training, I'm ready to compete for a spot on the Vancouver Olympic team. I want to show Mel, come September camp, just how hard I've worked and how good I can be.

But, one week before the 2008 September camp, news came via registered mail that I am completely released from the National Women's Hockey Team program. No phone call, no meeting, no explanation.

I am unceremoniously cut.

I break down and call Mel. I still feel I'm good enough to be there. Maybe I'm blind or just too full of pride, but I still feel I can contribute.

"Sorry, but we are going with the younger goalies."

I fight the decision both internally and externally. I am only 32. Would this happen in the NHL? I have no recourse. The cycle continues, and I am left out.

My National Team hockey career is over. There is no retirement party, no closure.

I just never get asked back.

·······

At first, I continued to play for the re-named (despite my protests) Mississauga Chiefs because I feel like I should. I have volunteered countless hours towards the success of the league, and I know having Olympians on the team helps generate fans.

I'm also at the height of my fitness, and I don't want the summer to go to waste. As the season progresses, my mindset gradually changes as hockey lures me back in. The joy of a huge save, the drenched shirt after a tough practice, the embraces after a big win — I still crave them all.

This is a transition year as the CWHL and Western Women's Hockey League merge but keep the CWHL name, thanks in large part to the gargantuan effort of my friend Samm Holmes, founder of the Strathmore Rockies who had moved out to Calgary in 2002 to pursue her National Team dream. She spearheaded the WWHL merger and we now have one North American league which includes a team from Alberta. A deal was struck with Governor General Adrienne Clarkson to award the Clarkson Cup to the *new* CWHL champions.

One league and one cup. Finally.

We finish the regular season in third place, once again behind Montreal and Brampton, but our Mississauga team is still strong. Unfortunately, Sarah Love ended up tearing her ACL, PCL, and meniscus in last year's final game, causing her to miss the entire 2008–09 season. I miss her at practices but have a new goalie partner O'Hara Shipe, from Alaska.

We lose our semifinal playoff series against Brampton in shootout overtime, with Jayna Hefford scoring the game winner, missing the chance to advance to the first ever Clarkson Cup finals.

Despite this, I still travel to Kingston, to volunteer my time behind the scenes with new commissioner Brenda Andress. Manon Rhéaume makes a return to the women's game suiting up in net for the Minnesota

Whitecaps. After being released from the National Team program in 2000 she returned a few years later, remarkably, for a stint on forward with the Montreal Wingstar in the old NWHL. I drop the puck for the final game that sees Montreal defeat Minnesota 3–1, realizing a dream for the league to finally play for one cup.

The most meaningful honour happens post-game, when Lisa-Marie Breton brings me into the euphoric Montreal dressing room. In front of her team she hushes the celebration to present me with a card signed by the whole team.

"Without you, none of us would be here. Thanks for all the hard work."

•••••••

I can't help but tune in to the 2009 World Championship in Finland; nearly the entire team is CWHL players. Delaney Collins, who now plays for Brampton and was on the team last year, has been left off the roster this time, as has Cherie Piper, which I think is a huge mistake.

Canada wins 2–1 in an exciting thriller against the Americans in the preliminary round, with Jen scoring the winner and Charlie Labonté providing excellent goaltending. Unfortunately, especially for Charlie, Team Canada once again loses for the second straight time in the finals to the Americans, 4–1.

The National Team announces its centralized roster that will compete for Olympic spots playing in Vancouver and decides once again to bring only three goalies to the Olympic centralization training camp — Kim St-Pierre, Charline Labonté, and Shannon Szabados. The roster includes Piper and Delaney, but leaves off long-time defenceman Cheryl Pounder, who, after giving birth last season, has been playing some remarkable hockey for our Mississauga team.

A hard centralization results in Delaney suffering an injury that ultimately leaves her off the final Olympic roster. Heart wrenchingly it's the third straight Olympic team she has narrowly missed making. Rookies Catherine Ward, Haley Irwin, and Marie-Philip Poulin crack the lineup. And Jennifer Botterill, Becky Kellar, Hayley Wickenheiser, and Jayna Hefford remarkably earn a spot on their fourth straight Olympic team.

The team trudges on. Team Canada is a well-oiled machine, capable of using a plethora of different cogs to make itself successful.

Huddled under my blanket, alone on my couch, the hockey final between Canada and the USA at the 2010 Vancouver Olympics is about to begin. Emotions have been oozing out of me all week; from sadness and jealousy, to anger and hurt, I have been all over the place. But today, I am transported back to being a fan. I am transported back to my parents' living room, watching the Olympics with my family, in awe of the spectacle and marvelling at the athletes.

Billy is away at a training camp in the interior of BC, preparing for his third Paralympic Games starting in a week. I'll be travelling back to Vancouver to watch him compete, along with some friends, including teammates Sarah Love and Tara French.

I went to Vancouver last week for Canada's last round robin game against Sweden. I was fortunate to receive an Olympic volunteer award and I couldn't pass up watching women's hockey while I was there. I wore a *BOTTERILL* jersey that I found at Jen's place and sat high in the rafters, unseen by most.

The game was a blowout. Interestingly, Charlie played the third period even though Kim started the game. I found out later that Kim, as the official backup, asked the coaches if Charlie, relegated to the third goalie position, could play the final period, knowing it would be Charlie's only chance to play in Vancouver. It was an incredible demonstration of friendship by an extraordinary individual.

As the final begins on TV, Wick wins the opening draw against American Jenny Potter. But more importantly, I am stunned that Shannon Szabados stands between the pipes for Canada.

I was sure it'd be Kim or Charlie, both extremely capable. I can't help but be sad for them. Though they have both served as my competitors for much of my career, there is no one else in the world that truly understands my story. I am forever intertwined in their lives, and the imprint they have left on me is permanent. Their hard work, their sacrifice, their drive to be the best pushed me at every turn. Never a sour word was ever said between us, but I know our friendship was stunted by competition, by constantly being pitted against each other by outside forces.

I have nothing but the utmost respect for these two individuals. I am me because of who they are: incredible athletes with an extraordinary drive to win. They are both extremely nice people and perhaps, had we met under different circumstances, we likely would have become best friends, which is why I admire their friendship through all the adversity.

I focus on the screen and at 14 minutes into the first frame, Jen circles the puck down low in the American end. She is a master at creating open space for herself, protecting the puck with her head up. American goalie Jessie Vetter watches intently as Jen drives below the goal line. As she skates behind the net, she covertly dishes the puck, same side to a waiting Marie-Philip Poulin in the slot, who one-times the puck high over an unsuspecting Vetter. I spill my drink as I jump to my feet. Jen hasn't been getting nearly enough ice time this tournament, and she just proved she is still amongst the best on the team, an invaluable asset. She makes the possible out of the seemingly impossible. I cheer alone in my living room, imagining myself along with millions across the country tuned in to this game.

Jen's been a constant in my life, and my best friend. She's been with me through all the ups and downs, rarely complaining and always providing encouraging words. She has the kindest of souls but is incredibly driven. She is successful because she gives herself no other options. She has rubbed off on me in numerous positive ways, and I am grateful to share this incredible journey together. This year hasn't been easy for her, mentally or physically, but on the grandest of stages, she once again proves she's one of the best in the world.

Canada scores again three minutes later, and incredibly once again it's 18-year-old rookie Poulin. This time it's the hard work of Meghan Agosta that provides the spark.

Shannon Szabados then shuts the door for Canada. The Americans outplay Canada for the final two periods, but Shannon keeps them in the game. She shows me why head coach Melody Davidson went with her today. With the game on the line, in the final frame, Cherie Piper, despite being cut last year, is often double-shifted. Her speed, tenacity, and ability to sacrifice her body in front of the puck are rewarded as she sees more ice time than nearly every other Canadian.

I cheer valiantly for Jen, for Megs, for Piper, and for every other girl with the privilege of wearing the Team Canada jersey. I stand for the final two minutes, willing time to pass, and as the buzzer sounds, I swell with pride, celebrating with the entire nation.

As Team Canada receives their medals on the blue line, it's a surreal experience of mixed emotions. It's not the same pain as Torino, my life has moved on since then. I wish I could have experienced this with them, but I feel like a proud parent as lifetimes of memories with each one of the players on the screen runs like a film script through my brain.

The staff fills the ice alongside the players. After the celebration they spread out in the players box directly behind the athletes. I see long-time staff members that have had a major impact on countless players over the years, including me. I see physio Doug Stacey, who kept me healthy, and equipment manager Robin McDonald, the very first face I ever saw with Team Canada. There's Dave Jamieson who once again guided the goalies through what must have been a tough season, being their shoulder to lean on and the constant in their lives. Sports psychologist Peter Jensen holds Becky Kellar's youngest son, Zach, who watches beside his older brother Owen as their mommy receives her gold medal.

Noah, Wick's son, is there too, looking all grown up. Also in the players bench is head coach Melody Davidson, the architect of this remarkable story, who extraordinarily has won her second straight gold medal behind the bench. Last, Lesley Reddon claps as the players receive their medals. Working for Hockey Canada, she has toiled diligently behind the scenes for years to keep this program successful. I once watched Lesley as an Olympian just as thousands of young girls now watch Shannon.

As each of the players bend down to receive their medal, their smiles are contagious. Many kiss their medal and point towards the stands, waving it high in the air.

They get to the end of the line, and there stand Kim and Charlie. The IOC representative places a gold medal around Kim's neck first as Charlie waits proudly smiling. Today, for the first time in women's hockey history, the third goalies will be awarded medals with their teammates on the blue line. *I fought for this.*

I watch Charlie, in full gear, side by side with her teammates, lean over to receive her gold.

I can't help but think I am a small part of her medal too.

Epilogue

Women's hockey sits in a precarious position. It's more popular than it's ever been, and participation is soaring at every level. With growth comes new pressures. There is a scrutiny that we have never had to face before that has forced the players, the game, and Canadian society that hasn't included women at many of the highest levels of sport to look inwards. To reflect on what is needed, what is in fact wanted, and how female sport at the highest level can be conceptualized.

I know how fortunate I've been to have made a living playing the game I love. Most were not as fortunate. I went from growing up with female peers who were never allowed to play to signing paid hockey contracts. I went from being yelled at for walking into rinks with a hockey bag to having full sized NHL arenas packed to watch me play.

Because I participated at a time when opportunity for female hockey players was limited, I am grateful for every step along the way. I am appreciative for every coach who said, "Yeah, you can be on our team," and indebted to every teammate who was inclusive of me.

I vividly remember the first time I walked into a Team Canada dressing room and they had free tape and gum. I was so excited, I had to call Dermot back in Winnipeg to tell him about our windfall. I remember the first time a sports company gave me a free set of pads, and then the first time a sports company *actually* paid me to wear their gear.

Whenever we received some sort of free swag, the National Team dressing room would light up. A free t-shirt was enough to send us into a frenzy. The first time two bags of Olympic clothes were sent to me in California, I invited all my friends over for a fashion show. I wore those clothes for years, incredibly proud to have earned the right to don the maple leaf, and we all felt tremendously fortunate for what we had.

Then we realized that our product was of some value. Thérèse Brisson helped us push the envelope. She created an advisory board and led the charge to ask, "Is this enough? Are free clothes enough?" For the first time, we started comparing our program to the men's program, and we started demanding more of the pie. We started to get paid not only by the federal government, but by Hockey Canada. And with that salary came more responsibilities, more expectations, and greater demands on our time and our training. The evolution of women's professional hockey had begun.

The first 10 years of the National Team, from 1987 (the first unofficial World Championship) to 1997, the decade prior to my time with the team, was comprised of players who took big risks to play hockey. Most had to buck social norms and were often ridiculed for being a woman who wanted to play hockey. There are countless stories of these women starting hockey later in life because their parents wouldn't let them play or there was simply nowhere for a girl to play. Many had older brothers whom they admired and watched at the rink, wanting to play hockey just like them. From a young age, often they had to speak up, and pave their own way to play. There were few female role models to emulate, no stories of other women who played — they were the firsts.

My friend Susie Yuen, from a Chinese immigrant family, started playing hockey in post-secondary school when she saw that the University of Manitoba had a women's club team. Manon Rhéaume wanted to play because she had a brother who played, and her dad coached the team. Danielle Goyette grew up playing on the outdoor rinks with her brothers but was prohibited from playing on the local organized boys' team. She wasn't able to find a women's team until she was 18. Jennifer Botterill, like countless before her, played ringette, a sport created for women in the 1960s because it was perceived then, and for many years after, that hockey was not for girls. Ringette has become an amazing sport in and of itself; however, as a sport its roots were established to keep women out of hockey. Jen made the switch at the age of 14 and went on to crack Canada's hockey lineup at 17.

Often players that played for Canada in that era had to embody a rebellious spirit. Many had to be the ones to change deep-seated beliefs in their families, their towns, and their communities.

My grandmother grew up when women first gained the right to vote. She in turn raised my mom to value education and to become the first woman in her family to earn a degree from University, however, she was not allowed to pursue sport past her early years. My mom then in turned raised me to dream beyond the societal norms, to push boundaries and believe I could accomplish anything regardless of my gender. I now have the privilege of raising a daughter who can see first-hand women being athletes, astronauts, and engineers, and just about every other conceivable job as those pursuits are normalized. My daughter will never know my mom's hardships, yet she too will still have ground to cover for equality.

Now, the players who don the red and white of the National Team, at a young age, start to dream about the Olympics, about representing their country, and about playing elite women's hockey. Girls are generally brought up to be strong, determined, and capable of anything boys are. Now, opportunities exist to play on boys *and/or* girls teams from a very young age, and there are camps and skills sessions for them to hone their skills with female role models and mentors. It's not parallel to the men's game — but the opportunities available to girls and women have increased significantly.

The pressures for these girls to be skilled in their teenage years is something my era never experienced. They must train harder and be more focused and more regimented than the generations before them. They are scouted at a young age to attend prep schools, for university scholarships, for local regional and provincial teams, all of which is intended to put them on the path towards competing at the National level.

The team is no longer a mish-mash of girls that hadn't been given opportunities to play. The team is now part of Hockey Canada's machine. Hockey Canada has begun to choose players who fit the mould, and the players with rebellious spirits are made to conform or left off rosters. Would players such as Cassie Campbell, with her bold, opinionated, and outgoing personality; or Geraldine Heaney, with her determination to train in her own way; or Thérèse Brisson, with her willingness to speak up; or Cherie Piper, with her fierce individuality, even make today's Team Canada? Because they have had to adapt their entire lives, they could have simply conformed, but our teams would never have been as successful, and they certainly would not have been as much fun.

With the demise of the Canadian Women's Hockey League in 2019, there is now, once again, the opportunity for great strides. Sometimes out of the most desperate situations are born the best ideas. Women have been playing hockey for over a century, and each new generation creates a legacy for the next to build upon. We must remember, uncover, and celebrate our unique history right across this country and around the world. At Norberry Community Centre, my local centre in Winnipeg, there was a women's team in the '60s, but then nothing for an entire generation. The rink I grew up on was renamed the Sami Jo Small Hockey Facility in 2016, so that girls for many years can know that they, too, belong on the ice.

Hazel McCallion, the former mayor of Mississauga and one of the strongest advocates of women's hockey in this country, played hockey professionally in the late '30s in Montreal and was paid five dollars a game — but much of women's hockey history is lost; what about all the other women in those leagues? Hazel continued to be an advocate and in 2007, when we won the National Championship with Mississauga, she held the team party at her house. A culmination of a lifetime of pride and advocacy. Then in 2019, in honour of "Hurricane" Hazel McCallion, the Mississauga Chiefs changed their club name to the Hurricanes.

My home province only inducted their first female player, Jennifer Botterill, in 2018 into the Manitoba Hockey Hall of Fame. Their second, Susie Yuen, was inducted in 2019. They are joined by official Laura Loeppky (Vanderhorst), who was my defensive partner at the '91 Canada Games. There should be many more alongside the hundreds of men who have been enshrined, including Delaney Collins and Margaret Hoban, a star goalie for the Winnipeg Olympics in the 1930s. Many stories are yet to be uncovered, but let's remember these women, celebrate their successes, and build upon their legacies.

Cassie Campbell and Hayley Wickenheiser have received the highest distinction, the Order of Canada, for their contributions to Canadian society — but they were our stars. They were the ones everyone always asked me if I knew. Rightly so, but, as more stories are told, more will be revered.

Numerous women have accomplished incredible feats, such as Jen getting a point in *every single* college game she played but one; or Becky Kellar coming back twice after giving birth to backstop our defensive core in four straight Olympics; or Kim St-Pierre asking if Charline Labonté could play a period so she could stand on the blue line and receive a medal. These are just a few of the incredible stories, unknown to the masses, that I hope become part of Canadian sport lore.

The Hockey Hall of Fame in Toronto only began inducting women in 2010; the first two were Angela James and Cammi Granato. Geraldine Heaney, Angela Ruggiero, Danielle Goyette, Jayna Hefford, and Hayley Wickenheiser have followed; they are all from my era but there is plenty of room for more. We need to uncover the stories of women who toiled away in obscurity and went on to dominate the leagues of their time and prove that women could play all along.

Jennifer Botterill will surely join the Hall — she's a shoo-in — as should Kim St-Pierre, Becky Kellar, Cherie Piper, Meghan Agosta, Caroline Ouellete, Marie-Philip Poulin, and Shannon Szabados. Along with several of the Americans I suited up against. And Kim Martin, the heroic Swedish goaltender who earned Sweden's first ever silver at the Olympic Games. The Hall of Fame is generally all about points or dominance at a position. If I were choosing, I'd also include Cassie Campbell for having captained two gold medal winning teams, Charline Labonté for having been a part of an incredible four Olympic gold medal winning teams, Manon Rhéaume for suiting up in an NHL game and inspiring a generation, Vicky Sunohara for being an integral part of the National Team for so long, and Colleen Sostorics for being a stalwart on defence for three straight Olympic gold medal performances.

Much has happened since my last National Team game, but through it all I played. I played long after most of my teammates retired because I still loved it. I played because I loved going to the rink, I loved pushing myself alongside younger teammates and against younger athletes as they pursued their National Team dreams. I played for another decade — until the age of 42, when I finally accepted the job of general manager of the Toronto Furies.

I never officially retired from the National Team (I'm still available, if needed?), that was something only the stars got to do. The only true retirements I ever saw were Geraldine Heaney's and Cassie Campbell's. Both hung it up at the height of their careers — the rest of us were simply replaced or unceremoniously cut. The machine chugs on.

Now I am simply a fan who happens to have played with or against most of the current stars on TV. I also never retired from the Toronto Furies. My playing time just dwindled, and I ended up watching more games than playing . . . forcing me to realize I could contribute more as a GM.

There are many more stories that have emerged from my last decade in the game about incredible people I was fortunate to meet and interact with, and the adventures that we pursued. But those stories are for another time. *For the next book.*

In 2011, I married Billy Bridges at a hockey-themed ceremony in Mississauga. It was July 1, Canada Day. Jen served as my maid of honour, with my long-time friends Gillian Russell, Kathryn McKenzie, and Dermot McDonald in the wedding party. Billy continues to play sledge hockey at the highest level as he attempts to play in his sixth Paralympic Games in Beijing in 2022. He is the all-time points leader and will likely be the first sledge hockey player inducted into the Hockey Hall of Fame (I might be biased . . .).

I gave birth to our daughter Kensi in November of 2015, and kept playing all the while. My dad says I'm too stubborn to give up. I don't think it was ever about hockey itself. It was about the feeling I get when I compete. The joy of being fully immersed in play.

I want to say thank you to all my coaches and teammates throughout my sports career. Circumstances brought us together; experiences made us friends. To my brother, thank you for being the inspiration to the story. To my dad for passing down his pathological optimism and to my mom for teaching me kindness, hope, and how to sacrifice for others. I owe my career to my parents and am forever grateful for their love and support on and off the ice.

To all those that pushed me, supported me, and allowed and encouraged me to play and to all those who were my friends in trying times, incredible times, and the times in between — I say thank you.